27/10/1988

Constitutional Law
Student text

Hutchinson Professional Studies Series (LLB)

Student texts
Constitutional Law
Contract Law
Criminal Law
English Legal System

Cases & Materials
Constitutional Law
Contract Law
Criminal Law
English Legal System

In Preparation
Administrative Law
Commercial Law
Company Law
Evidence
Family Law
Jurisprudence & Legal Theory
Land Law
Law of Tort
Law of Trusts
Public International Law
Revenue Law
Succession

HUTCHINSON PROFESSIONAL STUDIES SERIES

LLB

Constitutional Law

Student Text

Editorial Advisory Panel

Chart University Tutors

Hutchinson

London Melbourne Sydney Auckland Johannesburg

Hutchinson Education

An imprint of Century Hutchinson Ltd
62-65 Chandos Place, London WC2N 4NW

Century Hutchinson Australia Pty Ltd
PO Box 496, 16-22 Church Street, Hawthorn,
Victoria 3122, Australia

Century Hutchinson New Zealand Ltd
191 Archers Road, Glenfield, Auckland, New Zealand

Century Hutchinson South Africa (Pty) Ltd
PO Box 337, Bergvlei, 2012 South Africa

First Published 1988 by Hutchinson Education
© Chart University Tutors Ltd 1988

Printed and bound in Great Britain by Scotprint Ltd., Musselburgh

ISBN 0 09 182431 1

HELP US TO HELP YOU

The Hutchinson – Chart LL.B series is prepared to the highest possible standards. We have in preparing the student text borne in mind the needs of law students.

In our efforts constantly to improve the standards. We invite comments from you. If you feel there are ways in which the student text can be improved, please tell us. We will do our best to improve our next edition and will incorporate any helpful suggestions in our longer-term planning.

Thank you for your help. The comments form is set out below.

EDITORIAL PANEL
Jane Blessley
Charles Reed
Nicholas Bourne
Tracey Aquino
Sept '88

To: The Editorial Advisory Panel
Chart University Tutors
200 Greyhound Road,
London W14 9RY,
England.

Name_____

Address_____

_____

_____ Tel_____

Student Text title_____

_____

_____

_____

_____

_____

_____

_____

CHART UNIVERSITY TUTORS

200 Greyhound Road, London W14 9RY, Telephone: 01-385 3377
Telex: 266386 · Fax: 01-381 3377

FAR EAST SUBSIDIARY

Chart Tutors Sdn Bhd 58 Jalan Tuanku Abdul Rahman 50100 Kuala Lumpur, Malaysia. Telephone: 03-293 5337

Chart University Tutors has a long and distinguished record of training students in the legal profession and prides itself on the pursuit of academic excellence and this is reflected by our results and by the number of our students who gain places to research into Law and subsequently enter practice as first class advocates.

We are proud of our past students who have graduated with us and who are flying our flag in their professions.

Commitment and conviction in seeing to the progress of all our students rank top in our priorities and we invite students who are not yet part of Chart University Tutors to act today and become part of the growing tradition.

NICHOLAS BOURNE
PRINCIPAL

TRACEY AQUINO
DIRECTOR OF STUDIES

SONNY LEONG
REGISTRAR

Please send me further details (please tick)

	Full Time	Part Time	Home Degree
London LL.B (External)		Part Time	Home Study
'A' Levels	Full Time		
Bar Finals	Full Time		

Name ....

Address ....

Telephone (Home) ....

(Office) ....

LLB

CONSTITUTIONAL LAW

TABLE OF CONTENTS

LESSON 15 (REVISION)

LLB

CONSTITUTIONAL LAW

LESSON 1 (STUDY)

11. *OUT LINE OF CONSTITUTIONAL LAW*

12. *FEATURES OF BRITISH CONSTITUTION AND COMPARISON WITH OTHER SYSTEMS*

    12.1   AN UNWRITTEN CONSTITUTION
    12.2   CONVENTIONS IN THE CONSTITUTION
    12.3   FLEXIBILITY OF THE CONSTITUTION
    12.4   DOCTRINE OF SEPARATION OF POWERS
    12.5   SOVEREIGNTY OF PARLIAMENT
    12.6   THE RULE OF LAW
    12.7   UNITARY CONSTITUTION – THE POSITION OF NORTHERN IRELAND, SCOTLAND AND WALES
    12.8   PARLIAMENTARY GOVERNMENT
    12.9   CONSTITUTIONAL MONARCHY

13. *THE CONSTITUTIONAL POSITION OF NORTHERN IRELAND, SCOTLAND AND WALES*

    13.1   NORTHERN IRELAND
    13.2   SCOTLAND
    13.3   WALES

14. *THE EUROPEAN ECONOMIC COMMUNITY*

15. *THE EUROPEAN CONVENTION ON HUMAN RIGHTS*

16. *DOES THE UK NEED A BILL OF RIGHTS?*

11. *OUTLINE OF CONSTITUTIONAL LAW*

Constitutional law may be described as the law concerning the constitution of the country. It thus becomes necessary to know what is meant here by the word *constitution* and by the word *law*.

Law may be defined, in this context, as being those rules which the courts of the state will enforce as law. Such a definition is clearly a formula rather than an explanation. It raises many further questions. For the moment, however, this definition must suffice and consideration of the nature of law may be left to the science of jurisprudence which a student will encounter at a later stage in his studies.

The constitution is the system of rules, both formal and informal, which creates and regulates the Government and its departments and delineates the relationship of those departments both with each other and with the private citizen. The constitution of a country thus comprises its most fundamental and basic law, the law which *governs its Government*. The constitution lays down the ways in which the Government nay be changed and does not itself change with the Government.

12. *FEATURES OF BRITISH CONSTITUTION AND COMPARISON WITH OTHER SYSTEMS*

12.1 *An unwritten constitution*

A constitution is often visualised as being a single written document. Indeed the constitution of most countries is a single written document which has been enacted as law. The USA and the USSR both have written constitutions, as do most Commonwealth countries and the countries of Western Europe. It is sometimes said that the UK has no constitution. This is misleading because although the constitution of the UK cannot be found in a single written document it can be gathered from a number of sources: statutes and decided cases are the most important sources, custom and juristic writing also play a part.

(a) Statute law

Many statutes relating to constitutional law have been enacted. They do not form a complete constitutional code but there are few topics of constitutional law which have not been affected by legislation. *Legislation is the most important single source of constitutional law.* Some statutes have special constitutional law significance, even though that significance is sometimes a matter of historical and symbolic value rather than current legal force, e.g.:

(i) *Magna Carta 1215* – few provisions of Magna Carta remain today on the statute book, but it retains importance as being an early expression of the ideals of constitutional government. The Charter set out the rights of various classes in the community. Its most famous clauses lay down that no man shall be punished except by the judgment of his peers or the law of the land, and that justice should be denied to no one.

(ii) *Petition of Right 1628* – a petition by Parliament, (which was in conflict with the King), against taxation without Parliamentary consent, arbitrary imprisonment and the billeting of soldiers upon private persons.

(iii) *Bill of Rights 1688 or 1689* – enacted by Parliament after the Revolution of 1688 had brought about the downfall of James II and re-established the monarchy on terms which Parliament had laid down. Many of its principal provisions, or Articles, are still part of English law. The provisions include the establishment of the right of subjects to petition the King; that the raising or keeping of a standing army in time of peace is illegal without Parliamentary consent; that election of members of Parliament should be free; that freedom of speech and debates or proceedings in Parliament should not be impeached or questioned in any court or place outside Parliament; that excessive bail should not be required, nor excessive fines imposed, nor cruel and unusual punishments inflicted – and that all grants and promises of fines, and forfeitures of particular persons before conviction are illegal and void. For the full text see *Halsbury's Statutes, vol. 6, p. 489.*

(iv) *Act of Settlement 1700* – enacted by Parliament, to provide for the succession to the throne. It also provides, *inter alia,* that the Monarch must be a communicant member of the Church of England, that no one incapable of serving as a member of the House of Commons should hold an office under the Monarch or receive a pension from the Crown and that judges should be removable upon the address of both Houses of Parliament.

(v) *Statute of Westminster 1931* – granted legislative independence to the independent members of the Commonwealth, known at that time as the Dominions (Canada,

Australia, New Zealand and South Africa). Since that date there have been further independence statutes.

(vi) *Parliament Acts 1911, 1949* – enacted to prevent the House of Lords vetoing the legislative endeavours of the House of Commons by refusing to pass Public Bills which have already been passed by the House of Commons. These statutes will be discussed in more detail at section 32.9 (d).

(vii) *European Communities Act 1972* – enacted to make the necessary legislative changes to enable the UK to comply with obligations and to exercise rights arising under the Community treaties. The most important provision of the Act is *s.2(1)* which lays down that all those provisions of community law which, in accordance with Community law, are directly effective in the UK shall have the force of law in the UK without the need for enactment by Parliament in this country. Thus, for the first time a provision can become part of UK statute law without having first been enacted by the UK Parliament. (See for example *Macarthys Ltd. v Smith (1981) 1 All ER 111*).

(b) *Case law*

Case law may be a source of the constitution in two different ways:

Firstly, where statute does not cover the facts of the case and the judge makes his decision by reference to a law of nature or reason, the case becomes an *original source* of a constitutional principle. In *Dr. Bonham's Case (1610) 3 Ca Rep 1136*, Dr. Bonham had been required to pay a fine, half to the Crown and half to the Royal College of Physicians under the charter of the College which had been confirmed by Act of Parliament. It was held that the College had no jurisdiction over Dr. Bonham as he practised outside London. Coke, CJ, went on to say as an *obiter dictum* that *when an Act of Parliament is against common right and reason, or repugnant or impossible to be performed, the common law will control, and adjudge such Act to be void.* However, this dictum is no longer considered correct because under the doctrine of Parliamentary Sovereignty the will of the legislature supersedes that of the judiciary.

Secondly, where the courts are interpreting a statute, their decision may become a secondary source of a constitutional principle, the statute itself being the primary source. In the following cases the court made explicit or reinforced a constitutional principle which may only be implicit in the statute which the court was called upon to interpret. In the case of *McWhirter v AG (1972) CMLR 882* Mr. McWhirter had applied to the court for a declaration that the executive acts leading to the signing of the *Treaty of Rome*, by which the UK joined the EEC, were unlawful as being contrary to the *Bill of Rights 1688* which declares that the full power of government is vested in the Crown. His application was struck out as disclosing no reasonable cause of action. In giving judgment Lord Denning MR said that the courts do not let treaties signed by the Crown impinge on the rights or liberties of any man unless and until they are incorporated under our law by Act of Parliament. In *AG v Wilts United Dairies (1921) 37 TLR 884* an attempt by the Crown to levy money without express statutory authority was held *ultra vires*, i.e. beyond its powers. The Attorney General had sought to charge a fee of two pence on each gallon of milk purchased by the dairy from the Food Controller. The House of Lords held that neither the Act creating the Ministry of Food nor the regulations under which the milk had been supplied either directly or by inference enabled the Food Controller to levy a fee.

In *Waddington v Miah (1974) 2 All ER 377* the House of Lords, justifying its decision by reference to the Declaration of *Human Rights* of the United Nations and the *Convention for the Protection of Human Rights and Fundamental Freedoms*, took the view that it was hardly credible that Parliament would pass retrospective penal legislation and declared that offences created by the *Immigration Act 1971* were not retrospective in effect.

The fact that the British Constitution is not to be found in a single document has a number of important effects:

(i)   there is no difference between constitutional laws and other laws;

(ii)   no special procedure is required for the amendment of the British Constitution. Thus, the constitution is described as being flexible as opposed to rigid (see section 12.3 below);

(iii)   the courts have no power to declare legislation invalid as being unconstitutional. Thus, in *ex p Selwyn (1872) 365 P 54* it was said:

> there is no judicial body in the country by which the validity of an Act of Parliament can be questioned. An Act of the legislature is superior in authority to any court of law ... and no court could pronounce a judgment as to the validity of an Act of Parliament;

(iv)   there is no written guarantee of human rights. Thus in *R v Jordan (1967) Crim LR 483*, where Jordan sought legal aid to enable him to argue that the Race Relations Act was invalid as being in curtailment of free speech, his application was dismissed as it was said that the ground of application was unarguable -there is no general principle of free speech in English law. The UK is, however, a signatory to the European Convention on Human Rights (see section 15 below).

12.2 *Conventions in the constitution*

Much of the constitutional law of the UK has not been enacted by the legislature as law. Custom and convention are more important as sources of constitutional law in this country than they are in countries with a wholly written constitution. The British Constitution may be described as flexible in that change may come about without any legislative enactment as custom and convention gradually alter. However, even where the constitution is to be found in a single written document, custom and convention may still be used in the interpretation of that document. In that sense no constitution is ever wholly written and elements of flexibility may, by interpretation, be inserted into a rigid and formal constitutoin.

The extensive use of non-legal rules to supplement the legal framework of the British Constitution, although by no means unique, is a particular characteristic of the British Constitution.

Conventions are rules of political practice which are regarded as binding by those who operate under them. Conventions would not be enforced by the courts if the matter came before them, but they are regarded as being of so fundamental a nature that it would be unthinkable that anyone should transgress or fail to observe them.

Whilst the courts do not enforce conventions and no remedy for their breach would be available in law, they may nevertheless be taken into account when a court is reaching a decision on a point of law. Thus in *Carltona v Commissioner of Works (1943) 2 All ER 560* judicial notice was taken of the fact that civil servants customarily take decisions in the name of ministers and of the fact that ministers may be called to account by Parliament for those decisions. Again in *AG v Jonathan Cape (1976) OB 752*, Lord Widgery, CJ, held that the court had power in suitable cases to restrain the improper publication of information which had been received by a Cabinet minister in confidence and that the constitutional convention of collective Cabinet responsibility justified the court in restraining disclosures of Cabinet discussions. No injunction was grated in the Crossman case because the information was not sufficiently confidential to warrant this protection. However, in *Madzimbamuto v Lardner-Burke (1969)* (a case arising out of the unilateral declaration of independence in Rhodesia) the English court emphasised that no convention, however important, would limit the legal power of Parliament. Said Lord Reid in giving the judgment of the majority of the Privy Council:

> it is often said that it would be unconstitutional for the Uk Parliament to do certain things, meaning that the moral, political and other reasons against doing then are so strong that most people would regard it as highly improper if Parliament did these things. But that does not mean that it is beyond the power of Parliament to do such things. If parliament chose to do any of then the courts could not hold the Act of Parliament invalid.

Lord Reid's statement is important not merely for its clarity but also because it emphasises that the strength of a convention is a non-legal and informal strength. There is no legal sanction for breach of a convention; if the convention were broken. Is that sanction any less effective than a legal sanction enforced by the courts? The answer to this question has long been a matter of dispute. In the science of jurisprudence the view originally put forward by Austin (see *The Province of Jurisprudence Determined)* that the existence of a sanction was the reason for obeying a law, has now fallen into disrepute. It is now considered by many (see, for example, Hart: *Concept of Law)* that obedience comes about not through fear of the consequences of disobedience but rather as a positive act – a desire to behave according to the law and to gain general approval by acting in the generally accepted manner. If this analysis is taken to be true, there would seem to be little difference between a convention enacted as law and a convention which remains

informal but which is generally regarded as laying down a binding rule of political practice. Some of the most long-standing and hallowed rules of the British Constitution are rules of convention rather than of law and yet do not seem weakened by lack of legal enforcement. The general rule that the Monarch will exercise the Royal Prerogative, only with the advice of her ministers and the rule that ministers are collectively responsible to Parliament for the act of any one of their number in his capacity as a minister are both rules of convention. Other examples of conventional rules include that the Government must not impede the lawful activities of members of the Opposition and that the Prime Minister must resign immediately if it becomes clear that he has lost a general election, without waiting for the newly elected Parliament to meet.

Whilst breach of a constitutional convention may not result in a legal sanction, it would be unrealistic to disregard the informal sanctions which come about. The significance of public criticism in Parliament and in the Press when a convention is breached should not be underrated. The fear of criticism and controversy, especially where the convention in question is of long standing, is a very real deterrent. In certain cases breach of convention has given rise to enactment of the breached convention. One example is that the breach by the House of Lords of the convention that Money Bills from the Commons would not be vetoed gave rise to the *Parliament Act 1911* which enacted this rule and imposed further restrictions on the powers of the Lords.

The established conventions in the British Constitution have grown up over a period of many years. Each has gradually come to be regarded as an established and binding rule. Acceptance is sufficiently widespread that specific enforcement should not be necessary. Attempts to establish the rules of convention in newly independent Commonwealth countries have in general failed because the conventions have been imported wholesale and have not been allowed to evolve organically as gaps in the legal rules arose. In such situations, therefore, the immediate need must always be for clear legal rules. If a convention is to be used it must be a convention enacted in a legally enforceable form.

12.3 *Flexibility of the Constitution*

There is a second sense in which the British Constitution is flexible. It is usual in most countries for the law of the constitution to provide within itself for the method of its own alteration. Often the method for altering the laws of the constitution is different from,and more difficult to achieve than,that used to alter other laws which do not form part of the constitution. For example in the US, amendment of the constitution may only be carried out either by initiation of two-thirds of both Houses of Congress and ratification of the legislatures of three-quarters of the States, or by initiation of two-thirds of the States and ratification by conventions in three-quarters of the States. If the constitution may only be changed by following a specified procedure it is referred to as an 'entrenched' constitution. Alteration of the constitution of the UK is by contrast simple, for a law of the constitution may here be changed in precisely the same way as any other law, i.e. by Act of Parliament.

12.4 *Doctrine of separation of powers*

The functions of government have traditionally been divided into three classes – legislative (the making of law) executive (the making and application of policy and general administration) and judicial (the interpretation of law and adjudication on alleged breaches of law). The doctrine of the separation of powers is derived from Montesquieu, *L'Esprit des Lois (1748)* who argued that in order to maintain political liberty it was necessary that the three functions of government should be entrusted to three separate bodies so each would act as a check on the others. The jurist Blackstone was of the same opinion. In his *Commentaries* (1765) he said:

> in all tyrannical governments the right of making and of enforcing the laws is vested in one and the same man, or the same body of men; and where so ever these two powers are united together, there can be no liberty.

In the United States the Constitution provides for a strict, but not total, separation of powers. Legislative power is vested in the Congress, executive power in the President and judicial power in the Supreme Court. The separation is strict in that:

(a) no member of one branch of government may also be a member of another;

(b) the President cannot dissolve Congress;

(c) the President is not dependent on the support of Congress and holds office for a fixed term.

However, it is not total. Thus:

(i)   the President appoints judges to the Supreme Court subject to the approval of the senate;

(ii) the Vice-President presides over the Senate;

(iii) Congress must ratify any treaties the President may make before they can come into effect;

(iv) the President is empowered to veto legislation of Congress;

(v)   the Supreme Court can declare legislation unconstitutional and thus invalid.

There is, as can be seen above, a sort of see-saw arrangement which may formally be described as a system of checks and balances.

In the UK, broadly speaking, legislative power is vested in the Queen in Parliament, executive power in the Crown and judicial power in the courts of law. However, there is no formal separation of powers. For example:

(a) although there is a general rule that a person who is a member of one of the organs of government cannot be a member of another, e.g. civil servants or the police cannot stand for Parliament, professional judges cannot be MPs, there are many very important exceptions to the rule. Instances are that all ministers of government (with the one exception of the Scottish law officers) must by convention be drawn either from the Commons or the Lords. Thus, in the UK there is a Parliamentary Executive. Furthermore, senior judges are members of the House of Lords and so have legislative as well as judicial power; government ministers have a legislative capacity in Parliament, an executive capacity as officers of the Crown and sometimes also a judicial capacity in hearing appeals from administrative procedures within their departments;

(b) there are provisions designed to protect the independence of the organs of government and to prevent interference between the organs. Thus there are many provisions to protect the independence of the judiciary, e.g. the rule that judges of the High Court and above can only be removed from office by a joint address of both Houses of Parliament to the Queen. However, it is the Executive which is responsible for judicial appointments initially. The independence of Parliament is protected by the rules on privilege and the stance of the courts in refusing to consider whether a statute is invalid or unconstitutional and to review it on that basis;

(c) although Montesquieu envisaged that each organ of government would carry out only its own function, on examination of the facts this can be seen to be an inaccurate description of the position:

    (i) some legislative power is delegated by Parliament to the Executive in order that Parliament's time should be kept free for debate of the most important issues. Thus ministers frame statutory instruments of general application to the population;

    (ii) powers to determine justiciable disputes are confided in ministers and other bodies such as administrative tribunals and not simply the ordinary court system;

    (iii) the government is dependent upon the support of a majority of Members of Parliament (legislators) to retain office.

It is sometimes difficult to decide which of the powers is being exercised when a minister makes a particular decision is he acting in his executive or his judicial capacity? If it is established that he is acting in the judicial capacity, the high standard of procedure and impartiality expected of a judge will be required, for the lack of a strict separation of powers does not mean that the various functions are not recognised to be different. Attention is focused on the function being exercised rather than on the institution exercising it. The doctrine of ultra vires, framed by the courts, provides a means of control exercised by the courts over ministers exercising either a legislative or a judicial function (see Lesson 12) and this is a part of an informal system of checks and balances built into the UK Constitution. Whether or not the judiciary exercises any legislative function is a further problem. In a very limited measure, they certainly do (see the Rules Committee), but the question is a wider one and more in the realm of jurisprudence.

12.5 *Sovereignty of Parliament*

Parliament can pass any law whatsoever. However, no Parliament is bound by the statute of its predecessors, nor can it bind its successors. This topic will be dealt with in more detail in Lesson 2.

12.6 *The Rule of Law*

In 1959 the International Commission of Jurists meeting at New Delhi adopted the following definition of the Rule of Law:

> the principles, institutions and procedures, not always identical but broadly similar, which the experience and traditions of lawyers in different countries of the world, often having themselves varying political structures and economic backgrounds, have shown to be important to protect the individual from arbitrary government and to enable him to enjoy the dignity of man.

The Rule of Law, which has often been regarded as a peculiar characteristic of British constitutional law, was shown by the 1959 conference to be a principle recognised, in some form, all over the world.

The doctrine of the rule of law is of great antiquity in the British Constitution. Writing in the 13th century the jurist Bracton said the *king himself ought not to be subject to man but subject to God and to the law, because the law makes him king*. Bracton's statement was quoted to James I in 1607 by Sir Edward Coke, Chief Justice of the Court of Common Pleas. On being told that he was under the law and that it was the law that made him king rather than the king who made the law, James I was, Coke reported, *greatly offended: see The Case of Prohibitions (1607)*. This formulation of the doctrine of the rule of law in an attempt to prevent the monarch taking arbitrary action, i.e. action taken without regard to the law, ceased to be in point after the Revolution of 1688 had established the legislative supremacy of Parliament. However, the phrase *rule of law* lived on to

describe Parliament's supremacy in law-making and to show clearly that Parliament itself was governed by the law which it could change but which it could not *disregard*. In 1885 Professor AV Dicey published his *Law of the Constitution* based on lectures he had given at Oxford University. Dicey's new formulation of the Rule of Law has been of fundamental importance in the subsequent development of the doctrine.

Dicey divided the Rule of Law into three principles:

(a) *it means*, Dicey said, *in the first place, the absolute supremacy or predominance of regular law as opposed to the influence of arbitrary power, and excludes the existence of arbitrariness, or prerogative, or even of wide discretionary authority on the part of the Government. Englishmen are ruled by the law, and by the law alone; a man may be punished for a breach of the law, but he can be punished for nothing else*. Thus, in English law, nothing is contrary to law unless and until a specific rule forbids the act in question – our rights may not always be delineated, but our restrictions are;

(b) when we speak of the rule of law as a characteristic of our country, Dicey continued, we mean *not only that with us no man is above the law, but (what is a different thing) that here every man, whatever be his rank or condition, is subject to the ordinary law of the Realm and amenable to the jurisdiction of the ordinary tribunals*;

(c) *the general principles of the constitution (as, for example, the right to personal liberty, or the right of public meeting) are, with us, the result of judicial decisions determining the rights of private persons in particular cases brought before the courts; whereas under many foreign constitutions, the security (such as it is) given to the rights of individuals results, or appears to result, from the general principles of the constitution ... Our constitution, in short, is a judge-made constitution ... (it is) the result of the ordinary law of the land.*

Many criticisms may be made of Dicey's three principles. It must first and simply be said that much of what he wrote is now out-of-date. His chauvinistic catalogue of the virtues of the English law would not now be accepted by many English lawyers who are looking to foreign legal concepts to fill gaps in our domestic law. This change in attitude is demonstrated, for instance, by the recent strong advocacy of an enacted Bill of Rights for this country on the lines of that found in the US Constitution.

It is not merely Dicey's tone but also, often, his substance which is out-moded – government now has wide discretionary powers in some spheres, for government involvement in the lives of citizens has increased greatly in the years since the principles were formulated. There are now not merely *ordinary courts* but also what Dicey would, perhaps, have called *extraordinary courts* - special tribunals operating with special procedures and having exclusive jurisdiction over matters such as redundancy payments, national insurance and unfair dismissal. It is also no longer true to say that that body of the law which protects what may be called our civil liberties is judge-made law rather than statute law. The *Race Relations Acts* and the *Sex Discrimination Act 1975* are among many recent statutes giving new rights and protections in areas of civil liberties which had never been touched by judge-made law.

It may also perhaps be argued that if protection of civil rights was, in Dicey's day, the task of the courts, it was a task that they did not accomplish successfully. The recent calls for an enacted Bill of Rights stem from a realisation that civil rights in this country are unclear and undefined and largely unprotected. The reason that judge-made law is unsatisfactory in this area stems from the basic character of judge-made law. Judges can only give decisions on the facts of each case presented to them; they cannot legislate for the future. Unless a dispute goes to court, the judge cannot rule upon it. Those issues which have not been litigated in court must, therefore, perforce remain undetermined and uncertain. Dicey's third principle also ignores the doctrine of Parliamentary sovereignty for by that doctrine it is always possible for the legislature by a simple Act to overrule a decided case, e.g. the decision of the court in *Burmah Oil v Lord Advocate (1965) AC 75* was rendered ineffective by the *War Damage Act 1965*.

Whilst Dicey's three principles of the Rule of Law may be criticised as regards their detail, their basic substance was, and remains correct. In *Entick v Carrington (1765) 19 St Tr 1030* an attempt to justify a seizure of the plaintiff's books and papers, based solely on the ground that it was in the *interest of the state*, failed. The court noted that there was no legal authority for the seizure, and the concept of the interest of the state was not one recognised by the common law. In the case of *Wolfe Tone (1798) 27 St Tr 214* the court regarded the General Officer Commanding in Ireland and the Provost Marshal as being no less subject to the law than the ordinary citizen. Thus, despite their high offices, the court ordered that they should be taken into custody for failing to obey a writ of *habeas corpus*. In the more recent case of *Burmah Oil v Lord Advocate* the House of Lords held that the plaintiff company was entitled to compensation from the Government when the Government had destroyed their oil installations in Burma in 1942 to prevent them falling into the hands of the Japanese. The fact that the defendant was the Government did not mean that they were exempt from the normal duty to pay compensation in such circumstances. In fact the compensation was never paid. The sum involved was very large and the Government enacted the *War Damage Act 1965*, retrospectively authorising such destruction without payment of compensation.

In all these cases the basic idea of the Rule of Law has been upheld. The Government has been prevented from taking arbitrary action; the Government and its officers have been subject to the law no less than the private citizen; the courts have protected the rights of individuals in specific cases where the Government was in breach of the law. Thus the fundamentals of Dicey's formulation remain intact.

12.7 *Unitary constitution – The position of Northern Ireland, Scotland and Wales*

The British Constitution is *unitary* as opposed to *federal* or *confederal*.

A federal constitution is one in which a number of states form a unity so far as external affairs are concerned and in relation to certain laws applicable throughout the Federation, but where each state manages a large proportion of its own internal affairs. A confederation is a looser grouping of states which co-operate for a common purpose or purposes.

In law the *United kingdom* is a union of England and Wales with Scotland (forming Great Britain) and Northern Ireland; it does not include the Channel Islands or the Isle of Man (reaffirmed in the *Interpretation Act 1978*). The term *British Islands* was defined in the *Interpretation Act 1978* as meaning the UK, the Channel Islands and the Isle of Man. The term *United Kingdom and Islands* is used for immigration purposes

Wales was united with England by an Act of Parliament of the Tudors in 1536 and the common law of England has applied there since 1543. The judicial systems were amalgamated in 1830.

Scotland united with England and Wales by the *Treaty of Union of 1707*. It has, however, retained its own distinct system of private law.

Legislative union with the whole of Ireland occurred in 1800, but in 1920 the six northern counties were made into the separate entity of Northern Ireland and were given their own Government and Parliament. The remainder of Ireland became, at first, the Irish Free State, a self-governing dominion within the British Empire, and, later, the independent state of the Republic of Ireland. The system of government established for Northern Ireland in 1920 came increasingly to be regarded as unsatisfactory and in 1972, after several years of civil unrest, the constitution of Northern Ireland was suspended and the UK Government resumed direct rule. An attempt to establish a new Assembly in 1974 was unsuccessful and direct rule continues.

The Isle of Man has been under allegiance to the Crown since the time of Henry IV. The Channel Islands are possessions of the Crown and are all that remains to the sovereign of the old Duchy of Normandy. Neither the Isle of Man nor the Channel Islands form part of the UK and they have never been colonies. They retain their own legislatures.

Devolution. As a result of an increase in interest in Scottish and Welsh nationalism during the 1960's and the electoral successes of the Nationalist parties, the Labour Government in 1969 appointed a Royal Commission on the Constitution. The Commission's majority report, published in 1973, favoured *legislative devolution* for Scotland and Wales under which power to legislate, to settle policy and to administer in a number of fields would be devolved to assemblies elected by proportional representation.

Whilst the broad conclusion of the Report, that some devolution was desirable, was accepted by the Government, its detailed proposals were not. In the *Scotland and Wales Bill 1976-7* a very limited form of devolution, hedged about with numerous safeguards to be retained by the Government, was proposed. The Bill foundered.

In 1978 two Acts were passed, one for Scotland and one for Wales. These Acts established separate Scottish and Welsh assemblies to be elected by a form of proportional representation. The Scottish Assembly was given legislative powers in respect of 26 devolved areas which included health, transport, education and housing. Although the Assembly was given the power to amend or repeal Acts of the Westminster Parliament within those areas, ultimate sovereignty remained with the Westminster Parliament which would continue to legislate for Scotland and override Assembly Acts. Moreover, certain areas were expressly stated to be beyond the Assembly's legislative competence, e.g. revenue raising, foreign relations, and economic and industrial affairs. The Scottish Act also contained complicated provisions dealing with pre-Assent and post-Assent review of the *vires* of Assembly legislation both in the courts and at Westminster.

The Welsh Assembly was given only executive powers, including the power to make subordinate legislation. There were no provisions for judicial review.

In the event, the provisions of neither Act were implemented. Both Acts were repealed in 1979 after referenda had been held in Scotland and Wales. No new legislation concerning devolution is likely although with the loss by the Conservatives of many of their Scottish seats in June 1987 the Scots may again agitate for some form of devolution.

12.8 Parliamentary government

In all constitutional states there is a check or limitation upon the power of the Executive. In Britain executive powers are exercised by the Prime Minister and her ministers. The Cabinet is responsible to Parliament, which has the power to remove it if it has lost Parliament's confidence. Ultimately, therefore, the Executive in being responsible to Parliament is responsible to the people.

How Parliament is elected, its functions and the position of the Crown and Cabinet will be dealt with later in Lessons 3,4 and 6.

12.9 *Constitutional monarchy*

The UK is a monarchy. It is a constitutional, as opposed to an absolute, monarchy in that, although the Queen is the Head of State and government is carried on in her name, it is carried on in fact by the Executive, i.e. the Prime Minister and her ministers. Many of the limitations on the power of the monarch were laid down in the *Bill of Rights 1688* and the *Act of Settlement (1700)* (see earlier)' The sovereign retains certain personal prerogatives although these are limited in their scope.

The topic will be dealt with in more detail later. (See Lesson 4).

13. *THE CONSTITUTIONAL POSITION OF NORTHERN IRELAND, SCOTLAND AND WALES*

13.1 *Northern Ireland*

Prior to 1783 the whole of Ireland was subject to the rule of the kings of England. At this point the English Parliament purported to relinquish jurisdiction until 1801 when the two Parliaments, British and Irish, entered into union and a hundred Irish MP's were elected to the Parliament in London. There were also twenty-eight Irish peers in the House of Lords. Gradually, the demand for Home Rule grew and after a number of attempts the *Government of Ireland Act 1914* was passed setting up a self governing, undivided Ireland. The Protestant majority in the province of Ulster opposed it, and the Act was superseded by the *Government of Ireland Act 1920* setting up two separate Parliaments – one for Northern and one for Southern Ireland. Uprising followed in Southern Ireland and in 1922 the Irish Free State (now the Republic of Ireland) was formed and given Dominion status. Thus the constitutional position of Northern Ireland was set out in the 1920 Act (as amended) giving them a Prime Minister, Cabinet, Privy Council and a parliament composed of a Senate and a house of Commons (Stormont) and a Supreme Court. This did not bring total self government as the UK government retained a great deal of control – largely financial.

In the early seventies the Catholic minority's grievances came to a head and the unrest which followed led to large numbers of British troops being sent to Northern Ireland. In March 1972 the UK imposed direct rule on Northern Ireland and the government functions were placed into the hands of the Secretary of State for Northern Ireland – a Minister of the UK government. A plebiscite was held in 1973 and approximately 60% of the population of Ulster favoured remaining a part of the UK. A number of experiments followed in an attempt to substitute direct rule by some form of power-sharing between the Protestants and Catholics. All failed and Northern Ireland is still ruled from the UK under the *Northern Ireland Act 1974*. Further initiatives were attempted by Mr. Prior, the former Secretary of State for Northern Ireland, in the hope of breaking the deadlock all without success.

13.2 *Scotland*

When Scotland joined with England to become Great Britain in 1707-the Act of *Union* made the following provision regarding Scottish Law.

> The laws which concern public right, policy and civil government may be made the same throughout the whole United kingdom, but that no alteration be made in laws which concern private right except for evident utility of the subjects within Scotland.

The Act incorporated an Act for securing the Protestant religion and Presbyterian Church government in Scotland, which, it was said:

> shall be held and observed in all time coming as a fundamental and essential condition of any treaty or union to be concluded betwixt the two kingdoms.

The question therefore arises whether, by the Act of Union, the rules that Parliament cannot bind its successors and can repeal any statute were, in part, abrogated.

In *MacCormick v Lord Advocate (1953)*, the title of the Queen, Elizabeth was challenged on the ground that it contravened the *Act of Union*. It was held that the title had been adopted under powers conferred by the *Royal Titles Act 1953* and that the *Act of Union* did not forbid use of the numeral. But, in giving judgment, the Lord President, Lord Cooper said:

The Treaty (of Union) and the associated legislation, by which the Parliament of Great Britain was brought into being as the successor of the separate Parliaments of Scotland and England, contain some clauses which expressly reserve to the Parliament of Great Britain powers of subsequent modification, and other clauses which either contain no such power or emphatically exclude subsequent alteration by declarations that the provision shall be fundamental and unalterable in all time coming ..... I have not found in the Union legislation any provision that the Parliament of Great Britain should be 'absolutely sovereign' in the sense that Parliament should be free to alter the Treaty at will.

Thus Lord Cooper was clearly suggesting that Parliament was bound by certain clauses of the *Act of Union* and could not repeal or alter them.

The effect of Lord Cooper's opinion was reduced somewhat by his later admitting that *it is of little avail to ask whether the Parliament of Great Britain 'can' do this thing or that, without going on to enquire who can stop them if they do.* He agreed that perhaps no one could 'stop' them -short perhaps of Scottish resistance or the peaceable alternative of an *advisory opinion* of the International Court of Justice. However, the tentative principle remains that some fundamental legislation may bind Parliament's successors and may not be open to repeal. See further *Gibson v Lord Advocate*, where the same issues were explored (see section 23.1).

13.3 *Wales*

In 1284 Wales was annexed by the English King but not until 1536 did real integration take place. Welsh constituencies were given representation in the English Parliament. Virtually all Acts which apply to England equally apply to Wales. The legal system is identical and, essentially, so is the system of local government. There is a Welsh Office – a department headed by a Secretary of State with a seat in the Cabinet. Other ministries have Welsh departments, e.g. agriculture.

14. *THE EUROPEAN ECONOMIC COMMUNITY*

After the Second World War the western countries of continental Europe saw a need to establish friendly, mutually supportive relations and to that end a European Coal and Steel Community was founded in 1952. This was followed in 1958 by the European Atomic Energy Community and the European Economic Community, established under the Treaty of Rome 1957. Initially there were six members: France, West Germany, Italy, Luxembourg, the Netherlands and Belgium. During the 1960s successive British governments attempted to negotiate favourable terms for a UK entry to the EEC but failed. However, in 1972 The Treaty of Brussels was signed by which the UK accepted membership and the *European Communities Act 1972* was passed to implement the treaty.

On 1 January 1973 Britain together with the Republic of Ireland and Denmark entered the EEC. Greece joined on 1 January 1981. Spain and Portugal became members on 1 January 1986. Turkey now seeks membership.

The institutions of the EEC are as follows:

(a) The European Assembly or Parliament. This Chamber, unlike the UK parliament, is mainly a consultative forum and not a legislature. The Members of the European Parliament (or MEPs) are directly elected by the electorate of the country which they represent. In the UK, except in Northern Ireland, this takes place according to the usual first-past-the-post system but each European Parliamentary constituency exceeds the size of the UK Parliamentary constituencies. In Northern Ireland proportional representation is used. In the Assembly the representatives sit in party, rather than national groupings, and vote accordingly. Whilst the Council consults and ascertains the view of the Parliament on legislative proposals from the Commission the Assembly is in the end starved of power. It may veto the Budget proposals or vote by a two-thirds majority to remove the members of the Commission but it has little other control although questions may be raised in a similar session to Question Time.

(b) The Council of Ministers. This body is made up of one representative from each member state of the EEC. Usually the representative is the Foreign Minister but in meetings more closely concerning other departments of Government the representative may be a Minister from that department. Each of the Member States in rotation acts as President for a period of six months.

(c) The Commission. There are 17 members, one from each member state and a second member each for France, West Germany, Italy, UK and Spain. Members of the Commission are expected to act independently of the views of their home state and each member will be assigned a different area of responsibility. The Commission acts as a form of civil service in that it implements Community laws such as the competition rules in the Treaty of Rome. It also prepares the Community Budget and acts as a co-ordinator for the various community institutions. Finally the Commission makes proposals for community law and policy to the Council of Ministers which will then consult the Assembly before taking a decision to proceed.

(d) The European Council – This body is not recognised in any of the Treaties governing the Community. However, it is of considerable importance. Three times each year the Heads of Government of the EEC together with their Foreign Ministers meet. Decisions of paramount importance to the EEC are often made: e.g. it is at European Council meetings that the basis and size of contributions to the EEC and rebates have been decided.

(e) The European Court of Justice – There are 13 judges appointed by agreement between the member states' The court sits in Luxembourg and its proceedings are modelled on continental systems. Thus the litigation is conducted largely in writing and the proceedings are inquisitorial rather than adversarial. The Board of judges on any case gives one judgement and there is no provision for publication of a dissenting judgement. One of the most important of the functions of the court is to provide preliminary rulings under article 177 of the Treaty of Rome. In these cases a local court in a member state refers to the European court for clarification of the interpretation of community treaties and the validity of acts of the various community institutions.

A major disadvantage suffered by the European court is that it has no effective sanction against countries who choose not to implement its judgements. Thus in the 'Lamb War' France chose to ignore a ruling of the court that British sheep meat imports must be permitted.

15. *THE EUROPEAN CONVENTION ON HUMAN RIGHTS*

There are presently over 20 states which are members of the Council of Europe. This international organisation based in Strasbourg must not be confused with the 12-member, more highly organised and closely linked, European Economic Community (see section 14). The Council of Europe has the purpose of ensuring dialogue between the nations in Europe and minimum standards of human rights for the inhabitants of those states.

The European Convention on Human Rights was issued in November 1950 and has been added to by a number of subsequent protocols. An overwhelming majority of the members of the Council have ratified the convention although certain states have failed to approve the articles which permit individuals personally to bring a complaint and/or to accept the compulsory jurisdiction of the Court of Human Rights.

The Articles of the Convention, whilst binding in international law, are not automatically incorporated into the domestic law of the members of the Council (cf. the directly applicable parts of EEC law). Each individual state is left to judge how best the standards protected by the Convention can be enshrined in its domestic law. In countries such as the Federal Republic of Germany, with a written constitution, the terms of the Convention have been automatically incorporated into that constitution but in the UK no such incorporation has taken place although there are now calls for the European Convention to be used as the basis of a Bill of Rights to be incorporated into UK constitutional law (section 16).

The Convention is divided into Articles and these are of two sorts. There are first those Articles the purpose of which is to set out the basic human rights for protection and second those which provide a machinery for ascertaining whether there has been any breach of those rights.

The human rights covered in the Convention are those which are traditionally accepted as fundamental to a democratic State:

e.g.   Article 2   right to life (subject to certain exceptions).

Article 3   freedom from torture or inhuman or degrading treatment or punishment.

Article 5   right to liberty and security of person.

Article 6   rights to public and fair hearing etc.

Article 8   rights to respect for privacy, family etc.

Article 9   rights to freedom of thought, religion and conscience.

Article 10   rights to freedom of expression.

Article 11   rights to freedom of public assembly, association and to join trade unions.

Article 12   rights to marry and found a family.

First Protocol   rights to peaceful enjoyment of possessions, rights to education.

Fourth Protocol rights relating to freedom of movement within a state and from state to state.

More recently it has been suggested that rights to welfare benefits and other social and economic rights should be protected but this has not been done. Criticisms have also been levelled at the Convention on the grounds that-it is vague or out of date (for example how does the right to life apply to unborn babies? How can the right to join a trade union and the increasing use of the closed shop, which removes a man's freedom not to belong to one, be reconciled?)

The machinery for dealing with disputes provided by the Convention is as follows' The initial complaint that there has been a breach of the convention may usually be made either by an individual or another state but only after the domestic possibilities of redress have been exhausted. It is made to the Commission of Human Rights, which is staffed by one representative for each member state of the Council, who is required to act independently. The Commission decides whether a prima facie case of breach of one of the Articles is made out. If so, the complaint is reported to the state concerned and the Commission investigates and tries to reach a settlement. If this is impossible the case may be referred to the Court by another member state of the Council or by the Commission itself. Failing such a reference the case is dealt with by the Committee of Ministers by a two thirds majority. The court is staffed by one judge from each member state but only seven hear each case.

It is instructive to consider certain English cases in order to ascertain the effect of the European Convention on English law.

The European Convention on Human Rights is not part of English municipal law and cannot, therefore, be enforced directly in our domestic courts (see, for example, *Malone v Metropolitan Police Commissioner (1979) 2 All ER 620*). However, English courts do refer to the European Convention as an aid in interpreting English law (see, for example, *Waddington v Miah (1974) 2 All ER 377*: *R v Chief Immigration officer, ex parte Bibi (1976) 2 All ER 834*). As set out above provisions of the Convention are directly enforceable in the European Court of Human Rights in Strasbourg. In *Golders' Case (1975)*, for example, which concerned the right of a convicted prisoner in an English prison to have access to a lawyer for advice on a possible legal action against a prison officer, the European Court of Human Rights held unanimously that *Article 8* of the Convention, giving the right to respect for a person's private and family life, his home and correspondence, had been violated. More recently, in the *Sunday Times Thalidomide Case (1979)*, the European Court ruled by a narrow majority that English laws on contempt of court were incompatible with Article 10 of the Convention dealing with freedom of expression (contrast the earlier decision of the House of Lords in *Attorney-General v Times Newspapers Limited (1974) AC 273*). This decision of the European Court of Human Rights may have been influential in encouraging the House of Lords to take a narrower view of contempt of court in *AG v BBC (1980) 3 All ER 161* and it certainly influenced the drafting of the *Contempt of Court Act 1981*. The decision of the Court of Human Rights in the Malone case lent weight to public demands for a statute to regulate telephone tapping and the *Interception of Communications Act 1985* resulted.

16. DOES THE UK NEED A BILL OF RIGHTS?

Traditionally the view was taken that Britain required no Bill of Rights incorporated in a written constitution. This was because commentators considered that civil liberties were sufficiently protected by the common law developed in such cases as *Entick v Carrington (1765) St Tr. 1030.* Dicey certainly belonged to this school of thought. Recently there has been more debate and now there is a considerable body of opinion (including certain senior members of the judiciary such as Lords Scarman, Denning and Hailsham) which favours the introduction of a Bill of Rights setting out fundamental freedoms as a guarantee to the citizens of the UK. However there remain those who consider that the tradition of human rights in the Us sufficiently safeguarded for the future particularly in view of such recent watchdogs as the Council on Tribunals or the Ombudsman. The Bill of Rights' debate has been triggered by a number of factors including the civil unrest in Northern Ireland and Lord Scarman's 1974 Hamlyn lecture and kept alive by individual cases such as that of the Sunday Times or Mr. Malone. The discussion gave rise to a Select Committee Report in 1977 to 1978 and subsequently to the introduction of a Bill of Rights Bill by Lord Wade in the House of Lords in 1979 which, while passing all its stages in the House of Lords, never proceeded through the Commons and, therefore, never became law.

The difficulties of enactment of a Bill of Rights Bill include first the mechanics whereby such a Bill could be safeguarded against later repeal and second what fundamental rights and freedoms should be included in the Bill.

(a)   In most western democracies the Constitution, including a Bill of Rights, is written and is, in some way, entrenched. Some proponents of a Bill of Rights for the UK also believe that if the Bill is genuinely to prove a guarantee of fundamental rights entrenchment is required. However to do this would be introducing a new concept to the British constitution. Here constitutional laws are made in the same way as any other laws and the doctrine of Parliamentary Sovereignty specifies not only that Parliament may legislate on any subject but also that a later Parliament may repeal any legislation of any predecessor. Manifestly it can be argued that if entrenchment of a Bill of Rights were effective it would infringe all these principles and would amount to a revolution in constitutional thought.

Other supporters of a Bill of Rights believe that entrenchment is unnecessary and that it would be sufficient to adopt a wording similar to that in ss. 2(1) and 2(4) of the European Communities Act so as to state that the Bill of Rights overrode subsequent conflicting legislation unless the subsequent legislation made it expressly clear that a departure from the Bill of Rights was intended. However, there has been controversy over the effect of the sections in the European Communities Act and over the exact wording which would be needed.

If a Bill of Rights were adopted as an ordinary piece of legislation without entrenchment,it is argued by some that it would be worthless or at least devalued. However it is still strongly arguable that with a Bill of Rights on the statute book Governments would be wary of passing inconsistent legislation on the grounds that no party would wish to be seen to strike at human rights, for to do so would be likely to affect popular support at a subsequent General Election.

(b)   Whilst the European Convention on Human Rights is the document which many argue should be adopted for a British Bill of Rights (and is the only really serious possibility) others favour the United Nations' Charter and others again believe that certain provisions from the European Social Charter should also be included.

It has been pointed out (in the section on the European Convention) that this document is open to criticism as being outdated, very general in its terms and because it fails to protect the economic aspirations of the population. Some argue that to incorporate a Convention with such deficiencies into the domestic law would bring the law into disrepute by causing uncertainty and forcing the courts to make decisions of a more overtly political nature in deciding upon the validity of legislation.

In December 1983 leave was given to a private member under the Ten Minute Rule to introduce a *European Human Rights Convention Bill* supported by some MPs from all the political parties, but this attempt was unsuccessful. In late 1985 Lord Broxbourne introduced a Private Member's Bill in the Lords, the *Human Rights and Fundamental Freedoms Bill*, which passed all its stages in the Lords and on 19 June 1986 received a First Reading in the Commons. However, it failed because of lack of time for the other stages before the end of the session. In the 1986-37 Parliamentary session Sir Edward Gardner QC introduced a further Bill into the Commons but it failed at the Second Reading.

The political opposition to such reform means that the incorporation of the European Convention into domestic English law remains unlikely at the present time. In a letter to *The Times* on 5 June 1985 Lord Devlin lent his considerable authority to those opposing incorporation of the Convention and, in the same letters column, was supported by Mr CP Reed in the following terms:

> Lord Devlin once said that the British have no more wish to be governed by judges than they have to be judged by administrators. Yet government by judges is now taking place as a result of successful petitions to the European Court of Human Rights.

> The wide terms in which the European Convention is drafted means that the European judges must define the boundaries between conflicting rights. Inevitably they are faced with uncomfortably contentious policy choices. Those who argue for the incorporation of the European Convention into domestic English law are advocating the politicisation of our judiciary. If our citizens or residents dislike 'oppressive' or 'harsh' or 'inhumane' immigration laws they have many political means by which to protest against such laws, and a political forum (Parliament) in which to challenge and overturn such laws.

> However, if they lose in the political arena, they should not expect unrepresentative and unaccountable judges to act as a sort of court of appeal from Parliament. The fact that this expectation is now being realised through petitions to the European Court is no argument for transferring the powers of the latter to domestic English courts, since that would be to nationalise the evil rather than remove it.

Further reading

(i)   *General*

de Smith, *Constitutional and Administrative Law* (5th ed.), Chs.l-3, 5;
Wade and Bradley, *Constitutional and Administrative Law* (10th ed.), Chs.1-4,6, 8.

(ii)   *Bill of Rights*

Wade and Bradley, Ch.3l, pps 584-589;
de Smith, Ch.22, pps 457-461;
Constitutional Fundamentals, Wade, (Hamlyn Lecture 1980) pp 22 -40;
The Dilemma of Democracy, Lord Hailsham (1979);
Lord Fletcher Memorial Lecture, Lord Denning (1979), Law Society;
Oxford Essays in Jurisprudence, Heuston at pps 198 et seq;
Civil Liberties and a Bill of Rights, Wallington and McBride, (1976) at pps 11-41, 83-111;
English Law – The New Dimension, Lord Scarnan, (Hamlyn Lecture 1975), Sweet & Maxwell pps 9-21, 69-88;
Report of the Standing Advisory Committee on Human Rights, (Cmnd 7009,1977), pps 16-74;
Report of the House of Lords Select Committee on a Bill of Rights, (H.L. 176, 1977-78), pps 19-40;
The Political Constitution, Prof. J.A.G. Griffiths, (1979)42 MLR 1;
Lloyd (1976)38 MLR 121;
(1978)40 MLR 1; Jaconelli (1976) Public Law 226.

(iii)   *Conventions*

(1963) Public Law 401;
(1975) 91 LQR 218.

(iv)   *Rule of Law*

Essays in Constitutional Law, Heuston, ch.2;
Dahrendorf (1977) MLR 1;

for Trade Unions and the Rule of Law see:
The Discipline of the Law, Lord Denning (1978), Butterworths;
The Trojan Horse, John Burton, (1979), Adam Smith Institute.

(v)   *Separation of Powers*

Constitutional Theory, Marshall, (1971), ch.5;
Parliament and Congress, Bradshaw and Pring, (1972), Constable;
Government and Parliament, Herbert Morrison;
(1981) Public Law 105 (concerns the Separation of Powers in Nigeria).

(vi)   *European Convention on Human Rights*

1980 96 LQR pp 201-203;
1982 98 LQR p 183.

LLB

PARLIAMENTARY SOVEREIGNTY

LESSON 2 (STUDY)

21 *PARLIAMENTARY SOVEREIGNTY*

    21.1   HISTORY AND MEANING OF PARLIAMENTARY SOVEREIGNTY
    21.2   EFFECTS OF THE RULE

22. *SIGNIFICANCE AND VALIDITY OF ACTS OF PARLIAMENT*

    22.1   WHAT IS AN ACT OF PARLIAMENT?

23. *CAN PARLIAMENT BIND ITS SUCCESSORS AS TO THE SUBJECT MATTER OF LEGISLATION?*

    23.1   ACTS OF UNION
    23.2   THE STATUTE OF WESTMINSTER 1931 AND LATER INDEPENDENCE ACTS
    23.3   EUROPEAN COMMUNITIES ACT 1972

24. *CONCLUSION*

21. PARLIAMENTARY SOVEREIGNTY

21.1 History and meaning of Parliamentary sovereignty

What the parliament doeth, no power on earth can undo. Thus Blackstone summed up one of the fundamental doctrines of the British Constitution. Dicey considered the Rule of Law and the sovereignty of Parliament to be the twin pillars of the constitution. In a legal context the doctrine clearly asserts that there is no power in the state that can question the legality of an Act of Parliament. In this respect the UK is markedly different from most other countries where the supreme court of the state usually has power to pronounce on the constitutional validity of acts of the legislature and can, if necessary, declare them unconstitutional and void.

The traditional doctrine of Parliamentary sovereignty has a long history. When, during the reign of James I, the king wished to exercise the Royal Prerogative to legislate by means of proclamation, it was held by Coke, CJ, and his colleagues that no new offence could be created by proclamation where none had existed before, but that the King could issue a proclamation reminding his subjects of the existing law and that an offence would be more serious if committed after the issue of such a proclamation: *Case of Proclamations (1611) 12 Co. Rep 74.*

It was, at one time, established that the monarch had power to suspend and perhaps even to dispense with laws which had been duly enacted by Parliament. Thus in *Godden v Hales (1686) 11 St Tr 1165*, where the defendant, on accepting appointment as colonel of a regiment, had failed to take the oaths of allegiance and religious obedience required by statute, it was held that an action brought against him must fail as it was established that he had received a special dispensation from James II. However the *Bill of Rights of 1688* outlawed such suspending and dispensing powers and now the monarch retains only the prerogative right of pardon, a right which is clearly not inconsistent with parliamentary sovereignty. Note, however, that the right of pardon does not extend to civil actions.

Although the sovereignty of Parliament over the monarch was established by the end of the seventeenth century, the sovereignty of Parliament over the judiciary remained a matter for argument. In *Dr. Bonham's Case (1610) Co. Rep 118b* (for facts see Lesson 1) Coke had put forward the view that the court, as custodian of *common right and reason*, could declare void any Act of Parliament which did not accord with the precepts of such common right and reason. His statement was echoed by some later judges and found support in the argument propounded by Blackstone in the 18th century that there existed a *law of nature*, higher than any human laws, by which the validity of human laws must be tested. It must be emphasized, however, that although the idea of testing the validity of human law by reference to a higher and universal law of nature, or of reason, remained current for many years, there is no record of any judge attempting to strike down an Act of Parliament on this basis. Thus, Willes, J, in *Lee v Bude and Torrington Railway (1871) LR 6 CP 577:*

> If an Act of Parliament has been obtained improperly, it is for the legislature to correct it by repealing it; but so long as it exists as law the courts are bound to obey it. The proceedings here are judicial, not autocratic which they would be if we could make laws instead of administering them.

Willes, J, was in fact merely stating the traditional rule of law, if not of philosophy, by which judges had always operated.

21.2 *Effects of the rule*

It is thus clear that Parliament is sovereign over the monarch and the judiciary. The fact of Parliamentary sovereignty has a number of practical effects:

(a) *Parliament can legislate for any place or can change any law.* For example, by the *European Communities Act 1972* Parliament gave effect to British membership of the EEC; by *His Majesty's Declaration of Abdication Act 1936* Parliament altered the succession to the throne; and by the *Island of Rockall Act 1972* Parliament altered the territorial limits of the UK.

The *Canada Act 1982* 'patriated' the Canadian constitution – i.e. it terminated the power of the UK Parliament to make laws which extended to Canada.

Legislative power is thus apparently unlimited.

(b) *Parliament can repeal any statute.* Thus by the *Irish Free State Act 1922* the union between Great Britain and the whole of Ireland, established by the *Union with Ireland Act 1800*, was dissolved and by the *Northern Ireland Constitution Act 1973* and subsequently the *Northern Ireland Act 1974* the system of government of Northern Ireland set un in 1920 was radically altered. Similarly the *European Communities Act 1972* provides in *s.4* and Sch.3 & 4 for the repeal of much UK legislation consequent upon membership of the EEC.

(c) *Parliament can legislate to change its* own *procedure* or *composition.* Thus by the *Parliament Acts 1911 and 1949* the power of the House of Lords to withfold its assent to Public Bills was restricted, whilst by the *Peerage Act 1963* the composition of Parliament was changed in that it became possible for hereditary peers to disclaim their titles and thereby to lose the right to sit in the House of Lords.

(d) *Parliament can legislate retrospectively.* This is demonstrated by the *War Damage Act 1965* which retrospectively abolished the right to compensation of those whose property had been destroyed or damaged by acts of the Crown in time of war.

(e) *The courts can only interpret Acts of Parliament, they cannot question their validity.* In *Edinburgh and Dalkeith Railway v Wauchope (1842) 8 CL & F 710* Lord Campbell said:

All that a Court of Justice can do is to look to the parliament Roll: if from that it should appear that a Bill has passed both Houses and received the Royal Assent, no Court of Justice can enquire into the mode in which it was introduced into Parliament, nor into what was done previous to its introduction, or what passed in Parliament during its progress in its various stages through both Houses.

(f) *Parliament's power to legislate cannot be limited by international law.* The courts may not hold an Act void on the ground that it contravenes general principles of international law. Thus in *Mortensen v Peters (1906) 8f (3) 93* where an Act of Parliament had prohibited trawling in an area of the sea which lay beyond British territorial waters, the Act was held to be valid even though it might have been in contravention of rules of international law.

(g) *A later Act of Parliament can repeal the provisions of an earlier Act with which it is inconsistent.* This is known as the doctrine of implied repeal. The doctrine was explained by Lord Langdale in *Dean of Ely v Bliss (1842) 5 Beav 574* where he said:

If two inconsistent Acts be passed at different times, the last must be obeyed, and if obedience cannot be observed without derogating from the first, it is the first which must give way ... Every Act is made either for the purpose of making a change in the law, or for the purpose of better declaring the law, and its operation is not to be impeded by the mere fact that it is inconsistent with some previous enactment.

Thus in *Vauxhall Estates v Liverpool Corporation (1932) 1 KB 733* where the plaintiffs had claimed that compensation for land compulsorily acquired from them should be assessed on the basis of an Act passed in 1919 and not on the less favourable terms provided by an Act passed in 1925, it was held by the Divisional Court that the relevant provisions in the *Acquisition of Land (Assessment of Comgensation) Act 1919* must be regarded as impliedly repealed by the inconsistent provisions in the *Housing Act 1915* (see further on this point: *Ellen Street Estates v Minister of Health (1934) 1 KB 590).* (Note, however, the effect of the *European Communities Act 1972* on this doctrine. See page 2,302)

22. SIGNIFICANCE AND VALIDITY OF ACTS OF PARLIAMENT

22.1 What is an Act of Parliament?

It would not be true to say that Parliament is sovereign in everything it does. It is only sovereign when acting in a particular way prescribed by law. The legal rules governing the validity of an Act of Parliament are not themselves to be found in any statute; they are rules of common law. For a Bill to become law, it must follow the traditional procedure which has not altered since the time of Chief Justice Coke' He said (4 Inst 25).

> There is no Act of Parliament but must have the consent of the Lords, the Commons and the Royal Assent of the king, and as it appeareth by records and our books, whatsoever passeth in Parliament by this threefold consent, hath the force of an Act of Parliament.

The same is true today.

The rule laid down in *Edinburgh and Dalkeith Railway v Wauchope (supra)* that an Act of Parliament appearing on the Parliament Roll, nowadays simply an Act printed by the Stationery Office, cannot be challenged on the ground of procedural defects during its passage through Parliament, was reaffirmed by the House of Lords in 1974 in *Pickin v British Railways Board (1974) 1 All ER 609*. It was held in that case that it was not open to Mr. Pickin to argue that a private Act of Parliament was invalid because Parliament had been fraudulently misled by the British Railways Board in order that it should be passed. The clear words of Lord Morris show this strong principle has not been eroded in the 130 years since the *Wauchope* case. He said:

> It is the function of the courts to administer the laws which Parliament has enacted. In the processes of Parliament there will be just consideration whether a Bill should or should not in one form or another become an enactment. When an enactment is passed there is finality unless and until it is amended or repealed by Parliament. In the courts there may be argument as to the correct interpretation of the enactment: there must be none as to whether it should be on the Statute Book at all.

In reaching this conclusion the House of Lords unanimously reversed the decision of the Court of Appeal that the court might intervene where an Act of Parliament was shown to have been improperly obtained. In the Court of Appeal Lord Denning, MR, had said:

> Suppose the court were satisfied that this private Act was improperly obtained, it might well be the duty of the court to report that finding to parliament, so that Parliament itself could take cognizance of it, Parliament could put the matter right, if it thought fit, by passing another Act.

Thus, whilst Lord Denning was advocating a radical departure from the rule that the court should not investigate the proceedings of Parliament, he did not suggest that the court could itself declare an Act to be invalid but merely that the matter would be reported to Parliament, which could put the matter right, if it thought fit. To that extent, Parliamentary sovereignty emerges intact even from the Court of Appeal decision in Pickin.

However, although the validity of an Act of Parliament may not be questioned, it would seem possible to argue that an alleged Act is not an Act at all because it was not enacted by a properly constituted sovereign body. Thus if a purported statute had not had the threefold consent of Commons, Lords and Monarch declared necessary by Coke, it would not be a valid Act. Two colonial cases demonstrate the principle.

In AG for *New South Wales v Trethowan (1932) AC 526* the NSW legislature had enacted that the Upper House of the legislature could not be abolished by statute without a prior referendum. The requirement of a referendum could not itself be repealed except by the same process. However, a new government had attempted to abolish both the Upper House and the referendum provisions without holding a referendum on either issue. It was held by the Privy Council that the requirement of a referendum was binding on the legislature until it had been abolished by a law passed in the manner and form required, i.e. with the approval of a referendum. To put it another way, the referendum had been made part of the sovereign, part of the process of enactment for these purposes and so the sovereign body was not properly constituted unless a referendum was held.

Similarly in *Harris v Minister of the Interior (1952) TLR 1245* a statute passed by the two South African Houses of Parliament sitting separately was held to be invalid as the *South Africa Act 1909* provided that such a statute could only be enacted by a two-thirds majority of both Houses sitting together. The rules governing the composition of the sovereign body had not been observed and so the apparent statute was no statute at all.

In the UK nothing short of an Act of Parliament, enacted by the constituted sovereign body, can change the law. It was held in *Stockdale v Hansard (1839) 9 Ad & E1*, for instance, that a proclamation of the House of Commons could not render the publisher of Parliamentary papers immune from liability for libel. In giving judgement, Lord Denman, CJ, said:

> The supremacy of Parliament, the foundation on which the claim is made to rest, appears to me completely to overturn it, because the House of Commons is not the Parliament, but only a co-ordinate and component part of the Parliament. That sovereign body can make and unmake the laws; but the concurrence of the three legislative estates is necessary; the resolution of any one of them cannot alter the law.

The *Parliament Acts 1911* and *1949* provide that, in certain circumstances, public Acts may be passed by the Monarch and the House of Commons without the consent of the House of Lords. It may be questioned, therefore, whether Parliamentary sovereignty has ceased to rest in the triumvirate of Lords, Commons and Monarch. Is the sovereign body now composed merely of Commons and Monarch? The answer would seem to be *No*. The Parliament Acts merely provide a special procedure under which a special sort of delegated legislation may be enacted. Just as delegated powers to legislate are given to Government departments under various statutes, so under the Parliament Acts power is given to the Commons and Monarch to act alone in certain circumstances and provided certain specified procedures are followed. Again, under the *Regency Acts 1937-53* where a Regent is appointed if the Monarch is under 18 years of age, the Regent's assent to Bills creates another sort of delegated legislation. The identity of the sovereign body thus does not change although its powers may be delegated to other bodies.

23. CAN PARLIAMENT BIND ITS SUCCESSORS AS TO THE SUBJECT MATTER OF LEGISLATION?

23.1 *Acts of Union*

When Scotland joined with England to become Great Britain in 1707 the *Act of Union* made the following provision regarding Scottish law:

> The laws which concern public right, policy and civil government may be made the same throughout the whole United kingdom, but that no alteration be made in laws which concern private right except for evident utility of the subjects within Scotland.

The Act incorporated an Act for securing the Protestant religion and Presbyterian Church government in Scotland, which, it was said:

> shall be held and observed in all time coming as a fundamental and essential condition of any treaty or union to be concluded betwixt the two kingdoms.

The question therefore arises whether, by the *Act of Union*, the rules that Parliament cannot bind its successors and can repeal any statute were, in part, abrogated.

In *MacCormick v Lord Advocate (1953) SLT 255* the title of the Queen, Elizabeth II, was challenged on the ground that it contravened the *Act of Union*. It was held that the title had been adopted under powers conferred by the *Royal Titles Act 1953* and that the *Act of Union* did not forbid use of the numeral. But, in giving judgment, the Lord President, Lord Cooper said:

> The Treaty (of Union) and the associated legislation, by which the Parliament of Great Britain was brought into being as the successor of the separate Parliaments of Scotland and England, contain some clauses which expressly reserve to the Parliament of Great Britain powers of subsequent modification, and other clauses which either contain no such power or emphatically exclude subsequent alteration by declarations that the provision shall be fundamental and unalterable in all time coming.... I have not found in the Union legislation any provision that the Parliament of Great Britain should be 'absolutely sovereign' in the sense that Parliament should be free to alter the Treaty at will.

Thus Lord Cooper was clearly suggesting that Parliament was bound by certain clauses of the *Act of Union* and could not repeal or alter them.

The effect of Lord Cooper's opinion was reduced somewhat by his later admitting that *it is of little avail to ask whether the Parliament of Great Britain 'can' do this thing or that, without going on to enquire who can stop them if they do.* He agreed that perhaps no one could 'stop' them – short perhaps of Scottish resistance or the peaceable alternative of an *advisory opinion* of the International Court of Justice. However the tentative principle remains that some fundamental legislation may bind Parliament's successors and may not be open to repeal. In *Gibson v Lord Advocate (1975) SLT 134* the plaintiff argued that *s.2(1) European Communities Act 1972* was repugnant to the 1706 Treaty and therefore void on the ground that fishing regulations of the EEC would become a part of Scots law and that these permitted foreigners to fish in Scottish waters. This, it was argued, altered Scottish private law in a way which was not beneficial to Scottish citizens. The court decided that fishing regulations were a part of public law and that the Treaty was not therefore contravened. It reserved its opinion on what would have been the position had private law been involved.

It may be instructive to compare the attitudes taken to the Scottish Act of Union with those regarding the Act of Union with Ireland. The *Union with Ireland Act 1800* provided that the kingdoms and Parliaments of Great Britain and Ireland should be united 'for ever' as also should the Churches of England and Ireland. A little over half a century later the *Irish Church Act 1869* ended the union of the two churches and in 1922 the *Irish Free State (Constitution) Act* similarly dismantled the constitutional union. The 1869 Act was unsuccessfully challenged on the ground that it was contrary to the Act of Union, *ex p Selwyn (1872) 36JP54*, but no such argument was put forward regarding the 1922 Act. It is clear that the controversy which surrounded the passage of the two statutes was political rather than legal.

Thus far it can fairly be said that the question whether Parliament can bind its successors remains open. The issue arises not merely as regards Acts of Union, however. Two further situations must now be examined – the *Statute of Westminster 1931* and the *European Communities Act 1972*.

23.2 The Statute of Westminster 1931 and later Independence Acts

S.4 of the Statute of Westminster provides that no later statute should be deemed to extend to the Dominions, ie. Canada, Australia, New Zealand, the Irish Free State and Newfoundland, unless it was expressly stated in the Act in question that the Dominion had consented to its enactment. Had Parliament thus effectively limited its future right to legislate for the Dominions? In *British Coal Corporation v R (1935) AC 500* Lord Sankey LC answered the point succinctly: *Parliament could, as a matter of abstract law, repeal or disregard s.4 of the Statute (he said): But that is theory and Las no relation to realities.*

In the more recent case of *Blackburn v AG (1971) 1 WLR 1037* Lord Denning agreed:

> We have all been brought up to believe that, in legal theory, one parliament cannot bind another and that no Act is irreversible. But legal theory does not always march alongside political reality. Take the Statute of Westminister which takes away the power of Parliament to legislate for the Dominions. Can anyone imagine that Parliament could or would reverse that Statute: Take the Acts which have granted independence to the Dominions and territories overseas. Can anyone imagine that Parliament could or would reverse those laws and take away their independence: Most clearly not. Freedom once given cannot be taken away. Legal theory must give way to practical politics.

23.3 European Communities Act 1972

It has been said that the entry of the UK to the European Economic Community on 1 January 1973 resulted in a loss of the sovereignty of the UK Parliament. This statement has two aspects.

(a) It is argued that the effect of certain provisions of the European Communities Act 1972 is to undermine the doctrine of implied repeal. This needs further explanation. If Parliament may not bind its successors it follows that if Parliament passes an enactment which expressly repeals an earlier one the later statute is the one which will be enforced by the courts. If, however, a statute passed by Parliament is merely inconsistent with an earlier one (without expressly repealing it) the courts apply the doctrine of implied repeal and the later statute overrules the earlier. For example in *Vauxhall Estates v Liverpool Corporation* (the facts of which are set out in section 21.2(g) on page 2,102), the 1925 Act's provisions for compensation were preferred by the court to those of an Act of 1919.

Since 1972 the position has been less certain: *s.2(1) European Communities Act 1972* provides that certain provisions of the Treaties setting up the Community shall be directly applicable in the UK without the necessity for enactment by Parliament: *s.2(4)* of the Act has provided that legislation passed or to *be passed* shall be construed and have effect subject to *s.2(1)*. It is this that, it is argued, disrupts the doctrine of implied repeal and thus that of Parliamentary sovereignty.

The repeal of existing law which was inconsistent with EEC law on 1 January 1973 in no way affects the doctrine. However, the effect of the sections in relation to legislation enacted after that date which conflicts with EEC law has been a matter of debate. Some argued that in these circumstances the EEC law would prevail contrary to the doctrine of implied repeal. Lord Diplock has now made an *obiter dictum* in the House of Lords in the case of *Garland v British Rail Engineering Ltd. (1983) 2 AC 751* which was approved by the other Lords. He said that the question whether it was possible to imply an intention by Parliament that a post 1972 Act should operate in breach of an EEC treaty had yet to be decided and was open to argument. He also made it clear that he considered that Parliament could pass legislation inconsistent with EEC law with an express statement to that effect and it would be valid in the English courts.

In March 1987 in *Pickstone and Others v Freemans plc (1987) 3 All ER 356* the Court of Appeal considered the effect of European Community law on the *Equal Pay Act 1970* (as amended). It concluded that the wording of the Act was not ambiguous but that the changes made to the Act in 1982 had not been successful in harmonising UK law with EEC law. To achieve harmonisation the statute was read by the court as though extra words had been inserted by Parliament. However, the exact effect of this decision on what Lord Diplock said in *Garland's case* is not yet clear and leave was given to appeal to the Lords. The Lords heard the appeal in May 1988 but the result was not available for this edition.

In *Duke v G.E.C. Reliance Ltd (1988) Times 12 February 1988* the House of Lords decided that in construing UK Act of Parliament the circumstances at exactment had to be considered and that EEC Directives did not have to be followed in the course of interpretation of an Act's provision. Lord Templeman thought that Lord Diplock had been wrong in paying regard to an EEC Directive on *Equal Pay Act 1970* and *Sex Discrimination Act 1975* in *Garland v British Rail Engineering Ltd*. The treatment of regulations should be different in that these are directly effective whereas Directives are not.

(b)   Is the UK's entry to the EEC irrevocable?

In *Blackburn v AG* the plaintiff argued that Parliament was acting in breach of law in surrendering its sovereignty to the EEC. The Court of Appeal however, considered that the problem had not yet arisen. Said Lord Denning MR:

> What are the realities here: If Her Majesty's Ministers sign this treaty and Parliament enacts provisions to implement it, I do not envisage that parliament would afterwards go back on it and try to withdraw from it. But if Parliament should say so, then I say we will consider that event when it happens. We will then say whether Parliament can lawfully do it or not.

Thus it would seem that the question must remain open until and unless Parliament does decide to withdraw from the EEC.

In the Fletcher Lecture (December 1979) Lord Denning repeated a view which he asserted in *Macarthys Ltd v Smith (1979)*, namely, that if Parliament passed an Act withdrawing the U.K. from the E.E.C. (i.e. by repealing the 1972 Act) the court must and would give effect to such a repealing Act. This is because of another sort of political reality in such a situation, i.e. the power of an elected Parliament over an unelected judiciary.

Clearly Lord Diplock's statements in Garland's case uphold the view that withdrawal from the

EEC would be lawful and politicians negotiating entry seem to have envisaged that the step was revocable.

The Single European Act

On 1 July 1987 the *Single European Act* came into force. It is given effect in the UK by the *European Communities Amendment Act 1986.* The effect of the Act is that the EEC treaties are changed to allow for certain EEC legislation to be made in future by a qualified majority of the Member States, rather than unanimously as before. Under the voting system to be adopted legislation will have to be passed by 54 out of the total 76 votes and, since the UK is allocated only 10 votes, it can no longer veto legislative changes. This, of course, weakens the sovereignty of the UK but its exact effect in practice will only be revealed over the next few years. It is still true that unanimity is required where matters of national interest such as tax and social security are the subject matter of EEC legislation.

24. *CONCLUSION*

It is noticeable in each of the three situations which have been examined *Acts of Union, the Statute of Westminster*, and the *European Communities Act*, that the legal theory that Parliament cannot bind its successors may sometimes bow before other considerations. As Lord Denning, MR, said in *Blackburn v AG: legal theory must give way to practical politics*. Thus it would seem that Parliament is bound to abide by the *Statute of Westminster* and certain provisions of the *Act of Union with Scotland* because of the political consequences of any attempted repeal.

Even if it is admitted that political exigency is the true guiding factor, the doctrine of Parliamentary sovereignty is not necessarily thereby weakened. It has often been said that since Parliament is ultimately answerable to the people at election, sovereignty of Parliament is, in truth, sovereignty of the people. Since the courts do not admit to the power to strike down Acts of Parliament as being unconstitutional, the guardians of sovereignty must be the electorate. Lord Cooper in *MacCormick* remarked that the question was not what Parliament can do, but rather who can stop them. He suggested that the people could act as a brake on Parliamentary action. It must thus be admitted that the legal principle of Parliamentary sovereignty is based firmly upon political foundations; and that the true holders of sovereignty are also its guardians.

Further reading

Wade and Bradley, ch.5;
de Smith, ch. 4;
Heuston, *Essays in Constitutional Law*, (1964);
Marshall, ch.3;
Wade (1955) Camb. L.J. 172;
Fazal (1974) Public Law 295;
Mitchell (1963) 79 LQR 196;
Dike (1977) Public Law 283;
Winterton (1976) 92 LQR 591;
Trinidade (1972) MLR 375;
Mirfield (1979) 95 LQR 36;
Winterton (1979) 95 LQR 386;
Jacobs (1974) 90 LQR 486;
Freestone (1979) 42 MLR 220;
O. Hood Phillips (1979) 95 LQR 167;
O. Hood Phillips (1980) 96 LQR 33;
Ellis (1980) 96 LQR 511;
O. Hood Phillips (1982) 98 LQR 524;
Winterton (1981) 97 LQR 265.

LLB

PARLIAMENT AND PARLIAMENTARY PRIVILEGE

LESSON 3 (STUDY)

31. *PARLIAMENT*

31.1 *Parliament – Introduction*

It would be incorrect to regard Parliament as purely, or indeed primarily, a law-making body. It has also been called a *deliberative assembly for the redress of grievances* (Paul Johnson). Its original function was as a place of debate – a council summoned by the monarch for the discussion of important issues. Today, debate in Parliament, especially debate about proposed legislation, remains of paramount importance. It is the means by which the legislature can provide a check on executive action. Parliament may lack the ability to reach an independent decision on the legislative and other proposals brought before it, but it is the place where ministers,as the representatives of the Executive, can be made to account for what the Executive has done or proposes to do. In other words, the checking function is not one of mandatory controls, but of requiring explanation. It is said that the more a person has to explain his actions and ideas, the more deeply their merits and implications are probed and examined, the more likely is the resulting policy or action to be acceptable and efficacious.

Thus Parliament may be said to have three main functions: first, as a legislative body; secondly, as a debating chamber; and thirdly, as a court. The House of Lords remains the highest appellate court in the land for both civil and criminal cases, and both Lords and Commons have judicial functions in the sphere of parliamentary privilege (see sections 35 to 38)) and in committees dealing with private Bills.

32. COMPOSITION OF PARLIAMENT

32.1 House of Commons – Electoral Laws

The House of Commons is a representative assembly. It dates from the 13th century. The methods of providing representatives to sit in the House have altered considerably since its foundation.

32.2 Electors

By the *Representation of the People Act 1832 (the Reform Act)* the franchise was extended by means of property qualifications from the landed gentry to the middle classes. The growth in importance and influence of the House of Commons dates from this statute. The Reform Acts in 1867 and 1884 further widened the franchise and the Act of 1918 introduced adult male suffrage (without any property qualifications) and votes for women over the age of 30 whose husbands were qualified to vote in local government elections. In 1928 the vote was given to women over 21. In 1970 the law was changed by the *Family Law Reform Act 1969* so as to reduce the qualifying age of voters to 18.

Qualifications for the franchise are now as laid down in *the Representation of the People Acts 1983 & 1985*. Thus, in order to qualify as a parliamentary elector, a person must:

(a)   be 18 years of age on the date of the poll;

(b)   be a British subject (i.e. a citizen of the UK and Colonies or of any Commonwealth country) or a citizen of the Republic of Ireland;

(c)   not be subject to any legal incapacity (those incapacitated include aliens, persons under 18, peers and peeresses in their own right, convicted persons serving sentence in a penal institution, persons lacking the capacity to vote by reason of mental illness, subnormality, drunkenness or infirmity, and, in some circumstances, those convicted of corrupt or illegal practices at elections); and

(d)   be resident in the constituency on the qualifying date (10 October) or qualify as an overseas elector.

This last qualification has been the cause of some doubt. In *Fox v Stirk (1970) 2QB 463* it was held by the Court of Appeal that university students were resident at their hall of residence or college on October 10 and were thus entitled to register for those constituencies. The dictionary definition of residence, as requiring a degree of permanence, was used. It was said that students at their university address displayed a considerable degree of permanence. In May 1985 the Court of Appeal accepted that women encamped in tents at the gates of Greenham Common Cruise Missile Site were resident and thus entitled to be placed on the Electoral Register for the constituency. A person does not cease to be resident at his usual address by reason of temporary absence due to illness, holidays or business duties. The *Representation of the People Act 1985* reformed electoral law by extending the categories of those entitled to vote to overseas electors. They are British citizens under no legal incapacity who are not resident in the UK on the qualifying date, but who make a declaration that they intend to return to the UK, provided that they were resident in a UK constituency within the last five years.

It also provided for absent voters to vote by post or by proxy. Absent voters are those registered as service voters, those who cannot reasonably be expected to get to the polling station or vote unaided such as the blind or those with other physical handicaps, those who cannot reasonably be expected to get to the polls because of their own or their spouse's service or employment, those who can only reach their polling station by sea or air travel and overseas electors.

32.3 *Constituencies*

It was said by the *Committee on Electoral Machinery* (Cmnd 6408, 1942-3):

> The essential basis of representative Government in this country is that the main representative body of the legislature should consist of persons elected under conditions which confer on them an equal representative status. It is also a fundamental principle of our Parliamentary system that representation should be territorial.

By the *House of Commons (Redistribution of Seats) Acts 1949 to 1979* there are four permanent and independent Boundary Commissions for England, Scotland, Wales and Northern Ireland. Each commission has the task of reviewing the constituencies in that part of the UK with which it is concerned and of submitting reports to the Home Secretary, at intervals of not less than 10 or more than 15 years, proposing any necessary redistribution of seats. Changes in particular constituencies may be proposed from time to time according to need.

Appropriate sizes for constituencies in each part of the UK are laid down by statute and each commission must, so far as is practicable, ensure that constituencies are of the appropriate size. Reports from the Boundary Commissions must be laid before Parliament *as soon as may be (s.2(5) 1949 Act)*, together with a draft Order in Council giving effect, with or without modifications, to their recommendations. The draft Order must be approved by resolution of each House before the final Order is made by the Queen in Council.

General boundary reviews were made by the Commissions in 1954, 1969 and 1983. All proved controversial. The recommendations in the 1954 review that various constituencies should be abolished and others created in England resulted in the Commission's report being challenged in the courts. In *Harper v Home Secretary (1955) Ch 238* the mayor and a councillor in Manchester argued that the Boundary Commission had not abided by the statutory rules in drawing up their report. However, Evershed, MR, concluded it was clearly intended within the Act that:

> in so far as the matter was not within the discretion of the Commission, it was certainly to be a matter for Parliament to determine. I find it impossible to suppose that Parliament contemplated that, on any of these occasions when reports were presented, it would be competent for the courts to determine and pronounce on whether a particular line which had commended itself to the Commission was one which the court thought the best line or the right line – whether one thing rather than another was to be regarded as practicable and so on.

It should be noted, however, that the court was not here faced with a report drawn up in manifest disregard of the Act, but rather with one that arguably contained slight irregularities. Evershed, MR, admitted that the result might well be different where disregard was manifest. In *London Borough of Enfield v Local Government Boundary Commission for England (1979) 3 All ER 747* the House

of Lords upheld the decision of the Local Government Boundary Commission to give Enfield 66 councillors (in 35 wards) instead of 70 councillors (in 34 wards) as desired by the London Borough. The decision was based on the interpretation of the *Local Government Act 1972*.

The principle of out-of-date constituency boundaries was referred to by Mr Brittan in the 1979-83 Parliament:

> We are all too familiar with the scandal of the tiny constituencies in the heart of many of our great cities which boast more lamp-posts than electors ... the new boundaries will make

it certain that a vote cast in Bromsgrove is no longer worth a quarter of one in Newcastle, and that a vote in Suffolk is no longer worth a third of one in Salford.

In *R v Boundary Commission, ex p Foot (1983) 1 All ER 1099 & 1199* leading Labour politicians, including the party's leader, attempted to challenge the recommendations of the Boundary Commission on the grounds that they had placed too much emphasis on preventing the newly-recommended constituencies from crossing local boundaries and too little importance had been given to ensuring that the electorate in each constituency approached the electoral quota. However, in his judgment Donaldson MR in the Court of Appeal made the point that electoral equality was only one factor the Commission had to consider. It must also have regard, under the guidelines laid down by Parliament, to local boundary and other geographical considerations. Furthermore, it was in practice difficult for one challenging the Commission's recommendations to discharge the heavy burden of showing that the Commission had exercised its powers wrongly or improperly because the rules laid down by Parliament were really guidelines only, the Commission was required to give no reasons for its decisions and it could decide what was practicable. Despite the statistics in this case showing discrepancies of up to 48,000 voters between the largest and smallest revised constituencies, the Commission's recommendations could not be classified as unreasonable. The House of Lords subsequently refused leave to appeal to the Lords. The General Election of 1983 was held upon these freshly revised boundaries.

32.4 *Candidates*

The categories of those disqualified from sitting in the House of Commons are similar to, but more comprehensive than those of persons disqualified from the franchise:

(a) aliens;

(b) persons under 21 years of age;

(c) peers and peeresses in their own right;

(d) mental patients: *s.141 Mental Health Act 1983;*

(e) ordained clergy of the Church of England and Church of Ireland ministers of the Church of Scotland and priests of the Roman Catholic Church;

(f) persons guilty of corrupt practices under the *Representation of the People Act 1983;*

(g) prisoners serving a sentence of more than one year's imprisonment or detention, or unlawfully at large from such a sentence: *Representation of the People Act 1981;*

(h) bankrupts (whilst undischarged and for five years after discharge, unless discharge was accompanied by a certificate that the bankruptcy had not been caused by the bankrupt's misconduct);

(i) persons disqualified under the *House of Commons Disqualification Act 1975* (see *Schedule 1* to the Act – persons include judges (but not lay magistrates), civil servants, members of the regular armed forces and police force, and members of legislatures of non-Commonwealth countries).

It is finally also provided that no more than 95 holders of ministerial office may sit and vote in the House of Commons. This rule is intended to limit the Prime Minister's powers of patronage.

Anyone who does not come within the categories of disqualification may stand for Parliament. There is no limit to the number of candidates in each constituency, although each must give a deposit of £500 to the returning officer and will lose the deposit if he fails to poll at least one-twentieth of the total number of votes cast: *Representation of the People Act 1985*. He must also submit a nomination paper to the returning officer, which form must be signed by a proposer and seconder and eight other electors.

32.5 The election campaign

A candidate at a Parliamentary election is required to have an election agent, though he himself may be his own agent. Election expenses must be paid through the election agent and must be declared and published. The amount of expenditure which may be incurred and the ways in which it is incurred are both stringently controlled in order to prevent bribery and undue influence. However, whilst expenditure in *each* constituency is limited, national expenditure by political parties and interested groups, both before and during elections, is not. It was held in *R v Tronoh Mines Ltd (1952) (1 All ER 697)* that national advertising in support of one political party generally in all constituencies was permissible, provided it did not support a particular candidate in a particular constituency. McNair J added that the section of the *Representation of the People Act 1949* in question (s.63 (now *s.75 Representation of the People Act 1983)*) stated:

> does not prohibit expenditure, the real purpose or effect of which is general political propaganda, even although that general political propaganda does incidentally assist a particular candidate among others.

In the later case of *DPP v Luft (1976) 2 All ER 569* literature had been distributed in three constituencies by an anti-fascist group, urging voters not to vote for the National Front candidate. When members of the group were prosecuted under *s.63*, the House of Lords held that they had been acting in breach of the section as they had intended to prevent the election of a particular candidate, even though they had not acted to secure election of any other specific candidate.

Party political broadcasts on radio and television have been held to be intended to transmit information to the public, rather than to procure anyone's election. Thus, in *Grieve v Douglas-Home (1965) SLT 186* it was said that such broadcasts did not form part of Sir Alec Douglas-Home's election expenses as being intended to procure his election. The distribution of broadcasts as between the various parties is settled by agreement between the major parties and the broadcasting authorities. In the 1983 election campaign agreement could not be reached between the parties and the broadcasting authorities made their own allocation. Political advertising is banned on ITV and on commercial radio stations: *para.8 Sch.3 Broadcasting Act 1981*.

Voting in an election is by secret ballot (1983 Act) and a description of the candidate, not exceeding six words, generally giving the name of his political party, is permitted on the ballot paper: *Schedule I, Rule 6 Representation of the People Act 1983*. Each elector may vote only for one candidate and the successful candidate is the one receiving the highest number of votes, known as the *first-past-the-post* system.

32.6 Disputed elections

The procedure in cases of disputed elections is regulated by *Part III Representation of the People Act 1983*. An elector' a candidate or a person nominated by the candidate may present an election petition within 21 days of the election complaining of, for example, improper conduct or expenditure or that the successful candidate is disqualified as a member of the House of Commons. The petition is heard by an election court, consisting of two judges of the Queen's Bench Division, sitting without a jury. The court may sit in the constituency concerned and has wide-ranging powers, including power to hold the election void, power to hold the person elected to be disqualified, and, in some cases, to hold the person with the next highest number of votes elected in his stead. Appeal on a point of law lies with leave of the High Court to the Court of Appeal. The decision of the Court of Appeal is final. See further: *Re parliamentary Election for Bristol South East (1964). 2QB 257*

32.7 *The party system*

The two major parties in Great Britain are the Conservatives (in office since 1979) and the Labour party. Until 1988 when fusion of part of the Liberal party and Social Democratic Party took place the other two main parties were the Liberals and Social Democratic Party (SDP). The Liberal and SDP parties formed an 'Alliance' in the early 1980's because voters for both of these parties were drawn from the middle ground of the political spectrum and, if the parties were to compete electorally, both might be annihilated. The SDP was the newest party with the fewest MPs and its founders, the 'Gang of Four' were all former Labour Party Cabinet Ministers who could not reconcile their views with the more left-wing stance taken by the Labour Party after the 1979 General Election. Only one of them, Rt Hon David Owen MP, remains an MP.

After the June 1987 election Rt Hon David Steel MP by remarks he made during interviews triggered discussion of the fusion of the Liberal and SDP parties. After considerable wrangles between the two parties and a split between the pro-merger SDP members led by Mrs Shirley Williams and the anti-merger faction led by Rt Hon David Owen MP a new fused party the Social and Liberal Democrats (SLD), emerged and a leadership election takes place in summer 1988. Rt Hon David Steel MP will not be seeking election as leader, although he headed the Liberal party, remains in the Commons. It is likely that the SLD and SDP will face electoral setbacks as a result of the splits and demice of the Alliance.

In order to have a realistic chance of success in an election, a candidate needs to be a member of one of the nationally organised parties. Those who stand for election as independents are rarely successful and if successful at one election almost invariably lose their seats at a subsequent one.

An understanding of the party system is central to an understanding of the functioning of the House of Commons. Generally speaking all the members of a particular political party vote together and the Whip system is intended to ensure party discipline. Furthermore, since the mid-1960s, it has been accepted that the leader of the Conservative or Labour party in the Commons automatically becomes Prime Minister when an election returns a majority of members from his party.

32.8 *Suggestions for electoral reform*

There have been increasing calls for major reforms of principle in the electoral system. The present 'first-past-the-post' system has been widely criticised for the following reasons:

(a) it is possible for a government to have won a majority of seats without receiving a majority of the votes cast, and without the support of a majority of the electorate (see the 1983 and 1987 results below). Indeed, in February 1974 the Labour Party took office having polled fewer votes nationally than the Conservative Party;

(b) traditionally many constituencies are safe Labour or safe Conservative seats. In a safe Labour seat the Conservatives may poll very few votes and *vice versa*. There are a few marginal seats on which the outcome of an election depends and the votes of those living in these seats can, therefore, carry disproportionate weight;

(c) the national polling figures for the 1983 General Election and the table of seats won, show clearly how the 'first-past-the-post' system operates unfairly against the smaller parties:

Party	National poll figures	Seats in the House of Commons
Conservative	13,012,602	396
Labour	8,457,124	207
SDP/Liberal Alliance	7,780,577	23
Others	1,420,592	21

Although there is less than a one million difference between the votes cast for Labour and for the SDP/Liberal Alliance, the latter party won only a fraction of the seats because their nationwide support was more evenly spread and they came second to both Labour and Conservative candidates.

The election results for June 1987 tended to demonstrate again these defects as can be seen from the following table showing the votes cast for each party and the number of seats obtained in Great Britain (excluding Northern Ireland):

Party	No. of votes	Seats in the House of Commons
Conservative	13,738,899	375
Labour	10,033,633	229
SDP/Liberal Alliance	7,339,912	22
Others (various)		6

It should, however, be noted that the SDP/Liberal Alliance share of the vote has decreased;

(d) the June 1987 election results analysed in more detail show that increasingly the Conservative Party can be criticised as being the English party whereas the Labour Party has very strong support in Wales and Scotland:

Country	Conservative votes	Labour votes	SDP/Liberal Alliance votes
England	12,524,098	8,010,189	6,465,611
Scotland	713,499	1,258,177	570,043
Wales	501,302	765,267	304,258

In order to overcome these problems a number of alternative systems have been suggested:

(i) *Alternative vote*

Suitable for single member constituencies where there are more than two candidates. The voter marks in order of preference on the ballot paper. If no candidate obtains more than 50% of the vote, the candidate at the bottom of the poll is eliminated and his second preference votes redistributed and so on until one candidate exceeds 50% of the vote.

(ii) *Single transferable vote*

Suitable for multi-member constituencies where the voter marks his preferences numerically against the candidates' names. When one candidate obtains a large enough percentage of the poll to ensure he is elected his second preferences are re-distributed until a second candidate reaches the quota and so on until all the seats are filled.

(iii)   *Party list*

Each party has a national list of candidates. A voter has a single vote for a party and the percentage of the vote for each party nationally is calculated. Each party then fills the appropriate number of seats working from the top of its list downwards.

The main objection put forward to the above systems is that they would cause instability by necessitating coalition governments which would be constantly compromising to retain power.

It is unlikely that electoral reform will be introduced in the near future because this would be against the vested interests of the Conservative and Labour parties.

32.9   *House of Lords*

(a)   *Membership*

The House of Lords is not a representative assembly. It consists of 26 Lords Spiritual and over 1,000 Lords Temporal.

(i)   *The Lords Spiritual*

These are the Archbishops of Canterbury and York, the Bishops of London, Durham and Winchester, and twenty-one other bishops of the Church of England in order of seniority of appointment. These Lords cease to sit upon their retirements as Bishops and do not take a party political line.

(ii)   *The Lords Temporal*

(1)   *Hereditary peers*

Hereditary peers may be created by the Queen on the advice of the Prime Minister. Hereditary peers may be dukes, marquesses, earls, viscounts or barons. By *s.6 Peerage Act 1963* hereditary peeresses may sit and vote in the House of Lords (see the earlier decision in *Viscountess Rhondda's Claim (1922) 2 AC 339* which was overturned by this Act). From 1964 to 1983 no new hereditary peers were created and it was thought this would become the pattern for the future. However, in 1983 two new hereditary peerages were granted to men without heirs and in 1984 the former Prime Minister, Harold MacMillan was given an hereditary peerage. His grandson succeeded him as Lord Stockton in 1986.

No new *Scottish peerage* has been created since the Union of 1707. All surviving Scottish peers were, by *s.4 Peerage Act 1963*, admitted to the Lords. The Act of Union with Ireland in 1800 had provided that *Irish peers* should elect twenty-eight of their number to represent them in the Lords for life. The last surviving elected peer died in 1961 and it was held in the *Earl of Antrim's Petition (1967) 1 AC 691* that the right to elect Irish peers no longer existed since the whole of Ireland ceased to exist as a political entity in 1922.

By *s.1 Peerage Act 1963* the holder of an hereditary peerage may disclaim his peerage for his life. Disclaimer must take place, within one year of succession to the title or, if under age on succession within one year of attaining majority. By *s.2*, however, members of the House of Commons have only one month from succession or election to disclaim. Disclaimer is irrevocable. It does not affect any rights of property and does not affect succession on death.

(2) *Life peers*

The *Life Peerages Act 1958* enables the Queen to confer a peerage for life upon a man or woman. The object of the Act was to secure for the House of Lords the experience of distinguished men and women from many walks of life.

The eleven *Lords of Appeal in Ordinary*, the Law Lords, are appointed for life and retain the power to sit and vote even if they resign their judicial appointment. They must either have held high judicial office in the UK for two years or have practised at the Bar for fifteen years in order to be eligible for appointment. They do not take a party political line.

(b) *The Party system in the Lords*

Although many members of the Lords are members of the four main political parties, the Lords also has cross benchers. These are unknown in the Commons and are peers who have no political affiliation. They are called cross benchers because in the rectangular Chamber they sit at right angles between the Government and Opposition members who occupy benches along the length of the Chamber. They vote with or against the Government according to their conscience on each issue. Their role is an important one since they can perhaps provide more objective expertise and perhaps their presence helps to lend the House of Lords a less hectic and partisan atmosphere which enables it to examine Bills dispassionately, initiate non-controversial legislation, etc.

(c) *The functions of the Lords*

(i) Its most important function is as a part of the legislative process. It allows for prolonged and full debate of legislative proposals (e.g. 610 amendments were made in the Lords to the *Local Government Bill 1972*).

(ii) It provides a forum for debate on matters of public interest.

(iii) Less controversial but nevertheless important Public Bills may be initiated in the Lords (e.g. *Courts Act 1971*).

(iv) Consideration of subordinate legislation.

(v) Scrutiny of activities of the Executive.

(vi) Scrutiny of private legislation.

(vii) Appellate functions.

(viii) As a constitutional safeguard – the life of Parliament cannot be extended beyond five years without its consent.

(d) *Conflicts between the Lords and Commons*

In the early years of this century there was considerable conflict between the Conservative controlled Lords and the new Liberal Government. The Lords rejected a number of Government measures which had been approved by the Commons in 1909 and refused to pass the *Finance Bill* based on Lloyd George's budget to the Commons. Such a refusal was a breach of convention because it was recognised that the representative assembly, the Commons, should overrule the Lords on matters of taxation and gave rise to a constitutional crisis. In 1910 there were two general elections and after the second the Liberal Government made it known that the King was prepared to create four hundred new Liberal peers in order to end the constitutional crisis. This threat did not need to be carried out; instead, the *Parliament Act 1911* was passed. This Act removed the Lords' power of veto of money Bills and permitted a delay of two years only in the case of other *public* Bills: *s.2*. The period of permitted delay was reduced to one year in the *Parliament Act 1949*. It is essential to note, however, that the Parliament Acts have made no difference to the procedure for passing a private Bill, which *always* requires the consent of both Houses of Parliament. Additionally, a constitutional safeguard was written into the Act providing that only if the consent of the Lords was obtained could a Bill to prolong the life of Parliament beyond five years (a Public Bill, of course) be passed.

(e) *Proposals for reform*

In the *Parliament Act 1911* the preamble envisaged that, in due course, the House of Lords would be reformed so that it no longer reflected the hereditary principle. Agitation for reform has continued since. The main reasons for which it is felt reform is needed are:

(i) the majority of peers owe their seats to their succession to a hereditary peerage, they represent no constituency and have not qualified by personal merit to have a seat (cf life peers). This is outdated;

(ii) there is a constant in-built Conservative majority in the Lords which could, in theory, cause a Labour Government difficulties in effecting its legislative programme. Practically speaking, this rarely happens because the Lords fear abolition and are not therefore obstructive to Labour Governments. Indeed, the Lords may prove more obstructive to a Conservative Government's legislative programme since the Conservatives are unlikely to seek abolition. Examples in the present Parliament are the changes forced by the Lords in the *Local Government (Interim Provisions) Act 1984* to retain the elected GLC councillors between May 1985, (when their mandate expired) and May 1986, the date of abolition of the GLC and the alterations to the *Police and Criminal Evidence Bill 1984* making racial discrimination by the police a disciplinary offence. In 1988 the Lords are proving obstructive to the Government by rejecting provisions in an Education Bill and by threatening amendments to the 'community charge' legislation to replace the rating system.

(iii) many peers are not regular attenders in the House and are known as backwoodsmen but may be canvassed to attend and vote on controversial debates without the necessary information to make an informed decision.

In May 1988 the Conservative whips in the House of Lords contacted many backwoodsmen to attend when the Lords in Committee were considering the Local Government Finance Bill 1988 to introduce the community charge. The amendments being considered were to link the charge to the ability to pay and were defeated. The turnout in the Lords of some 500 peers was the second highest in 150 years and the opposition were highly critical of the Government's tactics.

There have been a number of proposals for reform. The Labour Government's *Parliament (No.2) Bill 1968* put forward a comprehensive plan for reform. Briefly, there was to be a two-tier system of voting and non-voting members. Voting members would be life peers and first holders of hereditary peerages. Additionally a voting member would have to be aged under 72, and attending at least one-third of the House's sittings. Non-voting members would be peers either over the age of 72 or those who could not attend the House regularly, together with all hereditary peers alive at enactment who wished to be non-voting members. New life peers would be created at the start of each new Parliament to ensure that the Government party had sufficient strength in the Lords. The Bill did not become law because of a rebellion by backbench MP's on both sides of the House.

Others would advocate more radical reform by, for example, replacing the present Chamber by one which was popularly elected perhaps on a regional basis or by proportional representation. However, the effect of such an action would be that the *Parliament Acts 1911 and 1949* would no longer be appropriate to regulate conflicts between the Lords and Commons and a new basis of cooperation would have to be reached. This might only be possible as part of a wider constitutional reform.

Finally, there are the abolitionists who believe that no second chamber is required. However, abolition would lead to the Commons, already overburdened, being forced to take on extra work, thus lowering the standard of, for example, legislation.

33. OFFICERS OF THE HOUSE OF COMMONS AND HOUSE OF LORDS

33.1 House of Commons

(a) Speaker

The Speaker is elected by the Commons from their own number at the beginning of each new Parliament. The Speaker of the previous Parliament is usually re-elected, if he is still a member and is willing to stand. Election is normally unanimous. The Speaker presides over the House, except when it is in Committee. He does not take part in debate and does not vote unless there is a tie, when the way in which he votes is set out by precedent. He rules on procedure and keeps discipline. His traditional role is as spokesman for the Commons to the Lords and to the monarch. On election as Speaker he detaches himself from his party affiliations and if he contests his seat at later elections he stands as an Independent and the two main parties will not usually oppose him.

The role of Speaker has been criticised because, it is said, his traditional impartiality effectively disenfranchises the electors in his constituency since their MP does not follow a party line and cannot ask a Parliamentary question. However, the Speaker may privately take up a constituent's grievance with a Minister and the traditional respect for the office may ensure that its holder is expeditiously answered on such occasions.

(b) The Chairman of Ways and Means

The Chairman of Ways and Means is a member elected by the House at the beginning of each Parliament to preside over committees of the whole House. He acts as deputy Speaker and when in the Chair acts impartially. However, he does not, at other times, resign his political affiliations.

(c) The Serjeant-at-Arms

The Serjeant-at-Arms is appointed by the Crown to carry out directions for maintaining order in the House and to execute warrants and carry out arrests.

(d) Government and Opposition Whips

The Whips have the duty to see that their parties are at full voting strength for important divisions (i.e. votes) of the Commons and they inform party members of the party line which is to be taken on a vote. They also keep leaders informed of feeling among backbench MP's.

33.2 House of Lords

(a) The Lord Chancellor

The Lord Chancellor is Speaker of the Lords, head of the judiciary and principal legal and constitutional advisor to the Government. The Lord Chancellor is a minister of the Crown and his appointment is a political one. Thus, he has less power as Speaker than the Speaker of the House of Commons and is not expected to be impartial He votes on a division and has no casting vote.

(b) Chairman of Committees

The Chairman of Committees acts as deputy Speaker of the House and takes the Chair when the House is in committee.

(c)   *Gentleman Usher of the Black Rod*

The Gentleman Usher of the Black Rod executes warrants of the House and summons the attendance of the Commons where necessary.

34. THE FUNCTION AND POWERS OF PARLIAMENT

34.1 Frequency of Meeting and Duration

Under the *Meeting of Parliament Act 1694* not more than three years must elapse between the dissolution of one Parliament and the meeting of its successor. By convention, Parliament must be summoned each year. Most taxes and grants of supply to the Crown are provided annually by Parliament, and the maintenance of the army and air force requires annual renewal. The two Houses of Parliament meet quite separately. A bill may be introduced in either House unless it is one authorising taxation or expenditure when it must be introduced into the Commons by a minister. Where private members' bills require public expenditure a minister must be persuaded to move a financial resolution in the House, otherwise the bill cannot be passed.

The *Parliament Act 1911* has enacted that the life of a Parliament shall not extend beyond five years, but Parliament may prolong its own life by another Act passed in the usual manner. The 1935 Parliament was extended until 1945 during the Second World War. Parliament may be dissolved before the five year term ends by exercise of the royal prerogative on the recommendation of the Prime Minister. The life of Parliament is divided into sessions - ~ usually of one year's duration, e.g. November to October. If adjournment for weekends and holidays, and the summer recess are taken into account, the Commons sits for 160 days. A session ends by prorogation – a short speech read on behalf of the Queen summing up the session's work. A new session is opened by the Queen in person.

34.2 Sources of procedure in the Commons

There are four sources of Parliamentary procedure:

(a) *practice*, i.e. unwritten rules learnt largely by experience;

(b) *standing orders;*

(c) *resolutions of the House* which are generally expressly provided to last beyond the end of the session; and

(d) *rulings from the chair* by the Speaker or Chairman of Committees as to interpretation of rules and Acts of Parliament.

34.3 Procedure

Here is a typical daily time-table of the House of Commons:

2.30 pm	Prayers
2.35 pm	Preliminary business, e.g. motions for new writs (to fill vacant seats), unopposed private business and, rarely, the presentation of public petitions.
2.40 pm	Questions for oral answer – *question time*, questions asked of ministers to obtain information or press for action on particular topics. Two days' notice of the question must be given
	Question Time gives members an opportunity to put forward the grievances of individual citizens, (see section 34.6(a)).
3.30 pm	Private notice questions – on matters considered by the Speaker to be urgent and thus submitted for an oral answer on the same day; and other preliminary

business, e.g. ceremonial speeches, statements by ministers and matters of privilege.

3.45 pm   Public Business – presentation of public Bills; Orders of the Day, including the stages of public Bills and Committees of the whole House.

7.00 pm   Possibility of interruption if a private Bill is down for debate.

10.00 pm   Interruption of Public Business – Government business motions exempted from the ten o'clock rule, e.g. Finance and Consolidated Fund Bills; Business taken after ten o'clock, e.g. proceedings on statutory instruments: Motion for adjournment – giving half an hour in which any matter not involving legislation may be discussed; when time runs out the House automatically adjourns.

10.30 pm   House adjourns.

34.4 *Legislation*

A distinction must be drawn between *public Bills* (including *private members' Bills*) which seek to alter the general law and which are introduced under the Standing Orders relating to public business, and *private Bills*, which relate to matters of individual, corporate or local interest and are subject to separate Standing Orders.

(a)   *public Bills*, other than money Bills, may generally originate in the Lords or Commons, although most originate in the Commons. A Bill goes through five legislative stages. These are:

     (i)   *First reading* – a purely formal and literal reading of the title of the Bill.

     (ii)   *Second reading* – where the main principles of the Bill are discussed.

     (iii)   *Committee stage* – a discussion of details and any proposed amendments taking place either in one of the Standing Committees, or, sometimes, in a Committee of the whole House, where all members have a chance to discuss it.

     (iv)   *Report stage* – the Bill as amended in Committee is reported to the whole House and further amendments may be made.

     (v)   *Third reading* – usually purely formal. There is debate only on the motion of at least six members, such debate being on the general principles of the Bill. If the motion *that the Bill be now read a third time* is carried, the Bill is deemed to have *passed* the House and is sent up to the Lords.

Procedure in the Lords parallels that in the Commons. If the Lords amend a Commons Bill it will be returned to the Commons for their further consideration. Once a Bill has passed both Lords and Commons it will be sent to the Queen for the Royal Assent. *It would now be unconstitutional, but not illegal, for assent to be refused.* Public Bills may be introduced by individual members of the House, in which case they are known as *Private Members' Bills*. Private Members' Bills may be introduced either in the Commons or in the Lords but, if public expenditure will be required, a government minister will have to be persuaded to move the necessary financial resolution. A private member may use one of three ways to introduce such a Bill:

     (i)   he must obtain a high place in the ballot for the right to introduce a Bill at the beginning of the session; or

(ii)   he may seek the leave of the House under the Ten Minute Rule (by which on Wednesday or Thursday he may make a speech supporting his proposal which is followed by an opposition speech and then a division on whether leave should be given); or

(ii)   he may seek to introduce the Bill without leave under Standing Order 37.

The major difficulty faced by private members seeking to introduce legislation is that they receive no governmental assistance in preparing the draft legislation unless the government decides to adopt the proposal and, furthermore, most Private Members' Bills fail to become law as they have not completed all their stages within the session and may be 'talked out'. eg. in Spring 1988 David Alton's Controversial Bill to limit abortions to foetuses under 18 weeks was lost by filibustering and other similar tactics. In other instances the government may by imposing a three line Whip defeat a Private Member's Bill eg. Richard Shepherd's Bill to reform S.2 Official Secrets Act was defeated in 1988. Despite these drawbacks a Private Member's Bill may become law if it has cross-party support and even if it fails to reach the statute book it may be useful in stimulating public opinion to demand reform or because the government decides to adopt its measure in the next session.

(b)   *Private Bills* are not initiated by MPs but by petition from persons or bodies outside Parliament. The procedure for them is very complex and is set down in special Standing Orders. The main argument on a Private Bill is likely to be heard at the Committee stage when proposers and opposers of the Bill will have a chance to argue their case before a Select Committee. A Private Bill goes through all the same procedural stages as a Public Bill.

(c)   *Hybrid Bills* are introduced as Public Bills but also affect private interests in some way. Their procedure is thus a combination of the Public and the Private Bills' procedure.

34.5 *Financial procedure*

Proposals to raise public money may be introduced only in the Commons and must be recommended by a minister. No levy can be made until the Bill has completed its procedure and has become an Act of Parliament. The Lords cannot alter such Bills, but may only assent to, or, theoretically, dissent from them.

Public expenditure is authorised by annual Acts. Government departments

prepare estimates in the autumn of their expenditure for the next financial year (running from the beginning of April to the end of the following March). These estimates guide Parliament in authorising expenditure and are debated on three days each session. Debates concern general principles only. The expenditure authorised by Parliament is laid down in the *annual Appropriation Act*. If government departments need money before the *Appropriation Act* is passed, then interim measures called *Consolidated Fund Acts* will be enacted.

Annually at the beginning of the financial year the Chancellor of the Exchequer introduces his *Budget* where he makes a financial review of the previous year, states government spending policy and proposes tax changes. The House then passes formal resolutions which enable immediate tax changes to be made. This practice was successfully challenged in *Bowles v Bank of England (1913) 1 Ch 57* but is now authorised by the *Provisional Collection of Taxes Act 1968*. The taxing resolutions are eventually embodied in the annual *Finance Act*. The effect of any tax changes may be made retrospective to the date of the Budget or some other chosen date.

The Commons influences government expenditure in a number of ways. First, debates on departmental work or public spending will indicate to the government what priorities the House favours and questions may be raised on expenditure at Question Time. Second, tax legislation must, as does all legislation, proceed through a Committee stage when backbenchers have a chance to contribute their views. Finally, there are more formal methods of control provided by the Treasury and Civil Service Committee, a new Select Committee, which in 1979 took over some of the work of the Expenditure Committee in acting as a watchdog over the Treasury and the 14 new departmental Select Committees which also monitor expenditure. The Public Accounts Committee is complementary to the other Select Committees. It examines the use of moneys voted by Parliament after the event and acts in cooperation with the Comptroller and Auditor-General. In 1983 the role of this officer was strengthened by an Act, which started as a Private Member's Bill, the *National Audit Act 1983*. It provided that in future the Comptroller and Auditor-General should be an officer of the Commons appointed by the Crown on a resolution of the Commons, proposed by the Prime Minister with the approval of the Chairman of the Public Accounts Committee. His independence is further protected in that he can only be removed in the same way as a High Court judge, by a joint address by both Houses of Parliament to the Crown. The functions of the Comptroller and Auditor-General include examining the accounts of government departments and, although he may not question the merits of policy decisions, he may, since the 1983 Act, undertake value for money and efficiency auditing. The Comptroller and Auditor-General has his own independent staff and his reports may be taken up by the 15-man Public Accounts Committee, a Select Committee chaired by an opposition MP, which can question the Accounting Officer of Government Departments (and sometimes the minister himself) about actions taken in the department. The Committee reports to the Commons and its reports may be debated by the Chamber.

34.6 *Scrutiny of the administration by Parliament*

The main ways in which actions of the Administration may be questioned are:

(a) *Question time* – takes place for forty-five minutes on four days each week when Parliament is sitting. The most important Government Departments answer questions in rotation and on Tuesday and Thursday in each week there is Prime Minister's Question Time. At Question Time any MP may ask a question but each MP is limited to two requests for an oral answer on one day (although he may ask for limitless written answers). Two days prior notice is required for a question unless there are special circumstances but having once posed a question MP's are allowed to ask 'supplementaries' of which no prior notice is given. A device used was to ask the Minister about his appointments for a particular day and then to follow this by a supplementary question designed to embarrass him. This has, however, now been curtailed for the Speaker made a ruling on 2 April 1984 that supplementaries must relate to the Question asked of the Minister.

A Minister may be questioned on any matter within his competence but he may decline to answer a question on grounds of national security or if the matter is *sub judice* and the Speaker is not satisfied that the issue is one of national importance. In relation to the nationalised industries the Minister cannot be required to answer questions on the day to day running of the business but the scope of this exemption is somewhat uncertain. In 1948 the Speaker gave a ruling that questions must not be posed in relation to public corporations, local government or the police. The Minister may also refuse to answer a question if to do so would be too costly.

Question Time is considered by some to be the most important means of control over the government, which is possessed by MPs, and it is, without doubt, a useful tool. MPs may obtain redress for the grievances of their constituents using the threat of a question being raised. However, Question Time has been somewhat discredited recently. In 1971 it was revealed that government departments were planting questions with Conservative MPs so as to minimise the time for Opposition oral questions. Furthermore, MPs are often poorly informed owing to lack of research assistance and their questions may miss the point. Finally, Question Time, particularly Prime Minister's Question Time, is fully covered by the media with the result that it may be used for political point scoring rather than its true purpose of Parliamentary control over the Executive.

(b)   *Adjournment debates* – which take place in the half hour after the motion for adjournment of the House. The nightly half-hour adjournment debate can be used to consider more fully issues raised at Question Time and MP's enter a fortnightly ballot the winners of which select the topic for debate. The Speaker is able to select the topic for debate from a list provided for him on one evening each week.

(c)   *Specialist Select Committees* – Fourteen new departmental Select Committees have been set up by the House of Commons to replace the old system, although the influential Public Accounts Committee has been retained under the traditional chairmanship of an Opposition M.P. (at present Mr. Robert Sheldon, Labour Party) as have a further seven of the old committees. The new committees will examine the departments concerned with the following areas:

> Agriculture; Defence; Education Science and the Arts; Employment; Energy; Environment; Foreign Affairs; Home Affairs; Industry and Trade; Social Services; Transport; Treasury and the Civil Service; Welsh Affairs and Scottish Affairs.

In theory, these committees will be able to scrutinise the policies and spending of Government Departments far more closely than the old system of select committees on specific topics allowed. There is also a Committee of Selection, an independent body of MPs, who will choose the members of each committee. (The chairman of this important and powerful new Committee is at present Mr Marcus Fox, Conservative Party). There is also a special Liaison Committee, which includes the chairmen of all the watchdog committees, and which acts as a coordinating body. Reports of each committee will be debated in the House, and each will have the power to send for official papers and civil servants to answer probing questions. Technically the committee cannot demand the attendance of a Minister, but it would be politically unwise for a Minister to refuse to attend.

The reforms were aimed at strengthening the control of Parliament over the Executive, and are based on the American system of Congressional Committee hearings. However, not all MPs have welcomed these reforms, because there is a fear that they might create first and second-class MPs (i.e. those who serve on the committees will command more power and respect than those who do not). The committees might also take power out of the Commons chamber, which had been the traditional place for bringing the Executive to account (through debates, Question-Time, etc. etc.).

In November 1983 in his Reith Lectures, Sir Douglas Watts considered the efficiency of the new Select Committee System.

He took the view that the new system had the following advantages:

(i)   it improved the quality of Ministerial decisions because Ministers carefully scanned all aspects of a problem knowing they might have to justify their views to a Committee;

(ii)   it had influenced Whitehall to publish more information and MPs were better informed;

(iii)   any Ministerial weaknesses were likely to be exposed.

On the other hand Sir Douglas had the following criticisms:

(i)   the questioning was sometimes superficial by poorly informed MPs;

(ii)   Ministers were often skilful in avoiding answering the questions put to them;

(iii) the special advisers to the Committees were sometimes poor.

His recommendations to improve the system included:

(i)   the provision of better briefing to Committee members;

(ii)   more informal sessions off the record devoted to information gathering.

(d) *The Parliamentary Commissioner for Administration, the Ombudsman* – appointed by the Crown to investigate complaints of maladministration by Government departments in the exercise of administrative functions. Complaints are addressed initially to MPs and the MP may decide to refer the matter to the Commissioner. If it comes within the Commissioner's field of competence, he will investigate and report back to the MP. If the Commissioner considers that injustice was caused by maladministration and has not been remedied, he may lay a special report before Parliament. See further *Parliamentary Commissioner Act 1967* and Lesson 14.

There have been recent criticisms of the Select Committee System prompted by events like the Defence Select Committee's investigation into the Westland Affair (see Lesson 6) when the Government refused to allow the civil servants, directly involved in the leaking of the letter from the Law Officers to Michael Heseltine, to be interviewed and instead gave access to Sir Robert Armstrong head of the Civil Service who had carried out an inquiry into the leaking of the letter. This, of course, hampered the most effective working of the Committee.

In the 1987/88 session of Parliament the departmental Select committees were not in place until December 1987 so that for the first six months of the session there was no Committee to monitor the workings of the main departments. Owing to disagreements over the membership of the Scottish Select Committee after the Government's electoral decline in June 1987 in Scotland there remains in June 1988 no Scottish Select Committee.

35. PARLIAMENTARY PRIVILEGE – INTRODUCTION

A legislature like the UK Parliament requires a certain freedom from interference if it is to function properly. For example, its members need to be able to travel to its meetings without hindrance and to speak in its proceedings with the utmost frankness. These advantages reflect the importance of the work of Parliament and are collectively described as the *Privileges of Parliament*. The description is not really appropriate because in law these advantages appear *not as privileges but chiefly as immunities from the ordinary legal process*, e.g. freedom from suit for defamatory remarks made in debate, or powers peculiar to Parliament, e.g. to punish those who offend against the privileges. These advantages place Parliament in a special position and they are therefore regarded with suspicion by the citizen and the courts. Equally, they are jealously guarded by Parliament itself. This conflict of interest has led to disputes between Parliament and the courts over who should be the arbiter of what Parliament's privileges are and what constitutes a breach of them.

The privileges of both Lords and Commons are similar and they will, therefore, be considered together.

36. RIGHTS AND IMMUNITIES OF INDIVIDUAL MPs AND OF PARLIAMENT IN ITS CORPORATE CAPACITY

36.1 *Freedom of speech and debate*

It is declared in *article 9 of the Bill of Rights (1688)* that *the freedom of speech and debates or proceedings in Parliament ought not to be impeached or questioned in any court or place out of Parliament.* This privilege is in fact much older than the Bill of Rights but was, in its early history, the subject of some dispute. Since, according to *Article 9*, it is *proceedings in Parliament* that are protected, it must be considered first what are proceedings in Parliament.

In 1957 GR Strauss MP wrote a letter to the minister responsible complaining of the methods used by a section of the nationalised electricity industry in disposing of scrap cable. The electricity board concerned began a libel action against him and Mr Strauss therefore raised the question of privilege. The matter was referred to the Committee of Privileges which decided that the letter to the minister was a proceeding in Parliament and was thus protected by absolute privilege from defamation proceedings and that a threat to start such proceedings amounted to a breach of privilege. The House, however, by a small majority, decided to disagree with the Committee. The Speaker subsequently ruled that such a letter, if arising out of a debate and made at the invitation of a minister, would be covered by privilege. A subsidiary issue which arose in the case was sent for opinion to the Privy Council. According to the *Parliamentary Privilege Act 1770* any person may bring a court action against a member of Parliament of either House and such action should not be challenged on the ground of privilege. The Privy Council held, however, that this Act only applied to actions against members in their private capacity: *Re Parliamentary Privilege Act 1770 (1958).*

Whilst the House's decision in the Strauss case shows that the scope of absolute Parliamentary privilege is limited, there would remain the defence of qualified privilege protecting members' communications on matters of public interest, made without malice, from action in tort: *Beach v Freeson (1971) 2 All ER 854 and R v Rule (1937) 2 KB 375.*

The absolute privilege rule clearly covers contributions to debates and to discussions in committee, to questions tabled and asked, and to their answers in Parliament. Acts unconnected with Parliamentary business but which happen to be done within the precincts of Parliament are not protected: *Rivlin v Bilainkin (1953).*

Parliamentary privilege attaches to official reports of the proceedings of Parliament and to other papers published by order of the House. This was laid down by the *Parliamentary Papers Act 1840*, a statute necessitated by the decision in *Stockdale v Hansard (1839) 9 Ad & E 1* that the publisher of Parliamentary papers was not immune from libel action. Unofficial reports of Parliamentary proceedings and articles about Parliamentary proceedings are not absolutely privileged but do have the defence of qualified privilege in tort: *Cook v Alexander (1974) QB 279.*

Interference with a member's freedom of speech in his Parliamentary capacity by means of threats, bribes or improper inducements may amount to a breach of privilege. Many MPs are sponsored by or act as spokesmen for trade unions or pressure groups. Problems of privilege may arise, as in the case of *WJ Brown MP (1947)*. Brown had been elected as an independent MP and entered into an agreement with the Civil Service Clerical Association to become their *parliamentary general secretary*. It was stated that he would retain full freedom to engage in his own political activities. The union later became dissatisfied with Brown's political opinions and decided to terminate the agreement. Brown argued that this amounted to a breach of privilege as he was being subjected to financial pressure. The Committee of Privileges, however, conclude that there was no breach of privilege on the facts of the case although it was recognised that the situation was one where privilege might be involved. In 1975 a clear case of breach of privilege arose. The Yorkshire branch of the National Union of Mineworkers, which sponsored a number of MPs, resolved to withdraw sponsorship from any MP voting on an issue contrary to union policy. The Committee of Privileges concluded that a breach had occured, although, in fact, the Yorkshire Branch's decision had already been overruled by the National Executive of the NUM.

On 22 May 1974 the House of Commons resolved that members must disclose any relevant financial or other interests when engaging in Parliamentary business. There is now an official register of MPs' interests. Every MP, save one (Enoch Powell) registered in the last Parliament; no sanctions are available for failure to register.

36.2   Freedom from arrest

Freedom from civil arrest exists during a session of Parliament and for forty days before and after the session. Imprisonment of defendants in civil proceedings, and more particularly of debtors, was common until the end of the 19th century and it is that situation which the privilege was intended to cover. It has now, therefore, lost its importance as arrest in civil cases is rare; indeed in 1967 the Committee on Parliamentary Privileges recommended abolition of the privilege. The immunity does not extend to arrest on criminal charges nor to preventative detention of security suspects in wartime: *Captain Ramsay's Case (1940)*.

36.3   *The right of the House to control its own composition and proceedings*

The House claims exclusive right to control its own proceedings and internal affairs. It is for this reason that the courts have shown such reluctance to investigate alleged defects of Parliamentary procedure in the passing of an Act of Parliament (see *Edinburgh and Dalkeith Railway v Wauchope* earlier). Thus, too, the courts will not concern themselves with matters arising within the walls of the House.

In *Bradlaugh v Gossett (1884) 12 QBD 271*, Bradlaugh, a militant atheist who had been elected member for Northampton, sought both a declaration that the Commons' resolution not to allow him to take the oath of allegiance was void, and an injunction to restrain the Serjeant-at-Arms from excluding him from the House in accordance with this resolution. The court refused to intervene. Said Stephen, J:

> I think that the House of Commons is not subject to the control of Her Majesty's courts in its administration of that part of the statute law which has relation to its own internal proceedings, and that the use of such actual force as may be necessary to carry into effect such a resolution as the one before us is justifiable.

See also *R v Graham-Campbell ex p Herbert (1935) 1 KB 594*.

The right of the House to regulate its own composition has a number of elements. It includes the right to regulate the filling of vacancies by ordering the issue of a writ for a by-election; the right to determine whether a person is legally disqualified from sitting as a member, although the House may seek the opinion of the Privy Council on the matter: see *Re MacManaway (1951) AC 161;* and the right to expel a member considered to be unfit.

In 1947 Mr Allighan MP was expelled as being unfit because he had committed gross contempts of the House. He had published a press article alleging that MPs had given details to the press of Parliamentary party proceedings held in the precincts of the House. He said that they had given the information for money while drunk. The matter was investigated by the Committee of Privileges and the article was held to be a contempt of the House. Since Allighan had himself received payment for giving information to journalists and had committed other contempts, the House voted to expel him.

Since there is no appeal process open to someone expelled by the House, the power is open to abuse. In the 18th century John Wilkes was expelled on a number of occasions by the House and was, each time, re-elected. Eventually the House accepted his election. It would thus seem that the remedy lies in the hands of the expelled member's constituents.

37.   *THE PENAL JURISDICTION OF PARLIAMENT*

The House has wide powers to enforce its privileges and to punish those who infringe them. It also has power to punish for contempt. Care must be taken to distinguish the terms *breach of privilege* and *contempt, for* while a breach of privilege is likely also to be a contempt, a contempt is not necessarily a breach of privilege. There are a defined number of privileges, but contempt is a far wider concept, covering any offence against the authority and dignity of the House. Thus in *Junor's Case* (1957, Report of the Committee of Privileges) the newspaper allegation that members were obtaining unfair allocations under petrol rationing, was a contempt, as was the disruption of a meeting of a Select Committee on Education hearing evidence about student relations. Other examples would include the refusal to give evidence, or the giving of false evidence, to a committee of the House, and disorderly behaviour by members or others within the precincts of the House.

Where a member has raised a matter of privilege and the Speaker rules that there is a *prima facie* case of breach of privilege or contempt, the matter is usually referred to the Committee of Privileges. This Committee is a Select Committee of the House, chaired by the Leader of the House. The Committee can summon members and others to give evidence. Its findings are reported to the House for decision. Apart from expulsion of a member, the House may decide to imprison a member or a stranger (i.e. anyone not a member), or to have the offender reprimanded or admonished. The old power of the House of Commons to impose a fine seems now to have fallen out of use. In practice today the Commons rarely imposes a punishment. In June 1986 the Committee of Privileges recommended that a *Times* lobby correspondent should have his pass withdrawn for six months and that *The Times* should be allowed no replacement, as punishment for the leaking of a draft Select Committee report, but the Commons refused to accept this recommendation.

The most common offence for which MPs are committed for contempt is use of unParliamentary language where no effort has been made to withdraw the remark or make an apology. On the first instance of disobedience of this type an MP is usually 'named' (suspended from attendance for five days). In May 1988 a Labour MP, Ron Brown, was suspended for 3 months for damaging the Commons ceremonial mace and refusing to apologise for his protest against Government Social Security cuts. An unusual feature of this case is that the Labour party has responded by removing the party whip for 3 months after the suspension ceases. This has not occurred since 1961.

38. PARLIAMENT AND THE COURTS

38.1 Parliament and the Courts in conflict

The House has always claimed to be sole judge of its own privileges. This right had been recognized by the courts at an early date. In *Ashby v White (1703) 2 Ld Rayn 938* Holt CJ said: *my brother says we cannot judge of this matter, because it is a Parliamentary thing. Oh: by all means be very tender of that.* The action concerned the refusal to allow someone to vote at an election. It was held by the House of Lords that the court would give a remedy, for Holt CJ had urged: *we are to exert and vindicate the Queen's jurisdiction, and not to be frightened because it may come in question in Parliament.* In the similar case of *Paty (1704) 2 Ld Rayn 1105*, however, the court denied that they had jurisdiction to intervene. The case is interesting for the dissent of Holt CJ' He stated the now-accepted principle that if Parliament states merely that the matter is one of privilege the court will not intervene;but if details of the alleged breach are given and are not, in fact, sufficient in law, the court will take jurisdiction.

In *Stockdale v Hansard (1839)* the Court of Queen's Bench extended this principle to declare that a publication authorized by Parliament was not, in law, covered by Parliamentary privilege. Damages for defamation were thus awarded to Stockdale. When the Sheriff of Middlesex attempted to levy execution on Hansard's property to recover the damages, the House responded by imprisoning the Sheriff for contempt and breach of privilege. In the subsequent *habeas corpus* proceedings the court held that the statement by the House that the Sheriff had been in contempt had to be accepted for, said Lord Denham, CJ: *it would be unseemly to suspect that a body, acting under such sanctions as a House of Parliament, would, in making its warrant, suppress facts which, if discussed, might entitle the person committed to his liberty.*

The dispute between the courts and Parliament remains largely unresolved. Since the Hansard case, both courts and Parliament had shown circumspection in their behaviour. In 1957, however, in the Strauss case, if the House had endorsed the report of the Committee of Privileges and had decided the letter was covered by absolute privilege, problems might well have arisen had a civil action been brought against Mr. Strauss.

38.2 Reform

In 1966 a Select Committee on Parliamentary Privilege was established. The Committee recommended that the expression *privilege* should no longer be used and that instead the House should speak of its *rights* and *immunities*, breach of which would be a contempt. Among other proposals it was considered that the House's penal jurisdiction should be exercised only sparingly and that trivial complaints of contempt should be dismissed without investigation. The House has never adopted these changes, however, so that the terminology and principles of Parliamentary privilege remain the same. There is, however, a noticeable trend for the House to ignore minor breaches and it is clear that the Committee of Privileges's conclusions in investigated cases are not automatically followed. For example, in 1975, when the Committee recommended that the editor of *The Economist* and a political correspondent should be denied access to the House for six months, the House voted to take no action. Thus the philosophy of the Select Committee's report may have been adopted even though the proposals were not. A further example occurred in 1986.

The Environment Select Committee of the Commons had prepared a draft report on the nuclear industry in which doubts about safety were expressed. This was leaked to a lobby correspondent of *The Times* and that paper published details in December 1985. The Committee on Privileges reported, recommending the Commons to punish the contempt by suspending the journalist from the House for six months and removing one lobby pass from *The Times* for a similar period. However, the Commons refused to mete out any such punishment in May 1986.

Further Reading

(i)   *General*

Wade and Bradley, Chs.9-12;

(ii)   *Electoral System*

Constitutional Fundamentals, Wade (Hamlyn Lecture 1980); (1971) Public Law 25;
Reform of the Electoral System (1983) Public Law 108.

(iii) *House of Lords*

The Reform of Parliament, Bernard Crick, Chs. 5 & 6.

(iv) *Parliamentary Privilege*

Some Problems of the Constitution, Marshall and Moodie (1967), Ch.7;
Heuston, Ch.4;
Zellick (1977) Public Law 29;
Freedom, the Individual and the Law, Street (1977), 4th Edn. Ch.6;
Freedom of Speech in Parliament, Its Misuses and Proposals for Reform, 1981 Public Law 30.

(v)   *The Party System*

Governing Britain: Hanson and Walles 4th Edn. 1984 Ch.3.

LLB

THE EXECUTIVE – PART I

LESSON 4 (STUDY)

41. *THE CROWN*

    41.1   THE CROWN – INTRODUCTION
    41.2   SUCCESSION TO THE THRONE
    41.3   ROYAL MARRIAGES
    41.4   TITLE
    41.5   REGENCY
    41.6   THE PRIVY COUNCIL

42. *THE ROYAL PREROGATIVE*

    42.1   THE ROYAL PREROGATIVE – INTRODUCTION
    42.2   PERSONAL PREROGATIVES OF THE MONARCH
    42.3   THE PREROGATIVE IN DOMESTIC AFFAIRS
    42.4   CONTROL OF THE PREROGATIVE

43. *THE PREROGATIVE IN FOREIGN AFFAIRS*

    43.1   INTRODUCTION
    43.2   ACT OF STATE IN RELATION TO ANOTHER STATE
    43.3   ACT OF STATE IN RELATION TO INDIVIDUALS

41.   THE CROWN

41.1   *The Crown – Introduction*

The three terms *Crown, Sovereign and Monarch* are often used interchangeably, and often the term Crown is used in a number of different senses. Usage has more or less ordained specific meanings for each term to avoid confusion, and these meanings are as follows:

(a)   The Queen in her personal capacity as Queen is usually referred to as such or as the Monarch.

(b)   The power in the state is referred to as the sovereign or the legal sovereign. Sovereignty is exercised by Parliament (see earlier).

(c)   The Crown generally describes the executive branch of Government; it is a generic term used to clothe those who carry on the Queen's Government with some sort of corporate identity. In this sense not only does the Crown describe the executive Government, but also the state itself.

The *State*, i.e. a corporate body of citizens, has no existence in this country. Public property is not owned by the state or the people, but by the Crown; public prosecutions are not brought in the name of the people but by the Crown in the name of the Queen.

The Executive has as its classic function the administration of the state. It implements the policies adopted by the legislature and gives effect to the decisions of the courts. It is concerned also with the development of proposals of policy and with giving the lead in affairs of state. The executive power resides in the Crown and historically this ensured that it was able to gain ascendancy in the business of Government, and this it has retained despite the rise of Parliament to legal supremacy.

41.2   *Succession to the Throne*

In 1689, following the departure of James II, Parliament invited William and Mary to become joint monarchs, and set out, in the *Bill of Rights* certain terms by which they were expected to abide. Title to the Crown thus became a matter for Parliamentary regulation.

(a)   *Act of Settlement 1700* provided that the Crown ... *shall remain and continue to the said most excellent Princess Sophia (Electress of Hanover and grand-daughter of James I) and the heirs of her body being Protestant.* It is further provided that Roman Catholics and those who marry Roman Catholics shall be disqualified from the succession and that the Monarch must swear to maintain the Churches of England and Scotland and must be a communicant member of the Church of England. The Crown descends according to the old property law rule of primogeniture. If the Monarch has a son or sons, the eldest will succeed and failing a male heir the oldest surviving daughter.

(b)   *HM Declaration of Abdication Act 1936.* The succession laid down by the *Act of Settlement 1700* has been altered only once. Alteration occurred in 1936 when, by *HM Declaration of Abdication Act*, Edward VIII ceased to be King and the member of the Royal Family then next in line of succession succeeded to the Crown. The abdication also necessitated amendments to be made to the Act of Settlement in order that the ex-king and his descendants should be excluded from the succession to the Throne.

41.3   *Royal Marriages*

Under the *Royal Marriages Act 1772* the Monarch's formal consent is required for the marriage of a descendant of George II unless the descendant is the issue of a princess married into a foreign royal family. In the following circumstances the Monarch's consent is unnecessary if:

(a) the person seeking consent is over 25 and

(b) gives 12 months notice to the Privy Council and

(c) Parliament does not object.

41.4 Title

The title by which the Monarch is known may vary in different countries of the Commonwealth, for each member state is free to enact its own form of title. It was laid down by the *Royal Titles Act 1953*, however, that in the UK the Queen's title should be *Elizabeth the Second by the Grace of God of the UK of Great Britain and Northern Ireland and of Her other Realms and Territories, Queen, Head of the Commonwealth, Defender of the Faith.* The title *Elizabeth the Second* was challenged in Scotland as contravening the Act of Union, for there had never been an Elizabeth the First there. The court held (in *MacCormick v Lord Advocate*, see earlier) that there was nothing in the Act of Union to prohibit such a title.

41.5 *Regency*

When a sovereign dies his successor succeeds to the throne immediately. The maxim *the King never dies* has been used to describe this practice. A person is never too young to accede to the throne and at common law there was no provision for a regency if the monarch was ill or under age. It has now been laid down in the *Regency Acts 1937-53* that a regent should automatically be appointed where the succeeding sovereign is under the age of 18, and that, on certain declarations of unfitness being made, a regent should be appointed where the sovereign is, by reason of infirmity of mind or body, incapable of performing the royal functions. Any such declaration must (to be valid) be made by three or more of the following – the Monarch's spouse, the Lord Chancellor, the Speaker, the Master of the Rolls and the Lord Chief justice. The regent will normally be the next person of full age in line of succession, provided that he is a British subject and is not excluded from succession by the conditions in the *Act of Settlement*. The regent is empowered to carry out all royal functions save that he may not assent to a Bill to change the succession or one to repeal the establishment of the Scottish church.

If the Monarch is not seriously incapacitated or is to be temporarily absent Counsellors of State may be appointed. These will be the Monarch's spouse, together with the next four persons in line of succession to the throne, who are of full age, and the Queen Mother. Powers may be delegated to them but unless specifically authorised they may not dissolve Parliament. They are not permitted to grant honours.

41.6 *The Privy Council*

The Privy Council has more than 350 members. By convention, all Cabinet ministers are sworn as Privy Councillors, as are the Archbishops of Canterbury and York, the Speaker of the House of Commons, the Law Lords, The Master of the Rolls and senior ambassadors. Privy Councillors are appointed for life although they may be removed on advice or at their own request. Cabinet Ministers of an outgoing Government therefore remain Privy Councillors. A Prime Minister may on the basis of the oaths taken by Privy Councillors give Members of Opposition parties who are Privy Councillors confidential information which is not otherwise available to those outside Government Privy Councillors are entitled to be addressed as *The Right Honourable* ... Meetings of the Privy Council are held, generally, in the presence of the Queen, at Buckingham Palace. The meetings are purely formal and have no real decision-making function. Usually only a handful of

Privy Councillors attend each meeting. The quorum is 3. Decisions of the meeting are called *Orders in Council*.

Although the Privy Council is largely of ceremonial and traditional significance and its duties could easily be re-distributed among other executive bodies, it retains one important function and that is the function exercised by the *Judicial Committee of the Privy Council*. The Judicial Committee consists of the Lord President of the Council (who does not sit) and those who hold or have held high judicial office and are Privy Councillors. The quorum is three. In practice it is usually the Law Lords who sit.

The Judicial Committee is the highest appeal court for the Channel Islands, the Isle of Man, the colonies and protectorates and for those independent Commonwealth countries which have retained this system of appeal. Although it is essentially a Commonwealth court, it also hears appeals from some UK professional disciplinary bodies (e.g. the Disciplinary Committee of the Institute of Chartered Accountants in England and Wales) and may advise the Crown on any matter which has been referred to it for opinion.

The Judicial Committee of the Privy Council still exercises the old prerogative right to hear appeals from the overseas dependencies of the Crown. The granting of independence to a colony does not, in itself, terminate the right of appeal to the Privy Council, but many Commonwealth states have, in fact, abolished this method of appeal after independence. Those countries which retain appeal to the Privy Council have often severely limited the types of appeal, considering that it is no longer appropriate for the Privy Council to be the final appeal court. Colonies and other dependent territories do remain within the jurisdiction of the Privy Council, but where they have some internal self-government they often also have power to limit the types of appeal going for Privy Council consideration.

The Privy Council originally had importance both as a constitutional court for the colonies and also as the upholder of fundamental standards of English law. Thus local excesses, particularly as regards criminal law, in all parts of the Empire could be controlled by the UK court.

Where the Privy Council jurisdiction survives, appeals may be of two sorts. There are those which can be brought without special leave and those which require special leave. Appeals without special leave are mainly civil matters. The conditions for appeal will be laid down either in a local Act or in UK legislation specifically applying to the place in question. The local court may be given a discretion as to whether the matter is one appropriate for the decision of the Privy Council.

Appeals with special leave apply mainly in criminal cases. The Privy Council does not here act as an ordinary appeal court but rather may give leave to a petitioner where there has been a clear departure from the rules of law or natural justice in the determination against him. This doctrine was explained by the Judicial Committee in *Arnold v King Emperor (1914) AC 644* where it was said that the Privy Council:

> is not guided by its own doubts of the appellant's innocence or suspicion of his guilt. It will not interfere with the course of the criminal law unless there has been such an interference with the elementary rights of an accused as has placed him outside of the place of regular law, or unless, within that pale, there has been a violation of the natural principles of justice so demonstratively manifest as to convince their Lordships, first, that the result arrived at was opposite to the result which their Lordships would themselves have reached, and, secondly, that the same opposite result would have been reached by a local tribunal also if the alleged defect or misdirection had been avoided.

Thus in *Ras Behari Lal v R (1933) 50 TLR 1* an appeal was allowed where a member of the jury in a murder trial had not understood the language in which the proceedings were conducted, and in *Knowles v R (1930) AC 366* appeal against a conviction for murder where the possibility of the lesser offence of manslaughter had not been considered was allowed. See also *Re Dillett (1887) 12 AC 459.* The principles on which the Privy Council will take jurisdiction are clearly narrow ones. The error must be manifest before it will give leave to appeal. Since criminal appeal in this country is now more widely available than when these principles were first enunciated it may be that the Privy Council also should widen its jurisdiction. However, although the Judicial Committee is free to alter its principles of jurisdiction, there is nothing to suggest that it will attempt to do so.

42. THE ROYAL PREROGATIVE

42.1 *The royal prerogative – introduction*

Historically the royal prerogative may be regarded as one of the attributes of kingship and may be compared with *Imperium* in Roman law. Before the development of legislation all executive government was carried out by virtue of prerogative powers; from the prerogative also was derived the validity of judgments given in courts of law and to some extent the authority of Acts of Parliament. With the development of a more sophisticated political system and the need for the king to impose heavier taxes and to take more control of national life, it became increasingly necessary for him to carry the support of Parliament, and executive powers became increasingly bestowed by Acts of that body. This process culminated with the triumph of Parliament over the king as expressed in the *Revolution Settlement of 1688* and thereafter new executive powers of Government always had to be contained in an Act of Parliament. Hence the scope of the prerogative today is much reduced. But after 1688 the king did retain certain prerogative powers most of which today are exercised on his behalf by his ministers. Some of the most important are the powers to conduct the State's foreign policy.

Blackstone's definition of the prerogative is as follows:

> by the word prerogative, we usually understand that special pre-eminence, which the king hath, over and above all other persons, and out of the ordinary course of the common law, in right of his regal dignity. And hence it follows that it must be in its nature singular and eccentrical; that it can only be applied to those rights and capacities which the king enjoys alone, in contra-distinction to others and not to those which he enjoys in common with any of his subjects.

The essential characteristics of the prerogative therefore are:

(a) that it is a part of the common law, but a part containing exceptions to the law that applies to ordinary citizens. It was said by Coke, CJ, in the *Case of Proclamations (1611) 12 Co. Rep 74* that *the king hath no prerogative but that which the law of the land allows him.*

(b) that it is unique and pre-eminent.

(c) that the exercise of the prerogative does not require the prior consent of Parliament.

(d) that prerogative powers are residual because it is now established that Parliament can take away any power, and, indeed, it has frequently done so. The first clear example of Parliament's limiting prerogative powers is to be found in the *Bill of Rights* (see earlier).

(e) that the exercise of the prerogative is discretionary. Thus in *Darnel's Case (1627) 3 ST Tr 1* the courts refused to examine the way in which an admitted prerogative power was being used; and in *Chandler v DPP (1964) AC 763* the House of Lords noted that the disposition and armament of the armed forces was one of the oldest prerogatives of the Crown and that the exclusive discretion of the Crown in the matter could not be challenged in court. However, in the Court of Appeal *Laker Airways v Department of Trade (1977) 2 All ER 182* Lord Denning indicated that he considered that courts should be prepared to review the exercise of the prerogative and this stance has been adopted by the House of Lords in November 1984 in *Council of Civil Service Unions v Minister for the Civil Service (1984) 3 All ER 935* (the *GCHQ case*), although the Lords indicated that the subject-matter of the prerogative would not always be suitable for review by the courts (for further detail see section 42.4).

42.2 *Personal prerogatives of the monarch*

The oldest personal prerogatives of the monarch have now largely been absorbed by what may be called the political prerogatives. The main personal prerogative that remains is that the monarch is the *fountain of honour*. The monarch grants the Order of the Garter, the Order of the Thistle, the Royal Victorian Order and the Order of Merit on purely personal discretion, but in all other honours acts on the advice of the Prime Minister. Some monarchs have actively supervised Prime Ministers' choices, but the monarch's role is largely a formal one.

It is important to note, however, that the monarch may still exercise great influence over the Prime Minister and other ministers. The monarch has the right to be kept fully informed. She has a weekly audience with the Prime Minister and receives Cabinet Papers and Minutes, Foreign Office despatches and telegrams and other State papers. Therefore, whilst having, in the last resort, to assent to ministerial advice, the monarch retains a *right to warn*, and to point out to ministers the disadvantages of proposed courses of action. Historically, such warnings have often been accepted by ministers, e.g. George VI directed Winston Churchill not to accompany the armed forces on D-Day. In an interview in April 1986 Mr Edward Heath (former Conservative Prime Minister, 1970-74) confirmed that on a number of occasions he had changed his government's policy on receipt of advice from the Queen although he gave no specific example.

In the earlier part of this century, the monarch retained a substantial degree of personal discretion when, by reason of death or resignation, it became necessary to choose a new Prime Minister. In such situations the monarch was free to seek such advice as he deemed necessary. Thus, in 1963, when Mr MacMillan resigned through ill-health, the Queen is said to have consulted only her private secretary and Mr MacMillan himself, before sending for Lord Home. However, now that each of the main political parties has a clearer leadership structure, such personal discretion will accordingly be limited.

There remains a possibility that the monarch might have to take a creative personal role by exercising the royal prerogative in emergency but the scope of the prerogative is vague in such situations and there are few precedents. It seems that the monarch might dismiss her government and call a General Election if the government had lost a vote of confidence in the Commons but refused to resign. However, the monarch is unlikely to interfere unless forced to do so because such intervention would be seen as apolitical act which might call the continued existence of the monarchy into question. The closest to a precedent is the situation in Australia in 1975 where Gough Whitlam's Labour Government was dismissed by the Governor-General because it failed to call a General Election after the Senate had refused to pass *Appropriation Bills* accepted by the House of Representatives, and Mr Fraser, leader of the Opposition, was asked to form an interim government which called a General Election, which it subsequently won. The Governor-General's actions gave rise to a storm of public protest and calls for Australia to be declared a Republic. No doubt, part of the outcry was prompted because interference was seen as emanating from a former colonial power, half a world away, but it is not difficult to surmise that a similar outcry could occur in the UK if the Monarch were to dismiss a Government.

Another example of a prerogative which might be exercised in emergency is if a Prime Minister, defeated in the Commons, asked for a dissolution of Parliament, the monarch could refuse if the national interest were against such a course. This power remains largely theoretical as it is unlikely that a modern monarch would attempt to use it.

42.3 *The prerogative in domestic affairs*

(a) *The Crown is the fountain of justice* – justice is administered in the Queen's name and the courts are the Queen's courts. However, it was established in 1607 that the monarch may not do justice in his own person, for, declared Coke, CJ:

His Majesty was not learned in the laws of his realm of England and causes which concern the life, or inheritance, or goods, or fortunes of his subjects, are not to be decided by natural reason but by the artificial reason and judgment of law.

The Crown through the Attorney-General exercises many functions in relation to criminal justice. Thus, prosecutions on indictment may be stopped by the AG entering a *nolle prosequi: R v Allen (1862) 1 B and S 850;* and it is necessary for a private citizen to be joined by the AG, called a *relator action*, if he seeks to enforce public rights at civil law: *Gouriet v U.P.W. (1978) AC 435.* The sovereign, acting by the Home Secretary, may also pardon convicted offenders.

The activities of the Crown in this sphere have not been open to review by the court. In *Hanratty v Lord Butler (1971) CLY 2975* the Court of Appeal refused to enquire whether a former Home Secretary had been negligent in the exercise of the prerogative of mercy; and in *Gouriet v Union of Post Office Workers (1978) AC 435* the House of Lords refused to allow a civil action brought by a private citizen who had tried, and failed, to get the AG's consent to a relator action. However the court's attitude to the review of the exercise of prerogative powers is changing and this may affect these prerogatives.

(b) *Control of the armed services* – by prerogative and by statute the monarch is commander-in-chief of the armed forces. Since the *Bill of Rights 1688* the raising of forces and their maintenance in peace-time has been a matter for Parliament, but the movement and disposition of lawfully raised forces is entirely within the prerogative and cannot be questioned in court: *China Navigation v AG (1932) 2 KB 197.*

(c) *Emergency and defence* – the Crown is responsible for the defence of the realm and is to be sole judge of the existence of danger to the realm from external enemies. In *Burmah Oil v Lord Advocate (1965) AC 75* Lord Reid said *the prerogative certainly covers doing all those things in an emergency which are necessary for the conduct of war.* However, it was held in that case that compensation would be payable for damage or loss caused by the exercise of the prerogative. Thus, the oil company whose installation in Burma had been destroyed by British Troops in order to prevent it falling into the hands of the enemy, became entitled to many millions of pounds. This decision was nullified by the *War Damage Act 1965* which retrospectively provided that no one was entitled to receive compensation for damage or destruction caused by lawful acts of the Crown *during, or in contemplation of the outbreak of, a war in which the sovereign is or was engaged.*

(d) *Prerogative immunities* – it is a principle of statutory interpretation that statutes do not bind the Crown unless it is clear, expressly or by necessary implication that Parliament intended the Crown to be bound. The Crown also has certain privileges and immunities when engaging in litigation, which are laid down by the *Crown Proceedings Act 1947* (see Lesson 13).

42.4 *Control of the prerogative*

(a) *By the courts* – the courts are only likely to consider prerogative powers which have been used directly to affect the rights of individuals.

The courts will not now recognise the existence of new prerogative powers. In *BBC v Johns (1965) Ch 32* Diplock, LJ, said:

It is 350 years and a civil war too late for the Queen's courts to broaden the prerogative.

The limits within which the executive government may impose obligations or restraints on the citizens of the UK without any statutory authority are now well settled and incapable of extension.

However, it is not altogether true to say that the limits of prerogative power are well settled and therefore an examination of a prerogative power to determine its existence could, in reality, be an examination of the power on its merits. Indeed in *Laker Airways v Department of Trade (1977) 2 All ER 182* Lord Denning, MR, went so far as to suggest that, since the prerogative was intended to be exercised for the public good, its exercise would be examined by the courts. However, this view was disapproved by the House of Lords in the *Gouriet* case.

The decision in the GCHQ case in November 1984 vindicated what Lord Denning said in *Laker Airways v Department of Trade.* The facts of the case were that in December 1983 the Government made an Order in Council the effect of which was to make trade union membership unacceptable in respect of civil servants working at General Communications Head Quarters in Cheltenham. The Government acted against the following background. After the Conservative Government was elected in 1979 there had been several disputes with civil servants, principally over pay. The Civil Service unions had operated a policy of selective strikes aimed at supporting their claims and had, on several occasions, chosen GCHQ as the venue for a strike, presumably believing its intelligence gathering operations to be so important that disruption might lead the Government to an early settlement. The Government viewed seriously the disruption at GCHQ but was not moved to bar Trade Union membership at GCHQ because it had not publicly acknowledged the existence of GCHQ. When the Prime spy case was heard in 1983 the existence of GCHQ became public knowledge and there was no further constraint to prevent the Government introducing its TU ban, which it did in December 1983, without prior consultation with the Unions. Each civil servant who gave up TU membership, or agreed in writing that in future he would not join one, received £1000 but those who refused, made themselves liable to transfer to less sensitive civil service jobs or, in the end result, to dismissal. The Council of Civil Service Unions challenged the Government action arguing it was invalid because the rules of natural justice were broken as the unions had not been consulted prior to the ban. Glidewell J in the High Court gave judgement in favour of the unions but this was reversed in the Court of Appeal and the House of Lords upheld the Court of Appeal ruling that the Government had acted legally.

The House of Lords' judgements were interesting for, although the Lords concluded that because national security was at stake the rules of natural justice did not apply to the Government's action, they speculated on the Courts' future attitude to controlling the exercise of the Royal Prerogative. The judgements indicate that the Lords consider there is no logical reason why the exercise of statutory powers should be reviewable by the Courts whilst those powers emanating from the Prerogative should not be. Nevertheless, the Lords pointed out that certain Prerogative powers are not, by the very nature of the subject matter involved, justiciable by the Courts. Examples of these areas, where the courts could not interfere, were given and the list was not an exhaustive one. It included declarations of war and peace, appointment and dismissal of ministers and the grant of honours.

In Rv S.S. for Foreign and Commonwealth Affairs ex p. Everett (1987) the Court was asked to consider the exercise of a prerogative power when Everett, applying abroad, was refused a passport, since there was an outstanding warrant for his arrest. He was granted only an emergency passport for a return journey to the UK. When he applied for judicial review of the refusal of the passport certiorari was granted to quash the decision since the Foreign Office had operated a fixed and rigid policy without regard to the merits of Everitt's case. The case shows the court's charged attitude to the review of prerogative powers.

(b) *By statute* – the question arises whether, where prerogative powers and statutory powers cover the same sphere of activity, the Crown should proceed under statute or prerogative power. In *AG v De Keyser's Royal Hotel (1920) AC 508* a hotel had been requisitioned for the use of the army in wartime. The Crown argued that possession had been taken under prerogative power, by which no compensation was payable, rather than under the *Defence of the Realm Acts* which made provision for compensation. The House of Lords rejected this argument and held that possession had been taken under statutory powers. Said Lord Moulton:

> When powers covered by this statute are exercised by the Crown it must be presumed that they are so exercised under the statute ... There can be no excuse for reverting to prerogative powers simpliciter ... when the legislature has given to the Crown statutory powers which are wider than anyone pretends were those that it possessed under the prerogative.

Thus while the statute was in existence, the prerogative power went into abeyance. See also *Laker Airways v Department of Trade.*

43.   THE PREROGATIVE IN FOREIGN AFFAIRS

43.1 *Introduction*

An *act of state* is the term given to an executive act done as a matter of within the allegiance of the Crown. It is often pleaded that an act is an act of state and that therefore the court does not have jurisdiction over it. As Lord Pearson said in *Nissan v AG (1970) AC 179* where the plea was not successful:

> the court does not come to any decision as to the legality or illegality, or the rightness or wrongness, of the act complained of: the decision is that because it was an act of state the court has no jurisdiction to entertain a claim in respect of it.

In *Salaman v Secretary of State for India (1906) 1 KB 613* Moulton, LJ, said:

> acts of state are not all of one kind, their nature and consequences may differ in an infinite variety of ways, and these differences may profoundly affect the position of the municipal courts with regard to them.

Where an act of state is pleaded, the mere fact of the plea does not oust the jurisdiction of the court. Rather, the court must examine all the facts and circumstances, and decide for itself whether an act of state was involved. No clear test has been used by the courts in determining whether an act of the executive is an act of state, but relevant factors would include the importance of the act as a matter of policy, the apparent intention of the executive in doing an act and the relationship of an act to any already accepted acts of state (see *Nissan v AG*, esp. *per* Lords Reid and Pearson). It is necessary that we should examine the concept of act of state under various different headings.

43.2 *Act of state in relation to another state*

(a) *Treaties* – treaties are merely international agreements. They are of many different sorts and may be given different names, e.g. conventions, agreements, pacts, etc. They may be bilateral or multilateral. In some countries treaties become part of the municipal law of the country as soon as they are concluded, but in this country it is almost always necessary for a treaty to be given legislative effect if it is here to be enforced as affecting private rights: see *Parliament Belge (1879) 4 PD 129*. European Community treaties are a possible exception to this rule, for, according to Community law, certain provisions are deemed to be *directly applicable* in the laws of member states. Many of these provisions have in fact been enacted in the *European Communities Act 1972* and under that Act future provisions must be authenticated by Order in Council, so that much of the directly applicable legislation will also expressly be part of English law.

The treaty-making power is a prerogative power and may not be impugned by the courts (see *Blackburn v AG (1971)* in section 23.3(b)). However, whilst the court must accept an act of state without question, the court must decide whether or not there has been an act of state and, if there has, what is its nature and extent.

There is also control by Parliament in some cases, for, where a treaty is expressly made subject to confirmation by Parliament, it cannot come into force unless an Act of Parliament is passed confirming it; and where a treaty involves an alteration of English taxation, authorisation by Act of Parliament, either before or after the treaty has been concluded, is again needed.

(b) *The declaration of war and peace* – by virtue of the prerogative the Crown is conclusively entitled to determine whether a state of war exists between the sovereign and a foreign country. Thus, in *R v Bottrill, ex p Kuechenmeister (1947) KB 41*, where the Crown sought to deport a German national after the end of World War II as being an enemy alien, the court was forced to accept a Secretary of State's certificate that the state of war had not been brought to an end.

(c) *Recognition of foreign states and their diplomats* – it is part of the royal prerogative to recognise and to withhold recognition from foreign states and their governments. By common law foreign states, governments and diplomats recognised by the Crown had immunity from the jurisdiction of the English courts (see *Duff Development v Government of Kelantan (1924) AC 797* and *Engelke v Musman (1928) AC 433*). However, this led to injustice and the *State Immunity Act 1978* reformed the law. It came into force on 22 November 1978 and provided for residual immunity to be accorded to recognised states, sovereigns or heads of such states and the government or government departments of such states. However, the Act removed immunity for a range of activities carried out by such parties such as transactions of a commercial, financial, industrial or similar character under contracts to be performed wholly or partly in the UK. It also removed immunity in respect of death, personal injury or damage to property caused by acts or omissions of the state in the UK and made further more detailed provisions.

The *Diplomatic Privileges Act 1964* divides members of diplomatic missions into three classes and gives different immunity to each class:

(i) members of diplomatic staff have full civil and criminal immunity (with a few exceptions);

(ii) members of administrative and technical staff have full immunity for official acts but are liable civilly (but not criminally) for acts outside their official duties;

(iii) members of service staff have immunity for official acts but full civil and criminal liability for acts outside the course of their duties.

The question of what category an individual comes within is one for certification by the Foreign Secretary, but the court has jurisdiction to determine whether or not someone was acting in the course of his duties.

Diplomatic immunity may be waived by the diplomat's head of mission or head of state, but waiver must be express and will only be a waiver of immunity for the jurisdiction of the court. A separate waiver of immunity is needed for the execution of a judgment.

(c) *Annexation or conquest of territory* – it is part of the prerogative for the Crown to decide what rights and obligations it takes over from the government of a state which it has extinguished by conquest or annexation. Thus, in *West Rand Central Gold Mining v R (1905) 2 KB 391* a refusal to accept responsibility for an allegedly wrongful seizure of gold bars by the former South African Republic was upheld by the court.

43.3 *Act of state in relation to individuals*

(a) *The act must be performed under the authority of the Crown* – thus, in *Buron v Denman (1848) 2 Exch 167* the captain of a British ship was held not to be liable for setting fire to a Spaniard's slave enclosure in West Africa and releasing the slaves, because he had general instructions to suppress the slave trade and his action was afterwards specifically approved by the Admiralty.

(b)   *The location of the act of state:*

(i)   *within the Dominions of the Crown* – act of state is *not* a defence to a tortious act done to a British subject within the Dominions: see *Entick v Carrington*. Thus, in *Walker v Baird (1892) AC 491*, where a commander of a British warship had taken possession of a ship belonging to a British subject in Newfoundland, it was no defence that the commander was acting under orders of the Crown. Aliens of *friendly* states are also protected when within the Dominions. In *Johnstone v Pedlar (1921) 2 AC 262* a US national in Dublin (then within the Dominions) was engaged in subversive activities. The seizure by the Crown of money in his possession was challenged by him and he was successful. The Crown could not plead act of state as a defence against an alien of a friendly country even when his actions were hostile if the alleged act of state occurred within the Dominions. A difficulty arises in that it is not clear what is meant in a modern context by 'within the Dominions' or 'inside the territory of the Crown'. Most of the cases referred to above occurred at a time when the British Empire still existed. Today it would be likely that the court would restrict the meaning of the phrases to the United Kingdom of Great Britain and Northern Ireland and perhaps such colonies as Hong Kong.

Enemy aliens are not protected and the plea of act of state will prevent investigation of action taken against them: *R v Bottrill, ex p Keuchenmeister* (section 43.2(b) above);

(ii)   *outside the Dominions of the Crown* – there is no clear judicial authority as to whether the defence of act of state would be available against British subjects. In *Nissan v AG* the House of Lords, in considering a claim in respect of damage to a requisitioned hotel in Cyprus belonging to a UK citizen caused by British troops on a drunken spree, did not have to decide the point as it was held that the act in question was not an act of state. The Lords took the view that whilst the despatch of soldiers to act as a peacekeeping force and to join UN forces had been an act of state, not every consequence of that decision would be so. Only an act which was part of, or reasonably incidental to, a high level policy decision would probably be treated as an act of state.

Lord Reid was of the opinion that a British subject *can never be deprived of his legal right to redress by an assertion ... that the acts of which he complains were acts of state.* Lord Wilberforce, on the other hand, could not accept such a broad principle, and the rest of their Lordships expressed no settled opinion. It therefore remains uncertain whether act of state can be a defence against a British subject in these circumstances.

What the House of Lords meant by 'a British subject' is also obscure. *Nissan v AG* was heard when the *British Nationality Act 1948* was still in force. The Act included in the definition of a British subject all Commonwealth subjects, but it has been doubted whether the court would today take this approach and it is thought that it might restrict the meaning to British citizens entitled to reside in this country and those who were settled here.

All that is clear is that the defence will stand against aliens outside British territory provided that the act of state was authorised by the Crown.

Further reading

Wade and Bradley, chs.13 and 18.
de Smith, ch.6.
MLR 42(1979) 72.
Markesinis (1973) Camb. L.J. 287.
Allott (1977) Camb. L.J. 225.
Gilmour (1970) Public Law 120.
Collier (1968) Camb. L.J. 102.
The English Constitution, Bagehot, ch. II.
Brazier 1982 Public Law 395.

LLB

CONSTITUTIONAL LAW

LESSON 5 (REVISION)

51. *REVISION OF LESSONS 1 – 4*

Read through each section of Lessons 1 – 4, pausing at the end of each paragraph to recall what you have just read. If you cannot recall it adequately and in detail, read and check your knowledge until you are satisfied.

When you have completed this task, test your knowledge further by working through all the questions on the next pages.

52. *REVISION QUESTIONS*

1. 'A Bill of Rights would give a power to the judges that they ought not to have and do not know how to exercise'. Discuss.

2. 'There is no logical reason why the United Kingdom Parliament should be incompetent so to redefine itself (or redefine the procedure for enacting legislation on any given matter) as to preclude Parliament as ordinarily constituted from passing a law on a matter' (de Smith, p.103). Discuss.

3. 'The legal sovereignty of Parliament has not been affected by the enactment of the European Communities Act 1972'. Discuss.

4. 'Parliament is legally sovereign, but only if it expresses its will in a way that the courts will recognize as a proper exercise of its sovereign power'. Explain and discuss.

5. 'The Parliament Act 1911 was, no doubt, a valuable democratic reform; but it did remove from our constitution an important check on legislative power and introduce an imbalance at its very centre'. Explain and discuss.

6. 'Whatever matters arise concerning either House of Parliament ought to be examined, discussed and adjusted in the House to which it relates and not elsewhere'. Do you consider this is still an accurate statement of the law?

7. Bland MP receives an annual retainer of £1,000 from the XYZ Trade Union, some of whose members are employed in the road construction industry. Bland declares in a debate in Parliament that certain firms are prolonging construction work on motorways in order to keep their work forces employed. The Minister for Transport in reply invites Bland to write to him with particulars, and Bland does so, naming Diggers Limited as an offending company and its directors as privy to the practice. In the same letter Bland writes that the directors have resorted to bribery in order to secure contracts from the Ministry. Bland is, however, unable to substantiate any of his allegations and the directors of Diggers Limited institute proceedings against Bland for libel.

   Employees of Diggers Limited picket the House of Commons, carrying placards demanding the expulsion of Bland from the House, and preventing commercial vehicles from making deliveries to the Palace of Westminster.

   The XYZ Trade Union write to Bland saying that they are dissatisfied with his parliamentary services to the Union and that if he does not give them an assurance that he will show greater zeal in defending the Union's interests in the future his retainer will be withdrawn.

   Bland asks the Speaker to rule that the actions of the directors of Diggers Limited and their employees and the letter from the XYZ Trade Union, are breaches of privilege.

   Discuss.

8. 'The King hath no prerogative but that which the law of the land allows him'. Explain and discuss.

9. A British aeroplane is hijacked in Ruritania, and the hijackers hold the passengers hostage at gunpoint while the plane is waiting at Ruritania Airport. By agreement with the Ruritania Government a platoon of British Commandos successfully storm the plane and release the hostages. In the course of the storming, Fosters an Australian citizen, is accidentally shot and injured and a grenade used by the commandos destroys valuable baggage in the hold of the plane belonging to Green, a UK citizen, and Harry, a US citizen.

Have Fosters, Green or Harry any redress in law against the Crown?

10. Is electoral reform needed in the UK? What alternative voting systems could be used and what are their defects?

11. How does the House of Lords' decision in *R v Secretary of State for Foreign and Commonwealth Affairs, ex p Council of Civil Service Unions* affect the courts' traditional view of the Royal prerogative?

12. Is the most important work of the House of Commons nowadays undertaken in its Committees?

LLB

PRIME MINISTER AND CABINET

LESSON 6 (STUDY)

61. *INTRODUCTION*

62. *THE CABINET*

    62.1   HISTORY AND DEVELOPMENT OF THE CABINET
    62.2   COMPOSITION ORGANISATION AND WORKING
           OF THE CABINET

63. *THE PRIME MINISTER*

    63.1   PRIME MINISTERIAL FUNCTION
    63.2   PRIME MINISTERIAL OR CABINET GOVERNMENT?
    63.3   MAIN CONVENTIONS OF THE CABINET SYSTEM

64. *THE CIVIL SERVICE*

    64.1   ORGANISATION OF GOVERNMENT DEPARTMENTS
    64.2   THE CIVIL SERVICE

61. *INTRODUCTION*

The House of Commons has 650 members and the Lords over 1,000. The party with the majority in the House of Commons forms the Government. Government Ministers may be drawn from the House of Commons or the House of Lords but by convention may *not* be co-opted from outside Parliament. There are approximately one hundred Ministers in a normal Government. A smaller group of the most senior ministers of state forms the Cabinet (about 20-25 in number). Mrs Thatcher's Cabinet appointed in June 1987 numbers 21 and there are approximately 110 Ministers in the Government.

62. THE CABINET

62.1 *History and development of the Cabinet*

The history of the Cabinet can be traced to Charles II's preference for consulting a small group of advisers in a private room (or Cabinet) rather than conferring with the full Privy Council. The practice was continued by later monarchs, although Parliament objected strongly to the by-passing of the Privy Council and attempted by the *Act of Settlement 1700* to bring it to an end. The provision in the *Act of Settlement*, that no one holding an office of profit under the Crown could sit in the House of Commons, was later repealed and thus the importance of the Cabinet continued.

In the 19th century it was said by Bagehot that the Cabinet was the *hyphen which joins the buckle which fastens* the administrative system to the political system. The Cabinet is of central importance constitutionally because the administration derives its authority from the Cabinet, which collectively derives its authority from the House of Commons, which derives its authority from the electorate. It is also at the pinnacle of the administration and the many decisions taken each week at Cabinet meetings lead to chains of action spreading out through the whole central administration.

62.2 *Composition, organisation and working of the Cabinet*

The Cabinet consists of a group of about 20 ministers, who, by convention, will all be members of either the Lords or the Commons and who have been invited by the Prime Minister to attend Cabinet meetings. The heads of certain important ministries will always be Cabinet members, but other members may be chosen because of their special expertise, their influences in Parliament or the country or the party. Some Cabinet Ministers will have few departmental responsibilities and are referred to as 'Ministers without Portfolio'.

The Cabinet generally meets twice a week throughout the year, with occasional emergency meetings. There is no set meeting place or quorum. The Prime Minister presides and decides on the agenda and much of the business is conducted on the basis of Cabinet papers which have been circulated in advance. This preparatory work is largely the responsibility of the Cabinet Secretariat, a group of senior civil servants.

The functions of the Cabinet are to discuss and decide policy and to co-ordinate between the departments of Government but the Cabinet do not discuss the Budget, the date of dissolution of Parliament for a General Election, Cabinet personnel, the grant of honours or the prerogative of mercy.

A note is made of the general discussion, but the views of individual Cabinet members are not usually publicised.

There are a number of cabinet committees responsible for specific areas of government (e.g. proposed legislation, draft legislation, defence). The committee system enables more work to be done by ministers and leaves the Cabinet as a whole free to discuss the most major issues. Note that non Cabinet ministers may be instructed to attend a Cabinet meeting or the meeting of a Cabinet committee.

Many modern Prime Ministers have had what is known as an *Inner Cabinet*, a group of three or four ministers close to the Prime Minister. This Inner Cabinet is generally unofficial and does not operate to a fixed agenda, nor does it have records or papers. The Prime Minister can consult informally with his Inner Cabinet to settle matters outside Cabinet meetings and power may thus move from the Cabinet as a whole to this smaller group, with the Cabinet acting as a sort of *Court of Appeal* in cases of dispute. The most recent example of an Inner Cabinet of sorts is that of Mrs. Thatcher's in the Falklands war.

The Cabinet does not generally initiate policy. Its function is rather to co-ordinate administration, to keep senior ministers in touch with all the various lines of governmental activity and to give the work of the Government a measure of unity. A formal vote is never taken at Cabinet meetings, although each member may give a statement of opinion. Those disagreeing with a decision of the majority of the Cabinet must, by convention, either support (in public at least) and accept the decision or resign.

63.   THE PRIME MINISTER

63.1   *Prime ministerial function*

The Prime Minister (PM) is chosen by the Sovereign although this choice is now purely formal and the leader of the majority party, or parties, in the Commons must be sent for. The PM has invariably taken the office of *First Lord of the Treasury*, and as the *Ministers of the Crown Act 1937* provided that a salary is paid to the person who is *Prime Minister and First Lord of the Treasury*, it would seem that the two offices are now inextricably linked. Some PMs have also taken some other office (e.g. Churchill was Minister of Defence, and Gladstone was Chancellor of the Exchequer).

The chief functions of the PM are to form a government, to choose and preside over the Cabinet and to act as the main channel of communication between the Cabinet and the Sovereign. It is the PM who advises the Sovereign on a dissolution for a General Election and on certain honours. Many Crown appointments (e.g. senior judicial offices, bishops, peerages) are made on his advice.

The PM also has functions in the House of Commons, speaking in debates, and answering questions on Government policy, and is traditionally responsible for the organization of business in the House (although this work is in fact delegated to the Leader of the House).

63.2   *Prime ministerial or cabinet government*

The position and power of the PM are the central features of modern cabinets. There are many reasons, within the British political system, to explain the PM's pre-eminence. The PM has a leading place in the eyes of the public and has control over appointments and promotion within the Government. Politicians are anxious for office and depend to a large extent upon the favour of the PM. In addition, a body of the size of the Cabinet, burdened with work as modern cabinets are, will fail to operate unless it is subordinated to a chairman who can guide, summarize and close the discussion. Finally, all the forces of party loyalty and organization tend to support the individual who is most closely identified with the success of the party, and this feeling is strongest when the party is in power and its leader is PM.

But the PM is not always master of his Cabinet and there is evidence to show that policies advocated by the PM have, on occasion, been modified or rejected. Also the PM may be won round to a point of view strongly argued by his senior colleagues. A recent example occurred in May 1988 when, it appears, a disagreement over exchange rare policy occurred between Mrs Thatcher, the Prime Minister, and Nigel Lawson, Chancellor of the Exchanger. Apparently the wholehearted support offered to the Chancellor by senior Conservative Colleagues and backbenches led Mrs Thatcher to compromise her views and expose her support for one Chancellor. However, the position of the PM is a special one with powers differing from those of his senior ministers. A PM soon puts his stamp upon a government, and if he fails to bind his colleagues together to cope with contemporary problems or to ensure action, then there is no one else who can do his job.

The exact relative positions of the PM and his Cabinet will vary according to the personalities of both the PM and his colleagues. But it is clear that the PM is not independent of his Cabinet and his relationship with his Cabinet may well affect his relationship with his party in Parliament.

63.3   *Main conventions of the cabinet system*

The two most important conventions of the cabinet system are those of *ministerial responsibility* and of *cabinet secrecy*.

(a) *Ministerial responsibility*

'Responsible' here simply means accountable. Every minister (whether in the Cabinet or not) is individually responsible to the Sovereign and to Parliament for the performance of his duties as minister. This means that he must answer questions about the working of his department in Parliament and also that he will be held accountable for the work of his department and must, in consequence, resign if serious blunders are exposed. A recent example of this was Lord Carrington's resignation as Foreign Secretary following the invasion of the Falkland Islands by Argentina. Ministers may also resign if a personal scandal becomes public, e.g. Profumo, Cecil Parkinson.

If a minister cannot satisfy the Commons with his answers to questions the Commons may show their lack of confidence by passing a motion to reduce the minister's salary.

In fact, resignations are rare and a minister who does resign is often appointed to another post although not always immediately. In June 1987 Mrs Thatcher selected Cecil Parkinson for the post of Minister for Energy.

Ministers are also collectively responsible to the Sovereign in that they must offer unanimous advice, and to Parliament in that they must demonstrate a united front in voting and speaking in support of government policy. The doctrine applies although rather less stringently to ministers not in the Cabinet and to Parliamentary Private Secretaries. Public unity of the Cabinet is an invariable rule although it is clear that there is sometimes private disagreement which does not result in resignation. Differences of opinion among leading members of the government would obviously afford ammunition to the government's opponents and so public harmony must be demonstrated.

The doctrine of collective ministerial responsibility has arguably been weakened in recent years. In 1975 Mr Wilson allowed members of his Cabinet to give their true views (rather than the Cabinet standpoint) during the campaign leading to the Referendum to decide on whether the UK should remain in the EEC but this freedom was limited to occasions when they were speaking outside Parliament about the EEC. In the same Parliament from 1974 to 1979 there were occasions when Mr Tony Benn (amongst others) made public his dissent from Cabinet policy in breach of the doctrine. Another factor undermining the doctrine is the increased use of 'leaks' by Cabinet ministers in recent times.

(b) *The Westland Affair 1986 and ministerial responsibility*

There were two resignations by senior Cabinet ministers, Michael Heseltine and Leon Brittan, in January 1986. These resignations exhibit the doctrines of collective and individual ministerial responsibility at work and raise other constitutional issues such as official secrets and the effectiveness of Select Committees. Both resignations were the result of the Westland Affair.

Westland Helicopters, a small British company, was in financial difficulty. Sikorsky Helicopters of the USA put together a rescue package and later a European Consortium with British and European participants offered an alternative. The European Consortium bid was preferred by Michael Heseltine, Defence Secretary, who made several statements from which his view was obvious. The Cabinet, however, decided to remain neutral and to leave the final decision with the Westland shareholders. When Michael Heseltine was informed in Cabinet that any future statement he might wish to make on the matter he must first clear with the Cabinet Secretary, he resigned, leaving the Cabinet meeting part-way through. He later explained that he could not tolerate a situation where no full discussion had been allowed in a full Cabinet meeting and criticised the Prime Minister's style of governing. He also then very strongly and publicly supported the European Consortium.

Leon Brittan faced two problems, one where he was alleged to have broken collective responsibility and the other, which eventually forced his resignation, was one of individual responsibility. First, Leon Brittan was accused by the Chief Executive of British Aerospace (a participant in the European Consortium) of having, during Sir Raymond Ligo's visit to the Department of Trade on another matter, had a meeting with him at which Leon Brittan was alleged to have said (contrary to the Cabinet's neutral stand) that British Aerospace should in the national interest withdraw from the European Consortium. Sir Raymond eventually withdrew his allegations but in the meantime they caused accusations of breach of collective responsibility and a howl of protest when Brittan in the Commons at Question Time denied receipt of a letter from British Aerospace when he knew such a letter had been sent to the Prime Minister.

Leon Brittan was eventually forced to resign because he had authorised a leak through his press department of a letter sent by the Attorney-General to Michael Heseltine alleging that Heseltine had given misleading information about the Westland Affair. Such letters from the Law Officers are always treated as highly confidential and the means of leaking the letter was particularly underhand. Although Mrs Thatcher and the Cabinet indicated that they would continue to support Leon Brittan, over half the backbenchers at a 1922 Committee meeting said they had lost confidence in Brittan and he therefore resigned.

Professor Zellick wrote to *The Times* about whether Leon Brittan had breached *s.2 Official Secrets Act 1911* and he took the view that there must be limits on a minister's power to disclose information and emphasised the very strong convention that it should not even be disclosed that the Attorney-General's advice has been sought, let alone the details of what it was. *(The Times, 1 February 1986).*

The government's refusal to allow the Defence Committee to question all the civil servants involved in the letter leak caused concern that the effectiveness of Select Committees would be impaired.

(c)   *Cabinet secrecy*

The operation of the Cabinet is surrounded by considerable secrecy and, by the *Public Records Acts 1958 and 1967*, Cabinet papers are only available for public inspection after 30 years or such other period as the Lord Chancellor may direct. Cabinet documents are protected by the *Official Secrets Act 1911*. Any serving Cabinet minister who was known to have revealed details of Cabinet meetings to the press would be likely to lose his office.

In *AG v Jonathan Cape (1975) 2 All ER 484* (the Crossman Diaries case) it was held that the court had power to restrain improper publication of information which had been received by a Cabinet minister in confidence, provided that it was clearly shown that the need for confidentiality continued. The doctrine of collective responsibility was said to be the justification for restraining disclosure and the *Official Secrets Acts* were not relied upon.

Since the court in the *Jonathan Cape case* decided that continuing confidentiality of the material in question had not been established, publication of Cabinet information less than ten years old was permitted. The government subsequently adopted the recommendation of a Privy Council committee that publication in such circumstances should not occur for 15 years, except with clearance from the Cabinet Secretary, but in the event of dispute it was ultimately a question for the ex-minister to decide as to what should be published.

64. THE CIVIL SERVICE

64.1 Organisation of government departments

At the head of each Government department or ministry is the *Secretary of State* or *Minister*. He is a member of the Government and changes with the Government. Under each minister will be one or more *Parliamentary Secretaries* or *Parliamentary Under-Secretaries;* they are junior ministers and again change with the Government.

The principal ministries are:

(a) *The Treasury*

Concerned with the supervision and control of national finance. It is the senior Government department and is headed by the First Lord of the Treasury (the PM) and the Chancellor of the Exchequer both of whom, by convention, are drawn from the House of Commons. Since the Treasury supervises finance, it is involved with the work of all the other ministries and is responsible for the allocation of money to each department.

(b) *The Home Office*

The Home Secretary exercises much of the royal prerogative to do with justice. He is responsible for the maintenance of the Queen's peace and supervises the police forces. He is responsible for legislation on criminal justice and controls the various state institutions of punishment. This department also deals with nationality and immigration matters.

(c) *The Foreign Office*

The Secretary of State is in direct contact with representatives of foreign and Commonwealth countries and with British diplomats overseas. The Office is concerned with the formulation and conduct of foreign policy. The Secretary of State is normally, although not invariably, drawn from the House of Commons.

(d) *Department of the Environment*

Formed in 1970 by the merging of the Ministries of Housing and Local Government, Public Buildings and Works and Transport (Transport has now been split into a separate ministry once again.)

(e) *Law Officers Department*

The Law Officers are legal advisers to the Crown and Parliament. The Attorney-General (one of the two English law officers) represents the Crown when it is involved in civil proceedings.

(f) *Other Ministries*

Other important ministries are the Ministry of Defence, the Department of Health and Social Security, the Department of Employment and the Department of Education and Science.

64.2 The Civil Service

(a) *Functions*

The Civil Service is regulated primarily under the royal prerogative. Civil servants carry out the detailed administrative work of a government department. Their appointment is non-political and so does not change with the Government. They perform routine administrative functions on behalf of the Minister, but the Minister remains responsible for their actions to Parliament and protects them even where a specific action was carried out without his knowledge see: *Carltona v Commissioner of Works (1943) 2 All ER 560*. This does not apply if the Minister's instructions have been disobeyed. Certain powers must be exercised by Ministers personally.

(b) *Political activities of civil servants*

Civil servants are disqualified by statute from sitting in the House of Commons and must resign office before standing as candidates in Parliamentary elections. Other political activities are governed by a code, the purport of which is to allow the more senior civil servants to take part only in local politics and to permit both national and local political activity by those at lower grades.

(c) *Civil servants and security*

In 1948 a purge was carried out on civil servants with communist or fascist affiliations. They were removed from participation in any secret work, but were, if possible, transferred to non-secret matters. Thereafter it was decided that civil servants employed on top secret work should be subject to a form of scrutiny known as *positive vetting*, which was concerned with general character defects which might make the civil servant more vulnerable to bribery or blackmail and therefore a security risk.

If a Minister decides that a *prima facie* case for the removal or transfer of a civil servant on security grounds has been made out, he can refer the matter to the *Three Advisers* (retired civil servants) who will investigate the allegation and hear evidence from the accused civil servant and any character witnesses he may produce. The accused person is not allowed to cross-examine those who have given information against him. The Advisers will present their findings, which remain secret, to the Minister and he may take action according to their advice, or not, as he wishes. The procedure is, in fact, used infrequently.

(d) *Terms of service of civil servants*

In order to understand the law applying to civil servants first the general law relating to employment must be explained:

The *ordinary employee* is nowadays protected in two ways:

(i) The common law (developing in this field from the 19th century) provides that each employee, who has not been in breach of his contract of employment, is entitled to a period of notice from his employer if the employer wishes to dismiss him. Such period of notice would be that set out in the contract between the employer and the employee or, if none, such a period as is reasonable in all the circumstances. There are now minimum notice periods set out by statute which depend on the length of service of the employee.

If the right period of notice is not given by the employer the employee may apply to the ordinary courts *for damages for wrongful dismissal*. The amount awarded to a successful employee will be calculated by ascertaining the gross amount which should have been paid by the employer to the employee during the notice period. Deductions are then made from this figure if the employee has found new employment within the notice period he should have received or if, had he made reasonable efforts to do so, he would have found such employment within that time.

e.g. X is entitled to 12 weeks' notice and his gross pay is £100 per week. He is dismissed without notice and subsequently finds a new job after 8 weeks at £100 per week. The damages he will be awarded are calculated as follows:

		£	
	12 x 100 =	1,200	
Deduct:	4 x 100 =	400	(for new job)
		800	wrongful dismissal damages

(ii)   by statute, the *Employment Protection (Consolidation) Act 1978*, provides a further protection. After an employee has served for one year (two years for jobs started on or after 1st June 1985), he may, if he is dismissed (even with the proper notice) apply to the industrial tribunal for *compensation* for *unfair dismissal*. He will obtain compensation unless the employer can show that he has dismissed the employee for a fair reason using a fair procedure and acting reasonably. The calculation of compensation for unfair dismissal is complicated and subject to various maxima.

These normal rules are modified in respect of civil servants.

At common law civil servants hold office at the pleasure of the Crown, but in practice they are not dismissed except for misconduct.

The relationship of a civil servant and the Crown has never been regarded as a traditional one of contract. Thus there has always been doubt as to whether a civil servant could recover arrears of pay as a contractual debt. In *Mulvenna v Admiralty (1926) SC 842* it was said that money could only be claimed on the bounty of the Crown and not as a debt. This decision was followed in *Lucas v Lucas and High Commissioner for India (1943) P 68* where it was held, therefore, that a salary owed to a civil servant was not a debt for the purposes of *garnishee proceedings*. In the earlier case of *Sutton v AG (1923)* it had been assumed, without argument, that a civil servant could sue for his pay and in *Reilly v R (1934) AC 176* Lord Atkin in the Privy Council had said:

> in some offices, at least, it is difficult to negative some contractual relations, whether it be as to salary or terms of employment on the one hand, and duty to serve faithfully and with reasonable care and skill on the other.

Again in *Terrell v Secretary of State for the Colonies (1953) 2 QB 482* it was said that a civil servant would recover salary owing to him, and the weight of authority is in favour of this view. However, the common law action of wrongful dismissal would not be open to a civil servant (although the statutory remedy in respect of *unfair dismissal* would).

Perhaps the most authoritative and recent statement of the position of a Crown servant at common law can be found in the judgments of the Privy Council in *Kodeeswaren v A-G for Ceylon (1970) AC 111*. In summary, it was said that a Crown servant has a contract of employment with the Crown, but subject to the condition (which, if not express, will be implied) that he is dismissable at pleasure. Thus no common law action could be brought for wrongful dismissal; but if other terms of the contract were broken (e.g. on pay) then the servant could bring a common law action for breach of contract (e.g. on a *quantum meruit* for work already done, i.e. arrears of salary). However, members of the Armed Forces are in a special position and cannot sue even for their accrued pay: *Leaman v R (1920) 3 KB 6631.*

Further Reading

Wade and Bradley, chs.14 and 15;
de Smith, chs.8 and 9;
The British Cabinet, Mackintosh (3rd ed.), Part VI, Sweet & Maxwell;
The Cabinet, P Gordon Walker;
The Diaries of a Cabinet Minister, Richard Crossman;
Brown, (1968) Public Law 28, 96;
Some Problems of the Constitution (1971), Marshall and Moodie, ch.4;
Finer,(1954) Public Administration 377;
Collective Ministerial Responsibility and Solidarity, Ellis (1930) Public Law 367;
Governing Britain, AH Hanson and M Walles (4th ed.), Fontana, ch.5.

LLB

CONSTITUTIONAL LAW

LESSON 7 (STUDY)

LOCAL GOVERNMENT (I)

71. *LOCAL GOVERNMENT*

71.1   INTRODUCTION
71.2   RELATIONSHIP OF LOCAL GOVERNMENT WITH
        CENTRAL GOVERNMENT

72. *STRUCTURE OF LOCAL GOVERNMENT*

72.1   STRUCTURE UNDER THE LOCAL GOVERNMENT ACT 1972
72.2   STRUCTURE UNDER THE LONDON GOVERNMENT ACT 1963
72.3 THE NEW STRUCTURE UNDER THE 1984/85 REFORM ACTS
72.4   FUNCTIONS TO BE TRANSFERRED TO LOWER TIERS
72.5   FUNCTIONS TO BE TRANSFERRED TO JOINT BOARDS
72.6   OTHER FUNCTIONS
72.7   COMPOSITION AND POWERS OF THE JOINT BOARDS

73. *GENERAL CHARACTERISTICS OF LOCAL AUTHORITIES*

73.1   PARISH AND COMMUNITY COUNCILS
73.2   COUNCIL MEETINGS
73.3   COMMITTEES
73.4   THE EFFECT OF THE LOCAL GOVERNMENT, PLANNING AND
        LAND ACT 1980
73.5   THE WIDDICOMBE REPORT ON THE CONDUCT OF LOCAL
        AUTHORITY BUSINESS

74. *FINANCE*

74.1   THE LAYFIELD REPORT ON THE RATING SYSTEM
74.2   REASONS FOR THE RATES ACT 1984
74.3   CRITICISMS OF THE RATES ACT 1984
74.4   JUSTIFICATION FOR THE RATES ACT 1984
74.5   RATES REFORM UNDER THE CONSERVATIVE GOVERNMENT 1987

75. *AUDITS*

71. *LOCAL GOVERNMENT*

71.1 *Introduction*

Local government permits a variation in government and administration to suit local needs and circumstances. Each area will have its own special problems and the inhabitants of those areas have the opportunity to elect local leaders who are familiar with those difficulties. Directly elected local government provides a check on the powers of central government, which is concerned with national policy and which might otherwise be tempted to over-ride local considerations in pursuit of the broader national interest. Civic consciousness is also aroused by the local community's interest in its direct responsibility for its own administration and therefore local government is an important means by which 'ordinary' people can participate actively in the decision-making process. Thus local government ensures a division of power between central and local authorities, and helps to preserve a healthy democracy in which local people have a direct say in local affairs and exercise a direct check over those immediately responsible for local decisions. It may be said that the essential feature of English local government is that it is both 'local' *and* 'government' within its own sphere; English local authorities are *not* mere organs of a central government, as in many Continental countries. Each local authority has a separate independent existence, and power to take decisions and make mistakes within the extent of the powers entrusted to it by the general law. The central government exercises a considerable control over the manner in which an authority may carry on its affairs, but local authorities remain independent entities and are in no sense organs of central government. However, the relationship of central and local government is a highly controversial subject and the abolition of the GLC and the metropolitan borough councils and the effect of the *Rates Act 1984* have led to strong criticisms that the Conservative Government are weakening local autonomy and causing a constitutional imbalance between central and local government (see sections 72 and 74.2 on 1984/85 reforms and the *Rates Act 1984*).

71.2 *Relationship of local government with central government*

In the provision of some services the local authorities have a great deal of autonomy. In other matters government departments regularly consult on matters affecting local interests so that there is a considerable two-way process of communication. Nevertheless, central government has a formidable array of methods by which it can control local authorities:

(a) *Orders, regulations, directions, circulars* issued by the Minister under the authority of statutes. E.g. under the *Education Act 1944* the Secretary of State may make regulations as to the standards of premises, etc. Orders, regulations and directions have force of law but circulars have no strict legal effect: they are the means by which policy is explained.

(b) *Appointment and dismissal*

Frequently the Minister must approve the appointment or dismissal of officers employed by local authorities, e.g. senior public health inspectors cannot be dismissed without the consent of the Secretary of State.

(c) *Inspection*

Largely this takes place in the three areas of social security, education and police.

(d) *Bye-laws*

These must be confirmed by the 'confirming authority' – usually a Secretary of State.

(e) *Confirming powers*

There are, in addition to bye-laws, many instances where the Minister's approval must be sought by local authorities, e.g. the establishment of new schools, clearance orders, compulsory purchase of land and the exercise of borrowing powers.

(f) *Audit*

This is largely through independent district auditors or approved professional auditors who must ensure that local government accounts are in accordance with law.

(g) *Grants*

Local authorities are encouraged to undertake certain services, e.g. health, slum clearance, house improvements, police and so on, by means of central grants. Therefore, they must satisfy the government that the services are being provided efficiently.

(h) *Borrowing powers*

Capital expenditure entails borrowing and this must be approved by the Secretary of State. Not only does this enable the Minister to see that the money is well spent but also the power may be used as an instrument of government financial policy.

(i) *Appeals to the Minister*

In a wide range of powers the local authority may affect the rights of individuals, e.g. condemn an insanitary house, refuse planning permission for development of land. In most of these cases there is usually a right of appeal to the Minister or the courts.

(j) *Default powers*

Where local authorities default in a particular duty the Minister may take over the duty if so empowered. These are few in number but a recent illustration is in the case of local authorities acting with unreasonable delay in the sale of council houses under the *Housing Act 1980*, e.g. Norwich District Council, threats by Patrick Jenkin to send Commissioners to run Liverpool if a legal budget was not passed by the Council.

72. *STRUCTURE OF LOCAL GOVERNMENT*

Local government in England and Wales (except London) underwent a major reorganisation on 1 April 1974, the date when the *Local Government Act 1972* came into effect, and a further massive reorganisation has been taking place during 1985-86 with the implementation of the *Local Government Reform Acts* passed in 1984 and 1985. The reforms that took place in 1974 will be briefly examined in order to show the impact of the 1984/85 reforms.

72.1 *Structure under the Local Government Act 1972*

England and Wales was divided into counties, each with a council; each county was divided into districts, each with a council, making 422 local authorities in total. Certain functions were assigned to the county councils (e.g. education and social services), others were assigned to the district councils (e.g. public health and housing). Six counties, because of their density of population, were classified as 'metropolitan counties' and their districts as 'metropolitan districts'. The six counties were South Yorkshire, West Yorkshire, Greater Manchester, Merseyside, the West Midlands and Tyne & Wear. (The remaining 47 non-metropolitan county councils covered less densely populated areas.)

72.2 *Structure under the London Government Act 1963*

Within London the *London Government Act 1963* had provided already for a similar two-tier system in which the 'upper tier' was the Greater London Council (GLC) with functions over the whole area, whilst the 'lower tier' comprised 32 borough councils with particular functions within their own area. For example, each borough council was the local planning authority for its area, responsible for granting or refusing planning permission for various kinds of local developments; but it was the responsibility of the GLC to draw up the 'Structure Plan' (the strategic development plan) for London as a whole, to which the borough councils were obliged to have regard when deciding whether or not to grant planning permission.

All the above local authorities were directly elected by the inhabitants of the areas covered by each body. The method of election was the same as that used for elections to the Westminster Parliament, i.e. universal adult franchise under the 'first-past-the-post' majority voting system.

72.3 *The new structure under the 1984/85 Reform Acts*

The Conservative Government had been re-elected in June 1983 on a manifesto which included a commitment to abolish the 'upper tiers' of the existing local government structure (i.e. the six metropolitan authorities and the GLC) mainly on the ground that the upper tiers were superfluous in that they did not perform as many functions as the non-metropolitan/borough councils and that, at a time when public expenditure cuts were an essential part of national economic policy, it was desirable to get rid of unnecessary layers of bureaucracy by 'streamlining' local government and by exercising greater controls over local authority spending (which would also be achieved under separate legislation controlling the rate-levying power of local authorities). The details of the proposed reforms had been spelt out in a White Paper in

October 1983: 'Streamlining the Cities' (HMSO, Cmnd 9063, £3.60) and were enacted in 1984/85, with the intention that they would be brought into effect during 1986. For this purpose the *Local Government (Interim Provisions) Act 1984* abolished the 1985 elections to the metropolitan county councils and the GLC and instead extended the life of those bodies for a further year.

The *Local Government Act 1985* was then passed to implement the structural reforms outlined in the White Paper. The 1985 Act was justified by the government on the grounds that it would remove a source of conflict and tension between the upper and lower tiers of local government, and between the upper tiers and central government; that it would save money through reductions in unnecessary staff; and that it would provide a system which would be simpler for the public to understand in that responsibility for nearly all local services would in future rest with a single authority.

The reforms took effect on 31 March 1986. On that date the GLC and the six metropolitan county councils ceased to exist. From April 1985 (the date on which fresh elections to that upper tier were due) there was a transitional period in which no elections took place, and instead the upper tiers enjoyed an extended period in office, without fresh elections, up to 31 March 1986.

From 31 March 1986, in place of the upper tier of local government, the functions formerly exercised by the GLC and the six metropolitan county councils are discharged either by the lower tier (i.e. the London borough councils)and (outside London) in the six metropolitan regions, by the metropolitan district councils or by specially-constituted Joint Boards and 'quango's' (quasi-autonomous, non-governmental organisations). There are expected to be about 20 of these bodies (none of them, of course, will be directly elected.)

72.4   *Functions to be transferred to lower tiers*

(a)   *Planning*

The borough and district councils already had responsibility for certain planning functions and they took over responsibility for the Structure Plan functions at present carried out by the GLC and MCCs. In view of the special problems posed by London in this area, there may also be a special 'London Planning Commission' (a quango) to supervise the overall development of London and to secure uniformity in approach from the 32 London borough councils. The borough and district councils also inherited those functions of the upper tier related to conservation, such as responsibility for historic buildings and ancient monuments. (The consequent abolition of the Historic Buildings Commission of the GLC has caused much disquiet in London because of the valuable work performed by that body in the past in preserving and protecting London's special architectural history.)

(b)   *Highway and traffic management*

Those functions previously exercised in this area by the GLC and MCCs are transferred to the borough and district councils, which had a degree of responsibility for such matters (London borough councils have always been highway authorities in their own right).

(c)   *Waste regulation and disposal*

The responsibility of the upper tier for these matters passed to the lower tier who are encouraged to increase private sector participation in the discharge of these functions in order to save money.

(d)   *Trading standards, etc.*

The consumer protection functions exercised by the MCCs pass to the metropolitan district councils, who are encouraged to ensure consistent standards of enforcement and to make appropriate arrangements for sharing equipment and specialist staff. (The London borough councils already had responsibility for trading standards and consumer protection.)

(e)   *Civil defence*

This responsibility becomes entirely that of the lower tier.

72.5 *Functions to be transferred to Joint Boards*

(a) *Police*

The existing police authorities of the six metropolitan counties were replaced by Joint Boards consisting of district council representatives and magistrates. (London has its own Metropolitan Police Force, answerable directly to the Home Secretary because of the special security and policing problems posed by the capital city.)

(b) *Fire*

The existing fire brigades in the metropolitan counties and in London are retained with Joint Boards responsible for administration in place of the MCCs and GLC.

(c) *Public transport*

This responsibility passes to Joint Boards in the metropolitan counties (London already has a special London Regional Transport Board, separate from the GLC, with responsibility for the administration of the capital's 'bus and underground services'. The members of the Board are appointed by the Secretary of State for Transport, and are accountable directly to him and to no-one else: *London Regional Transport Act 1984*).

72.6 *Other functions*

(a) *Education*

This was already a responsibility of the Metropolitan district councils and remains in their hands. In Inner London, education was the responsibility of the Inner London Education Authority (ILEA), which was a special committee of the GLC and not a separate local authority (see *ILEA v Secretary of State for the Environment (1984) The Times*, 26 May (CA)). The government was persuaded that a unitary education service, administered by a single education authority, would offer the best prospect of meeting the special educational needs of inner London and in improving the standards and cost-effectiveness of the education service. In a surprise concession the government announced that the ILEA would be directly elected.

(b) *Land drainage and flood protection in London*

This was the unique responsibility of the GLC which in May 1984, amid great pomp and ceremony, put into operation the massive Thames Flood Barrier. Responsibility for land drainage and flood protection (including the ownership and operation of the Thames Barrier) passed to the Thames Water Authority (a nominated body).

It is not possible to go through every detailed change that was effected by the structural reforms, but the above changes are generally regarded as the most significant in the package of proposals presented to Parliament. In addition the creation of Joint Boards to run certain local services merits further consideration because it is here that local democracy is said to be undermined, with people who are not directly elected to the Boards taking important decisions on matters affecting the everyday lives of local people. It is feared that such Boards, being accountable to central government, may give greater priority to following national policy on public expenditure cuts, thereby sacrificing local services and refusing to meet local needs.

72.4 *Composition and powers of the Joint Boards*

The government's desire is to constitute these Boards in such a way that they will be as representative as possible without being too large or unwieldy. The number of members nominated by each borough and district council will, if possible, bear a relationship to the size of each council's electorate.

In the metropolitan counties the boards for fire, public transport and police will probably be composed of two members from the district council with the smallest electorate in each area, with the other district councils in the area having further members in proportion to the size of their electorates. On this basis boards would vary in size from 12 members in South Yorkshire to 30 in Greater Manchester. For London a similar basis of nomination would not be practicable because of the large number of constituent councils (32) so, instead, in order to secure a membership which could be capable of effective management, the government proposed that there should be one member from each borough council and from the Common Council of the City of London (a special corporation independent of the 32 councils).

All the new Joint Boards would have the power to levy precepts on their constituent authorities. Those precepts would be set on a uniform basis, and the yield from each local authority would be proportional to its rateable value.

In London there is an additional specialist body, created by statute, to take over the GLC's management of existing debt and residual legal liabilities.

The precepts issued by each Joint Board will be subject to approval by the appropriate Secretary of State for the first three financial years in order to prevent extravagant or expensive use of the new organisations. The Secretaries of State will also have the power to specify levels of manpower because, in the government's view, the key to achieving savings will be the elimination of duplication of work and an increase in efficiency from a slimmer work-force.

Whether these reforms will achieve the stated aims of the government remains, of course, to be seen. One thing seems certain: the 'boom' years of local government (the early and mid-1970s), which witnessed a massive increase in staff levels and new layers of bureaucracy, are at an end, and contraction, not expansion, is now taking place. For many of those in local government it could be said that 'The party is over'.

73. GENERAL CHARACTERISTICS OF LOCAL AUTHORITIES

Local authorities are multi-functional. In addition to functions already mentioned there are libraries, smallholdings, recreation facilities, and weights and measures. In this sense a local authority may be distinguished from gas, electricity and water authorities which are concerned with one service only.

Each local authority is a body corporate, created by statute and dissolvable only by statute. Being a statutory corporation means having only those powers granted by the statute which created that particular corporation. In order to obtain other powers individual local authorities may have to ensure the passage of private Acts of Parliament which confer the additional powers.

73.1 Parish and community councils

About 10,000 small towns and villages have parish councils (in England) or community councils (in Wales) in addition to their two principal councils.

73.2 Council meetings

The chamber where the council meets is usually semi-circular and members of the same party sit together in a group. The chairman sits in the middle with the chief executive at his side. The chief executive is the principal paid official and he can speak but not vote. Below the platform sit committee clerks who make an accurate record of the meeting. There are special galleries for the press and public.

73.3 Committees

You will find an Education Committee and a Social Services Committee on every list of county council or metropolitan district committees. These are *statutory committees* compulsory by Act of Parliament.

Most councils have a central Policy and Resources (or Management) Committee of leading councillors who try to look at the council's work as a whole. Their recommendations must go before a full council meeting where every councillor has a chance to debate them.

When committees meet at least one chief officer is present and ready to give information and service.

The council decides how much freedom its committees shall have. They may be allowed to make their own decisions except on finance; or they may be told to submit nearly all their proposals to the council meeting; or usually something in between the two.

Any committee (except finance) may co-opt non-councillors up to one-third of its total membership. These co-opted members take a full part in discussion and voting.

All committees must allow the press and public to attend their meetings unless they pass a special resolution to exclude them from a particular meeting, e.g. because members of the public intend to disrupt the meeting so as to prevent the transaction of business: *R v Brent Health Authority ex parte Francis (1985) 1 All ER 74.*

Any attempt to exclude councillors of minority parties will be an abuse of power and void, and the same will apply to any attempt to deny council information to such councillors: *R v Hackney LBC, ex parte Gamper (1985) 3 All ER 275.* However, in regard to the receipt of council information, the burden will be on the individual councillor to prove a 'need to know' the information in question, and for this purpose idle curiosity is not enough: *R v Birmingham City DC, ex parte O (1983) 1 AC 578 (HL)*.

73.4 *The effect of the Local Government, Planning and Land Act 1980*

The *Local Government, Planning and Land Act 1980* increased the accountability of local authorities to their electors by requiring them to publish key information about their activities in a form which will make comparisons between authorities easier, and by requiring improved accountability of local authority direct labour organisations, so that they are run as separate and accountable trading bodies in fair competition with the private sector, and with a reasonable rate of return on the capital they employ.

73.5 *The Widdicombe Report on the Conduct of Local Authority Business*

This reported in June 1986 making 88 recommendations. Some of the more important follow:

(a)   Councils should have standing orders about their committees which should be balanced to reflect the party strengths on the Council unless the parties waived this right. There would be no public right of access to purely deliberative committees and on the decision-making committees there should be no non-elected members. Advisers should not be allowed to vote and those disqualified from being members of a committee should not be present.

(b)   Every council should provide a Council Question Time and time for minority business.

(c)   Twin-tracking (being a councillor for one council but employed by another) should be stopped.

(d)   Above the rank of principal officer employees of local authorities should have restrictions placed on their political activities.

(e)   There should be a statutory public register of the pecuniary and non-pecuniary interests of councillors.

74. FINANCE

The average council gets about half of its income from central government grants (66% in 1975-76). There is a large 'Rate support grant' to each council, and much smaller *specific grants* for certain services such as clean air schemes. In addition the government pays housing subsidies which are not tied down to a total figure.

Under the *Local Government, Planning and Land Act 1980* a new system for the distribution of rate support grant to local authorities in England and Wales is introduced with a single block grant in place of the needs and resources elements of the old grant, while ceilings are prescribed for the level of total local authority capital expenditure. The new system is designed to relate each local authority's entitlement to grant more closely to its 'standard expenditure' so that any authority spending significantly above this level would have to bear an increasing proportion of the burden itself. Authorities receive annual capital blocks for housing, education, social services, transport and other services but, having received these allocations, they are free to determine their own spending priorities by the transfer of resources between spending blocks.

When local authorities need to borrow money for works of a permanent nature they may do so only with the approval of the Secretary of State and in accordance with any conditions laid down; this 'loan sanction' was devised in order to ensure that local authorities adhere to principles of sound finance and to facilitate the government's management of the national economy.

Finally, approximately 48% of local authority income today is derived from rates. Rates are a form of local government tax calculated by reference to the rateable value of property occupied by the ratepayer (i.e. how much he would pay in rent for the property on the open market). The rate is an amount expressed as so many pence in each £ of rateable value. The amount of money raised by way of rates is nothing like enough to meet the cost of the services which local authorities are now required to provide; hence the need for the rate support grant (above).

74.1 *The Layfield Report on the rating system*

The Layfield Report (1976), Cmnd 6453, criticised the rating system on the following grounds:

(a) It is regressive in the sense that the amount paid by way of rates does not properly reflect the ability of the ratepayer to pay (although this may be offset to some extent by rate rebates and other supplementary benefits). Many wage-earners do not pay rates (e.g. because they reside as lodgers), yet have the right to vote in local elections and thereby determine how rates should be spent. By contrast many commercial and industrial enterprises pay heavy rates for their premises, yet have no say in the way rates are levied and spent (although the people who individually comprise those enterprises will do so if they are householders).

(b) Assessments are often uneven and there is no direct link between the rate paid and the use made by the ratepayers of the local government services provided. For example, libraries and swimming pools ('public baths') may be maintained out of rates levied from people who do not use those facilities. Conversely, users of those facilities may not be ratepayers.

(c) The inadequacy of rates necessitated central government support in the form of grants, and the large proportion of local government income represented by such grants defeated the principles of accountability, in the sense that the authority incurring expenditure should be responsible for finding the income necessary to finance the expenditure.

The *Layfield Report* recommended improvements to the rating system which would include future assessment (based on revaluations at frequent regular intervals) on capital values rather than (as at present) on rental values. The Report also advocated the introduction of a local income tax, to be collected by the Inland Revenue at levels determined by each local authority.

However, the *Layfield Report* was not implemented because no government has been able to produce a satisfactory alternative scheme, despite some manifesto commitments by the major parties aimed at either abolishing rates or radically reforming the way in which they are levied. Yet the problems caused by the system remained as great as those which prompted the establishment of the Layfield Committee. The enormous increase in the rate burden in some areas, coupled with disturbing evidence of the way in which rates were being spent (on seemingly frivolous or non-viable projects which represented a huge waste of resources) acted as the spur to government intervention. In a measure which provoked as much political controversy as the Acts re-structuring local government, the Conservative government passed the so-called 'Rate-capping' legislation: the *Rates Act 1984*.

74.2   *Reasons for the Rates Act 1984*

The government explained that the rating system, although defective, must be retained because there were serious objections to the various alternatives which had been proposed:

(a)   a poll tax would require significant exemptions and be hard to enforce. It would need the compulsory registration of all who were liable to pay;

(b)   a sales tax would be complex and impose new burdens on retailers;

(c)   a local income tax would be expensive to run and increase the marginal rate of income tax.

Further, none of these alternatives would deal with the problem of excess spending by local authorities; and central government would still have to help authorities with low resources and high expenditure needs. For those reasons the government decided that the rating system must be retained. However, it pointed out that some improvements had already been made under the *Local Government, Planning and Land Act 1980*, which had extended domestic rate relief to most mixed businesses and domestic properties, as well as extending to small businesses (among others) the right to pay rates by instalments. In line with the recommendations of the *Layfield Report* the Act has also conferred on ministers new powers to order revaluations when appropriate and, if necessary, for certain classes of property only. Further, the government intended to require councils to consult business representatives before fixing their rates. (See further *Green Paper on Rating*, reported in *The Times*, 17 December 1981.) In the government's view these reforms would go some way to redressing the grievances underlying the widespread hostility to the rates. Further, the burden of rates should be significantly reduced following the abolition of the GLC and MCCs. As a back-up power to all this the government intended to take much closer control over the way in which local authorities levied rates by exercising, where necessary, a power 'to cap' (i.e. put a limit on) the amount of rates that could be raised by any single council. (A previous idea to force councils to hold referenda if they wished to overspend was dropped by the government in the face of strong back-bench opposition in Parliament.) The new law removed the powers of councils to levy supplementary rates once the demand notes for the main rate have been issued at the start of each financial year. Since councils would be allowed only one opportunity each year to set a rate there was a danger that they might set a high rate in order to allow for higher than expected costs so, in order to meet that danger, the government would set a maximum allowable percentage increase in the rate for each year in order to 'cap' high-spending councils from levying unfairly high rates. The 'guilty' councils which exceeded the set limits would be listed by the Secretary of State after full consultation with Parliament. Any council that is 'capped' may apply for a redetermination allowing it to levy a higher rate than that first proposed by ministers. However, a council which obtains a redetermination must accept any extra controls imposed by ministers. (This may mean being told how much to spend on particular services.) The rate-capping powers came into force in the 1985-86 financial year.

74.3 *Criticisms of the Rates Act 1984*

The rate-capping plan attracted widespread criticism, mainly on the grounds that it would undermine the accountability of elected local authorities, destroy local autonomy, and upset the delicate balance of power between central and local government by enabling a centralisation of decision-making. Opponents argued that MPs and central government civil servants would be unable to make rational or fair decisions about local needs, since those are understood only by locally elected representatives who live in the community and who are directly accountable to local people. The very idea of a councillor embodies the notion of someone who balances what the community needs against what it can afford to pay; if the councillors get that judgment wrong, they may not be re-elected. *The Times* (21 December 1983), in a leader entitled 'Parish Pump Imperialism', criticised the rate-capping legislation on the ground that if, as the government argued, it was needed in order to curb a few high-spending councils who were responsible for exceeding the Treasury's targets year after year, why should the government desire a general power to set the spending of each and every council in England and Wales? (Presumably, other methods of persuasion and grant manipulation by which central government could put pressure on the guilty local authorities could be used; no doubt the government would argue that all those methods have been tried in the past and proved ineffective.) *The Times* also criticised the very wide discretionary powers which the Secretary of State would enjoy in naming overspending councils. Further, without a significant increase in central government staff so as to cope effectively with the details of local spending,the legislation posed grave dangers of maladministration. In an earlier leader on this subject, entitled 'The Wretched Ratepayer' (16 September 1983) *The Times* indicated that the real problem at the heart of local authority overspending was the weakened financial accountability of councils to their electorates, so that instead of treating that disease, the government would instead be suppressing only the symptoms of that disease. Some authorities have subscribed the lack of real political accountability of councils to the electoral system used for local elections, under which, on a very low turnout, political extremists are able to garner sufficient votes to secure election and then dominate some councils for the rest of their period of office, without any further political accountability to their electorate as a whole for the way in which they spend the rates. (There is, of course, an audit system, but that does not deal with the problem of the lack of political accountability of councils for their spending decisions to their electorate.) (Some who pay rates have no votes, and *vice versa:* see above at 74.1.)

74.4 *Justification for the Rates Act 1984*

Supporters of the legislation would emphasise the need to control rampant inefficiency and waste in local government. The independence of local government from central government, which is no doubt an essential part of the diffusion of political power in the UK, cannot be relied on in order to resist reform from a government elected on a manifesto containing clear commitments to carry out such reform, for the principle of Parliamentary sovereignty overrides all other constitutional conventions. The fact that central government, through grants, meets a large part of local spending inevitably blurs accountability and reduces autonomy: at one time the rate support grant accounted for 66% of local authority spending; the fact that it has now fallen to around 51% merely indicates the ever-changing nature of the relationship between central and local government. The rate-capping legislation should therefore be seen as simply another stage in the development of this relationship, in which local government will continue to enjoy independence within variable limits set by legislation and administrative practice. Local authorities will not lose the broad discretion they have always enjoyed for running their own services and in deciding how best to provide for them. Further, under *s.137 Local Government Act 1972*, as amended by the *Local Authorities (Expenditure Powers) Act 1983*, councils may, in defined circumstances, levy up to a 2p in the £ rate in order to make grants for purposes which are of general benefit to the community, including the provision of financial assistance towards the acquisition of land and the carrying out of building work, so this power will go some way towards off-setting the loss of the councils' old power to levy a general supplementary rate in order to finance particular projects.

In October 1984 the Secretary of State for the Environment announced a further comprehensive review of local government finance.

74.5 *Rates reform under the Conservative Government*

Before the June 1987 General Election the Conservatives hastily pushed through Parliament a Bill to reform the Scottish rates system. Following the Conservative election victory the Government has indicated that it will fulfil its manifesto commitment to reform the rating system. The Local Government Finance Bill 1983 is in its Committee Stage in the House of Lords in May 1988.

It proposes to abolish rates, replacing them by a community charge per head of the adult population, including pensioners, students and those on social security. The rate of charge will vary with the area but everyone will be subject to it. There will be some exemptions for example for the mentally ill, those living permanently in hospital or in prison. In addition for the poorest rebates of up to 80% will be provided. The community charge is to be introduced in 1989 in Scotland and in 1990 in England and Wales but for nine inner London Boroughs and the City of London there will be arrangements to phase the charge in over a longer period as it is likely to be at a high rate and to cause considerable hardship in these areas if this is not done.

The supporters of the charge believe that it will increase accountability in that those who use and receive local authority services will in future be paying for them but those who criticise the charge as a 'poll tax' believe it is enequitable since it is not dependant on the ability to pay and even the poorest will have to pay 20% of the charge. Conservative backbenchers in both the Commons and the Lords sympathised with this view but were unable to obtain an amendment to link the charge to a person's income. The opponents to the charge believe that the charge will be expensive and very difficult to collect. The system of business rating is also to be changed and a single unified business rate will be set by central government.

After the introduction of community charge and the new business rate these will produce approximately 50% of local authority funding, the rest being provided by central government grants.

75. AUDITS

The spending of money by local authorities is subject to an annual external audit. Until recently local authorities had the right to choose their own auditors, but now they are chosen by a special body called the Audit Commission, which was set up in July 1981 and which began work in 1983. The Commission's members are chosen from industry, commerce, local government and the professions, with an independent chairman. (A previous idea that responsibility for district audits should be assumed by the Comptroller and Auditor General was rejected by the government on the ground that it might clash with the constitutional position of local authorities.) The Commission may appoint 'district auditors' (who usually come from the Department of the Environment) or, with the approval of the Secretary of State, 'approved auditors' from the private sector firms of professional accountants if that seems desirable. Both sets of auditors have the right of access to local value for the money which has been spent on their behalf. Local authority electors have rights to attend before the auditor and make objections to any items of expenditure disclosed by the accounts. For this purpose any 'person interested' may inspect the accounts at each audit. The auditor's main function is to ensure that proper accounting practices have been followed in the compilation of accounts, but he is also under a general duty to report anything which he thinks ought to be reported in the public interest, such as the possibility of loss due to waste or extravagance or poor value for money, etc. Reports are sent to the Audit Commission and to the local authority in question. The reports must be published in the press, if the press so desires. The district auditor (but not the approved auditor) has the power to apply to court for a Declaration that any particular item of account is 'contrary to law' (i.e. *ultra vires*, beyond the local authority's legal powers). If the Declaration is made the court may order responsible councillors to repay the unauthorised expenditure and, if it has exceeded £2,000, may disqualify such councillors from the council for a specified period (this will happen only if the councillors had acted unreasonably or in the knowledge that the spending was contrary to law). The approved auditor lacks these powers; he may, however, report to the Commission who may direct the district auditor to hold an extraordinary audit. It must be emphasised that the district auditor cannot challenge in court any matter of policy which was within the legitimate discretion of the local authority; he may challenge issues of policy only where they involve questions of law and it seems that *ultra vires* decisions have been taken: *Crown v Roberts (1908) 1 KB 407* per Farwell J.

The Local Government Act 1988 gives the auditor a new power to intervene if he reasonably believes a council is acting or is about to illegally. Formerly the power was only retrospective now there is a prospective power too. This was introduced to deal with makes like the Liverpool City Council's declaration of an illegal budget in 1985.

Further reading

Wade and Bradley, Chapter 21 and Appendix B.
de Smith, Chapter 20.

Further advanced reading

Municipal Empire, David Walker (1983), Temple Smith, £8.95.
'Freedom of Information and Local Government', *Public Law* (Winter 1981), at p.545.

LLB

CONSTITUTIONAL LAW

LESSON 8 (STUDY)

LOCAL GOVERNMENT (II)

81. *JUDICIAL CONTROLS OVER LOCAL AUTHORITIES*

    81.1   LIABILITY IN TORT
    81.2   LIABILITY IN CONTRACT
    81.3   LIABILITY OF COUNCILLORS
    81.4   PUBLIC LAW LIABILITY OF LOCAL AUTHORITIES

82. *LIABILITY FOR MALADMINISTRATION: LOCAL GOVERNMENT COMMISSIONERS*

81. *JUDICIAL CONTROLS OVER LOCAL AUTHORITIES*

It may be said that local councils, like individuals, have to obey the ordinary laws of the land. Originally it was argued that local authorities, being creatures of statute, were subject to the doctrine of *ultra vires*, so that they could not be liable in tort for anything arising out of an *ultra vires* act (i.e. an act beyond their legal powers). But that argument was rejected by the court in the case of *Campbell v Paddington Corporation (1911) 1 KB 960* in which it was held that the District Council was liable in damages in respect of injuries caused by the erection of a stand in the road (for the purposes of viewing King Edward VII's funeral procession), an act which the Council had no legal power to carry out. Even though *ultra vires*, it was still their act.

The nature of local authority liability is *vicarious*, i.e. local authorities are responsible for the wrong-doing of their employees because it is the employee who acts on behalf of the council. The extent of liability can be very wide, e.g. for breaches of contract and for torts.

81.1 *Liability in tort*

See *Anns v Merton LBC (1977) 2 All ER 492* where the owner of a block of maisonettes sued the council because their inspector had approved the building work which later turned out to have faulty foundations, making the buildings unusable. The House of Lords held that the council were vicariously liable for their inspector's negligence, because the council had a duty to inspect the premises *and* a duty of care to the owner of the premises to ensure that the inspection was properly carried out. On the facts they were in breach of that duty of care, causing damage to the plaintiff.

However, in the leading judgment in this case, Lord Wilberforce drew a distinction between the exercise of statutory discretion on the one hand, and operational acts performed in the discharge of decisions on the other. Private law liability will attach only to the negligent operation of statutory powers and not to the exercise of the discretion as to whether or not to operate those powers, for that will be a question of public law and the *ultra vires* rule and, although public law remedies embrace a right to compensation, this will not be the same as a right to damages in a private suit for common law negligence.

Lord Wilberforce said that, in deciding on the extent of a council's statutory duty to inspect building foundations, it was not enough simply to apply the common law 'neighbour' principle of *Donoghue v Stevenson (1932)*, because to do so would be to neglect the essential factor that the council was a public body, whose powers and duties are definable in terms of public not private law. The problem, said Lord Wilberforce, was to define the circumstances in which the law should impose, alongside those public powers and duties, a duty in private law towards individuals so that they might sue for damages.

Lord Wilberforce went on to explain that most statutes relating to public bodies contain in them a large area of policy or discretion to be enjoyed by the public body in question and not by the courts, which were neither competent nor well-equipped to make those sorts of policy judgments: policy must be left to the politicians. However, Parliament also intended that those policy decisions should be made *bona fide*, within the powers granted, and reasonably in the sense that a particular decision was one which any reasonable public body of the kind in question might make. However, if a decision was *ultra vires* for infringing any of those principles, the remedy lay in public law only and did not create a right of private action to sue for damages in respect of injury sustained as a result of the *ultra vires* decision.

In so far as policy decisions had to be implemented, different considerations applied, said Lord Wilberforce. This 'operational area' might well embrace common law duties of care towards those 'neighbours', who might be affected by the practical execution of the policy decisions and, although it would not always be easy to draw the line between policy and operation, nevertheless 'it can safely be said that the more operational a power or duty may be, the easier it is to superimpose on it a common law duty of care'.

Thus it seems from Lord Wilberforce's words that if a council gives proper consideration to the question of inspection (taking into account all the relevant factors, not acting from improper motives, etc.) and decides that inspection is not necessary, then there is no basis in either public or private law for attacking that decision.

Lord Wilberforce's principle has found expression in several cases, sometimes with the result that a public authority escapes liability, e.g. *West v Buckinghamshire CC (1984) The Times, 13 November*, where it was held that the decision of a highway authority not to place double white lines on a road was a matter of policy and discretion, giving rise to no duty of care to road users, and which could not be attacked in the courts unless it could be shown that the authority had exercised its discretion negligently.

Contrast *Bird v Pearce (1979) 77 LGR 75*, where it was held that once the authority had placed road markings on a road they were under a duty of care to all road users to take reasonable care to ensure that those markings did not deteriorate so as to create a hazard, so that the authority in question was liable in negligence for an accident which had been caused when road markings placed by the authority had been obliterated by the authority's road resurfacing work.

See also *DHSS v Kinnear (1984) The Times, 7 July (QBD)*, where it was held that the health authorities have discretion as to whether arrangements should be made for the immunisation of persons against certain diseases, and that this discretion cannot be challenged in private law provided it is exercised *bona fide;* but that any negligent advice given by the health authorities as to the manner and circumstances in which immunisations were to be performed fell within the 'operational category' and could form the basis of a private action for negligence against the Department.

See also *Levine v Morris (1970) 1 All ER 144* (negligence in siting a road sign, because such siting was an operational, not policy, decision); contrast *Haydon v Kent CC (1978) 2 All ER 97* (no breach of statutory duty to maintain a path because the decision whether or not to clear ice from it was a policy, not operational, one).

There are many other cases in which local authorities have been held liable for various torts such as occupiers' liability, nuisance, and breach of statutory duty (see *Harris v Birkenhead Corp (1976) 1 All ER 341* on occupiers' liability; *Pride of Derby Angling Society v Derby Corp (1953) Ch 149* on nuisance; contrast *Smeaton v Ilford Corp (1954) 1 All ER 923* on

nuisance; and *Southwark LBC v Williams (1971) 2 All ER 175* on breach of statutory duty; contrast *Read v Croydon Corp (1938) 4 All ER 631* and *Governors of Peabody Fund v Sir Lindsay Parkinson (1984) The Times, 19 October (HL))*.

81.2 *Liability in contract*

In respect of contractual liability, local authorities can be sued only on contracts which they had power to enter. They are forbidden to enter any contract which fetters their future discretion as a bye-law making authority. Such a contract is void, e.g. *William Cory Ltd v City of London Corp (1951) 2 All ER 85* where there was a contract under which a company agreed to remove refuse collected by the council in its barge. Later the council made a bye-law restricting the size of barges used on the Thames. As a result the company found that it was illegal for them to use their own barges. They sued the council for breach of contract but failed because the contract was *ultra vires* the council.

It would be contrary to public policy to allow councils to pay damages for breaches of *ultra vires* contracts, which both parties are assumed to know was a void agreement. See also *Triggs v Staines UDC (1968) 2 WLR 1433* where the council had purported to enter a contract to the effect that it would not exercise its statutory compulsory purchase powers. This was declared void on the ground that the powers to take land compulsorily were entrusted to the council and their successors to be used solely for the furtherance of that object, which the legislature regarded as being for the public good. Hence any contract purporting to bind them and their successors not to use those powers was *ultra vires* the council as being contrary to public policy.

Similarly, in *York Corporation v Harry Leetham & Sons Ltd (1924) 1 Ch 557* the corporation purported to make two long-term fixed charge contracts with the company. By doing so the corporation fettered itself in that the statutory power given to it allowed it to vary its charges annually so as to match the running costs of the service. It followed that the agreements were *ultra vires* the corporation.

Specific power to enter contracts is conferred on local authorities by *s. 135 Local Government Act 1972*, and this power may be delegated to committees, sub-committees or officials. The power is exercisable through standing orders, and if the council fails to comply with the relevant standing orders when deciding whether or not to enter a contract, any person aggrieved may apply to the court for an order compelling compliance with those orders. However, the court will give the council the opportunity to vote to suspend those standing orders so as to remove the breach: *R v Hereford Corp, ex parte Harrower (1970) 3 All ER 460*.

81.3 *Liability of councillors*

If the council is vicariously liable for the acts of its employees, it would be unnecessary to sue individual councillors, though it would be possible to do so if they voted for the resolution which authorised the unlawful activities. Usually, however, their liability as individuals is invoked in the fields of financial impropriety, e.g. their liability for authorising unlawful expenditure.

In addition they are under a statutory duty to disclose any 'pecuniary interest' which they may have as individuals in matters coming up for decision by the council: *ss. 94-98 LGA 1972*. A breach of that duty exposes a member to criminal proceedings. If a member has a pecuniary interest, direct or indirect, in any CONTRACT or other matter and is present at the council meeting when it is discussed, he MUST:

(a)   disclose his interest; and

(b)   refrain from discussion AND voting.

The *de minimis* rule applies; a member is not treated as having an interest if it is so remote or insignificant that it could not reasonably be regarded as likely to influence him in discussion and voting. Also any interest he has as a ratepayer, etc. is disregarded.

'Pecuniary interest' means more than pecuniary ADVANTAGE: Parliament has NOT said that they may vote AGAINST their interest; it has said that they must not vote on ANY matter in which they have a pecuniary interest: per Lord Goddard CJ in *Brown v DPP (1956) 2 All ER 189*. Hence voting in a matter which is to the financial detriment of a member is just as illegal as voting in one which is to his financial advantage!

If he does vote, the whole decision may be void as contrary to natural justice on account of bias, but it is more likely that his vote will simply be treated as invalid and not cast, and not affect the validity of the vote as a whole: *Nell v Longbottom (1894) 1 QB 767.*

81.4 *Public law liability of local authorities*

Insofar as the administrative decisions of local authorities are concerned, it is well established that (per Lord Greene MR in *Associated Picture Houses v Wednesbury Corp (1948) 1 KB 223*) 'a judge must not substitute his own policy decision for that of a local authority'. Provided the authority acts within 'the four corners of its discretion', without bad faith or fraud, then the decision is not *ultra vires* just because the judge disagrees with it. It will be *ultra vires* if it is a decision which is so unreasonable that no reasonable local authority would have come to such a decision, e.g. a decision to dismiss all red-haired teachers – per Warrington LJ in *Roberts v Hopwood (1925) AC 578.* (Also see R v Liverpool City Council ex p Ferguson and Others (1985) Section 121.3 of the Manual) This judicial control is effective so far as legality of decisions is concerned. On policy questions the authority is answerable to central government and, of course, its own electorate.

82. *LIABILITY FOR MALADMINISTRATION: LOCAL GOVERNMENT COMMISSIONERS*

In 1974 Local Government Commissions were established by the *Local Government Act 1974* (one for England and one for Wales). These commissions allocate members of their body to particular areas and these Local Government Commissioners (LGCs) investigate complaints of 'injustice' suffered as a consequence of maladministration in connection with the exercise of administrative functions by a local authority, a police authority or a water authority. Complaints must be passed on by councillors, so the 'filter' system is retained. After investigation, the LGC must make a report to the relevant authority which must be made available to public inspection: if the LGC finds injustice the report states the relevant adverse findings and the authority must then inform the LGC as to the remedial action it has taken or proposes to take.

From 1 June 1984 complaints made direct to the Local Commissioners are sent to the Lord Mayor, Mayor or Chairman of the Council, in the hope that the complaint may then be settled locally. If not, the councillor will be asked to send the complaint to the Local Ombudsman to consider whether it should be investigated. (The procedure for making a complaint to the Local Ombudsman is explained in a free booklet, *Your Local Ombudsman*, obtainable from council offices or Citizens' Advice Bureaux or direct from the Commission at 21 Queen Anne's Gate, London SW 1).

An interesting case on the work of the Local Government Commissioners is *R v LGC for the North and North East Area of England, ex parte Bradford Council (1978) The Times, 1 August*, where it was held *inter alia:*

(a)   that a 'faulty decision may amount to maladministration' (per Eveleigh LJ), but that 'maladministration' is something which relates essentially to the manner of taking a decision and does not touch the merits of the decision, which the LGC may not question; and

(b)   it is not necessary, in a complaint under the *Local Government Act 1974*, to identify the exact action which is alleged to amount to maladministration; it is enough to state generally what act of the local authority gives rise to the complaint.

In addition, Lord Denning MR commented on the LCC's powers to act on his own initiative, if a councillor of the local authority whose decision is complained of does not act; Lord Denning said the reason for this distinction from the Parliamentary Commissioner for Administration (who operates only under the 'filter system') is the need to circumvent the supposed tendency of councillors to identify with their authority and therefore to be unwilling to entertain complaints against it, in contrast to the MP who (unless he is himself a Minister) owes no allegiance to any central government body which is complained against.

In the winter of 1984 Professor Yardley, the distinguished academic and expert in administrative law, gave a lecture to Chart University Tutors law students about his new appointment as Local Government Commissioner for Greater London and South East England (see also his article in *Public Law*, Winter 1983, at p.522). As a follow-up the institution of Local Ombudsman was subject to critical analysis by one of Chart's lecturers in the student magazine *Vision* (Summer 1984) and it is reproduced here:

ON OMBUDSMEN

by

Charles P Reed

Listening to Professor Yardley's talk on ombudsmen to CUT students and staff (16 February 1984) my general impression was of a kind and decent man who, in his public office of Local Commissioner for Administration, is probably doing little bits of good in an unspectacular but generally effective manner. Unfortunately we live in a country of finite resources, which is currently experiencing the evil of mass unemployment and where the social and welfare services are under increasing threat from the lack of adequate public investment. In those circumstances it is fair to ask whether taxpayers' money should continue to be spent on such institutions as local ombudsmen.

In every survey which has been taken since the introduction of 'ombudsmen' in this country it has been demonstrated that they are less well known and less popular in public opinion than other comparable institutions such as the Director General of Fair Trading (an office set up at about the same time as local ombudsmen, i.e. 1973/74). Professor Yardley ascribed this fact to public apathy, but that does not accord with the general nature of the modern British people, who have become much better informed on aspects of public life than their counterparts in, say, the 1950s. Today ordinary people expect to take an active and intelligent part in the decision-making process. Therefore it is, perhaps, more likely that the failure of the local ombudsmen to make a favourable impact on British public opinion is due to the nature of their work, rather than public apathy. There is no doubt that, on the whole, the local ombudsmen deal only with the 'small change' of administrative failures and accordingly lack the ability to be a really powerful force for individual civil liberties. To that extent (and to keep to the analogy) the abolition of local ombudsmen would be about as significant as the abolition of the half-penny coin.

There are also criticisms that can be made concerning the way in which the office of ombudsman operates in practice. To the extent that he is a 'peoples' grumbles-man' he is a mere duplicate of an MP or local councillor, but lacking the element of election which makes the MP/councillor representative 0-f and accountable to his constituents. The fundamental reason for the existence of the ombudsman is his ability to go where MPs/councillors are unable to go, i.e. 'behind the administrative curtain' into the dark recesses of Whitehall and its provincial offspring. Therefore, since the ultimate strength of an independent ombudsman is his power 'to get at the books', surely an ex-civil servant is better qualified than anyone else in knowing where to look for possible instances of maladministration? A person with no experience of the civil service and who cannot find his way round the departmental files will be of no use. Is it not a good working rule to recruit gamekeepers from the ranks of former poachers? Nor is it good enough for the ombudsman simply to rely on his professional staff to do the investigative work for him, for the fact is that it is he who was designed to be the major investigator.

In both his lecture to CUT students and in his article in 'Public Law' (Winter 1983) Professor Yardley estimated that there are now around seven different institutions of ombudsman operating in the UK (though admittedly some of these offices are held by the same person). There is speculation that more ombudsmen may be created in the future, e.g. for the nationalised industries, even though representative consumer councils already exist to monitor their operation. The Labour Party is in favour of an ombudsman to investigate alleged abuses of police powers. It seems, therefore, that ombudsmen are enjoying a growth industry at the moment. Professor

Yardley has spoken encouragingly of the increased co-operation between the existing ombudsmen, but why not go further and have a merger of the various offices, thereby creating an integrated system for complaints against government departments, local authorities, health authorities and so on? In that way public money might be saved through the concentration of resources and the standardisation of procedures.

At the moment there is little, if any, control over the way in which the ombudsman exercises his discretion on the question of whether to take up, continue or discontinue an investigation into a particular complaint. There is an obvious danger that such discretion could be exercised in an arbitrary way and, possibly, undermine some of the jurisdictional barriers which Parliament decided, as a matter of public policy, to erect around each office of ombudsman. To take one example which Professor Yardley gave in his lecture: the local ombudsman is forbidden to investigate a complaint where the complainant has an alternative remedy in the courts and where it is reasonable to expect the complainant to pursue that alternative remedy. Professor Yardley said that, on this matter, he exercises his discretion in a very generous way so as to regard it as unreasonable for the complainant to go to court where, for example, such action would cause great worry to that complainant. Since most ordinary people are literally terrified (and rightly so) at the prospect of going to court, Professor Yardley's locus standi test comes perilously close to being no test at all.

Professor Yardley referred to the relatively small number of cases in which a finding of maladministration had been ignored by the local authority in question. He gave very persuasive reasons why he was against using sanctions to compel the local authority to take appropriate remedial action. He thought that moral persuasion and political pressure constituted the best way in maintaining a friendly working relationship with all local authorities. But there is, perhaps, a more fundamental reason why the ombudsman should not have such enforcement powers; it may be that, just occasionally, the ombudsman gets it wrong. Although there is no precise definition of maladministration, nevertheless there is a clear statutory embargo on any challenge to the policy of the authority by the ombudsman. Provided that the policy has not been formulated or implemented in such a way as to involve maladministration, the contents of that policy cannot be challenged by the ombudsman no matter how wrong or unjust or 'immoral' he may believe it to be. In the few cases where local authorities have resisted his findings, it has been on this ground, i.e. that the ombudsman has overstepped the mark and condemned them, not for maladministration, but for their policy. The most famous example of this occurred in 1975 when the Parliamentary Commissioner alleged maladministration against the Industry Department over its handling of the Court Line Holiday Company. But the Industry Secretary (Mr Tony Benn) rejected the finding and persuaded Parliament to support him by successfully arguing that the PCA had infringed s.12(3) Parliamentary Commissioner Act *1967*, which precludes the PCA from questioning the merits of a decision taken without maladministration.

Finally, other critics, such as Professor Mitchell, have contended that the institution of ombudsman is a mere palliative which fails to deal with the central problem, namely the lack of a comprehensive body of administrative law and a rational system of administrative courts to enforce it. I agree. Personally, I would prefer to see Professor Yardley sitting in the House of Lords in its judicial capacity, helping to formulate and develop administrative law on an imaginative and civilised basis. As for ombudsmen, well, their continued funding must depend on the value that can be attached to their work and whether they provide sufficient evidence to show that they should enjoy priority over youth training schemes, kidney dialysis machines, law centres, etc. etc. etc. etc.

The *Widdicombe Report* of June 1986 recommended changes to the role of the local ombudsmen:

(a) they should be allowed to receive complaints direct from members of the public;

(b) they should be empowered to investigate matters on their own initiative;

(c) a remedy should be provided via the county court if a local authority would not follow an ombudsman's recommendation;

(d) the jurisdiction of the local ombudsmen should be increased to cover commercial transactions and the appointment of local authority employees.

Further advanced reading

Public Law, Winter 1983, at p.522 (Professor Yardley).
New Law Journal, 11 June 1981, at p.635 (C Bell).

LLB

CONSTITUTIONAL LAW

LESSON 9 (STUDY)

91. *FREEDOM OF EXPRESSION*

    91.1   INTRODUCTION
    91.2   CIVIL LAW
    91.3   CRIMINAL LAW

92. *FREEDOM OF ASSOCIATION AND ASSEMBLY*

    92.1   FREEDOM OF ASSOCIATION
    92.2   FREEDOM OF ASSEMBLY

93. *DISCRIMINATION*

94. *EMERGENCY POWERS*

    94.1   EMERGENCY POWERS – USE OF THE ARMED FORCES
    94.2   EMERGENCY POWERS IN PEACE AND WAR

95. *THE ARMED FORCES*

    95.1   *INTRODUCTION*
    95.2   MEMBERS OF THE ARMED FORCES
    95.3   MILITARY LAW

91. FREEDOM OF EXPRESSION

91.1 Introduction

Freedom of expression is nowhere defined in English municipal law. The broad principle, as with most civil liberties in England, is that whatever is not illegal is legal – a proposition which was turned on its head in *Malone v MPC (No. 2)* (telephone tapping). It is, therefore, necessary to examine the various civil and criminal law restrictions on freedom of expression. (For an excellent summary, see Roskill LJ's judgment in *Re X (a minor) (1975) Fam 47)*. It should be noted, however, that Britain is a signatory to the *European Convention on Human Rights, Art. 10* of which provides that *everyone has the right to freedom of expression* subject to certain protection of health and morals, and so on. Any civil or criminal restriction on freedom of expression which does not fall within those categories as defined by the European Court of Human Rights, is unlawful: see, for example, the Court's ruling in the *'Sunday Times' Thalidomide Case (1979)*. It has already been seen that the Convention is not directly enforceable in English courts of law (see Lesson 1).

91.2 Civil law

The law of defamation protects a person from false statements which expose him *to hatred, ridicule, or contempt, or which tend to lower him in the estimation of right-thinking members of society generally* (Lord Atkin in *Sim v Stretch (1936))*. If such statements are made in writing or other permanent form, they are libel, otherwise slander. Where the defamatory effect of statements was unintended, a correction and apology may be published to stay the action. Certain communications, e.g. in Parliament and the courts, are absolutely privileged and no action can be brought in respect of them. Other statements may attract qualified privilege and are protected if they were made without malice. Where the defence of privilege does not apply, the most usual defences raised are that the statement was true or that it constituted a fair comment on a matter of public interest.

It should be noted that libel proceedings must be brought in the High Court and that no legal aid is available for such proceedings. Therefore, those who wish to protect their reputation need wealth to proceed. The ordinary man in the street who may be defamed has no effective remedy.

A device sometimes used to prevent further publication of an allegedly defamatory statement is to issue a writ for defamation in order to take advantage of the law of contempt of court which prohibits prejudicing civil as well as criminal proceedings (see 91.3(f) below). The courts are conscious of the serious ramifications of 'gagging writs' for freedom of expression, and a plaintiff who applies for an interim injunction in these circumstances to silence his critics is unlikely to succeed unless he can establish that the usual defences to defamation are inapplicable to his case: see, for example, *Bonnard v Perryman (1891) 2 Ch 269; Wallersteiner v Moir (1974) 1 WLR 991; Woodward v Hutchins (1977) 1 WLR 760*. In addition, owing to the *Contempt of Court Act 1981* contempt can only occur when proceedings are active and *civil* proceedings do not generally become 'active' within the Act until a date for hearing is set.

Breach of confidence is a comparatively new ground of action. It is based on the principle that one person should not unfairly take advantage of another's confidence. The action is generally used to protect business and commercial secrets, but it has been used to prevent the publication of marital confidences *(Argyll v Argyll (1967) Ch 302)* and might also apply to prevent the publication of confidential information received by a cabinet minister, the disclosure of which would be contrary to the public interest in under-mining the doctrine of collective responsibility (see *A-G v Jonathan Cape Limited (1976) QB 752)*.

91.3 *Criminal law*

(a) *Censorship and control of the media*

The media are, of course, subject to the usual civil and criminal constraints on freedom of expression. In addition there is a non-statutory Defence Press and Broadcasting Committee with representatives from the Civil Service and the media. It operates a non-statutory 'D-notice' system whereby editors may by letter from a government department approved by the Committee be requested not to publish any information which may adversely affect national security. Disobedience to such a request is not an offence *per se*, but it may invite a prosecution under the *Official Secrets Acts 1911-39*. Even if no prosecution results, disobedience to a D-notice may result in a less cooperative attitude from Whitehall in the future so it is not a step lightly to be undertaken.

The Charter of the BBC empowers the Home Secretary to censor material broadcast by the Corporation and to direct that certain matters should be broadcast. (However, the BBC retains the liberty to explain what information is broadcast as a result of a Government direction to do so.) The IBA is under a statutory duty to satisfy itself that its programmes comply with certain statutory standards (see *s.4 Independent Broadcasting Authority Act 1973);* but it is doubtful whether that duty may be enforced by a member of the public acting without the Attorney-General's fiat (compare *Gouriet v UPW (1978) AC 435* with the earlier decision in *Attorney-General, ex rel McWhirter v IBA (1973) QB 629)*. Again the Home Secretary can prevent broadcast of certain matters. A Broadcasting Complaints Commission has now been set up to cover the BBC and IBA operations.

Theatrical performances are no longer subject to prior censorship, but they remain subject to special rules against obscenity and other criminal offences (see *Theatres* Act *1968)*. Prior restraint does exist with films. The *Cinematograph Act 1952* authorises the licensing of films and their classification. Films are now also subject to the *Obscene Publications Act 1959, s.53 Criminal Law Act 1977,and* the common law principles of obscenity and public indecency apply (see, for example, *R v Greater London Council, ex parte Blackburn (1976) 3 All ER 184)*.

Newspapers are no longer officially censored but no newspaper is under any duty to take an impartial stance (cf. the television operators) and most newspapers have a quite clear political leaning. Although there is no censorship the law does provide that certain matters (e.g. details of trials of juveniles) should not be printed. There has been a Press Council in operation since 1953 which has several times been reformed and now contains lay members as well as professionals in the newspaper world. There have been further calls for reform and a suggestion that persons described in newspaper articles should have a right of reply.

(b) *Obscenity*

The *Obscene Publications Act 1959* provides that it is an offence to publish obscene matter. The test of obscenity is not dissimilar to that which was adopted in *R v Hicklin (1868) LR 3 QB 360*, i.e. something is obscene where its effect is, taken as a whole, such as would tend to deprave and corrupt persons who are likely, having regard to all the relevant circumstances, to read, see or hear the matter contained or embodied in it. The tendency to deprave must, therefore, be tested according to the persons likely to come into contact with the material. Whether material is obscene is a question for the jury, as is the possible defence of 'public good', i.e. that publication is justified for the public good on the grounds of scientific, literary, artistic, educational or other merit. It is clear that obscenity is not limited to sexual matters: see, for example, *R v Calder and Boyars Limited (1969) 1 QB 151* (book advocating drug-taking held to be obscene); *DPP v A and BC Chewing Gum Limited (1968) 1 QB 159* (obscenity included violence).

There have been many recent judicial criticisms of the current law on obscenity (see, for example, *R v Metropolitan Police Commissioner, ex parte Blackburn (No. 3) (1973) QB 241; DPP v Jordan (1976) AC 699.* A *Home Office Committee on Obscenity and Film Censorship* has been appointed to examine the present law (see also *Law Commission Report on Conspiracy and Criminal Law Reform*, HC 176 (1976)).

It should also be noted that apart from the *Obscene Publications Act 1959*, there are many other statutes under which summary proceedings may be brought, e.g. *s.4 Vagrancy Act 1824; Indecent Advertisements Act 1889; Child Pornography Act 1978;* as well as various common law offences such as indecent exposure, obscene libel, conspiracy to corrupt public morals or outrage public decency (see, for example, *Shaw v DPP (1962) AC 220* and *Knuller Limited v DPP (1973) AC 435* and *s.5(3) Criminal Law Act 1977).* There are also many laws permitting seizure of obscene matter by, for example, Customs and Excise officers.

Finally, not only is it possible to challenge English laws of obscenity as being contrary to *Art. 10 European Convention on Human Rights* (see Lesson 1), but it is also open to argue in English courts that action is contrary to EEC law: see, for example, *R v Henn and Darby (1980) 2 All ER 166* where it was argued unsuccessfully that *s.42 Customs and Excise Act 1952*, dealing with confiscation of *indecent or obscene* material was contrary to the freedom of movement provisions of the *Treaty of Rome.* The law is also unsatisfactory in that it is too vague as to the meaning of 'deprave' and 'corrupt' and that for a matter to be obscene it must be likely to affect a 'significant' proportion of its likely readership (again a vague concept).

An attempt to reform the law on obscenity was commenced in the 1986-87 session of Parliament but lost because, *inter alia*, of the General Election.

(c) *Sedition, incitement, criminal and blasphemous libel*

It is a common law offence to publish a seditious libel or to utter seditious words. There must, however, be evidence of intention to promote violence and disorder over and above strong criticism of public affairs (see *R v Aldred (1909) 22 Cox CC1).* It is an offence under the *Incitement to Disaffection Act 1934 maliciously and advisedly to endeavour to seduce a member of the armed forces from his duty or allegiance* (see, for example, *R v Arrowsmith (1975) QB 678).* Even more importantly, it is a criminal offence to incite racial hatred: *s 18* and *s 19 Public Order Act 1986* provide that it is an offence for any person either to publish or distribute written matter which is threatening, abusive or insulting, or to use in any public place or at a public meeting words which are threatening, abusive or insulting, where (in either case) hatred is likely to be stirred up or intended to be stirred up against any racial Coloured or nationality group in Great Britain. No prosecution can be brought without the Attorney-General's consent.

There has been a recent revival in the old common law offences of criminal and blasphemous libel. A number of successful private prosecutions for criminal libel have drawn attention to the width of that offence (see, for example, *Goldsmith v Pressdram Limited (1977) QB 83).* Criminal libel does not depend on evidence of the likelihood of a breach of the peace arising from publication (see *R v Wicks (1936) 1 All ER 384).* It was generally believed that this was an essential ingredient to the offence of blasphemous libel, but the position is now quite uncertain (see *Whitehouse v Lemon (1979) 2 WRL 281).*

(d) *Insulting words and behaviour*

S.4 Public Order Act 1986 makes it an offence to use threatening, abusive or insulting words and/or behaviour in a public place or public meeting with an intent to cause a person to believe immediate unlawful violence will be used against hem or another by any person or to provoke that person or another to use immediate unlawful violence or whereby the person is likely to believe such violence will be used or it is likely such violence will be provoked. It is probably the most significant constraint on freedom of political expression and will be discussed in greater detail later (section 92.2).

(e) *Official Secrets Acts 1911 to 1939*

Until 1889 there was no legislation to protect State secrets but it then became an offence wrongfully to communicate information received as a civil servant. In 1911 during the increasing tension between Britain and Germany a new *Official Secrets Act 1911* was introduced and passed within 24 hours. It was a reaction to a series of scandals where German agents had been watching defence installations but could not be convicted of any offence under the current law. Perhaps its rapid passage and the background of international tension help to explain why the Bill was so sweeping in its effect and so ambiguously and widely drafted. It creates over 2,324 offences. *S.1* of the Act is entitled 'Penalties for Spying' but the ground it covers is undoubtedly wider than that commonly regarded as spying. For example, nuclear protesters approaching a military airfield with a view to immobilising it peacefully were convicted under the section. The wording of the section makes it an offence for a purpose prejudicial to the safety or interests of the State to approach any military or other prohibited place or obtain or communicate to others information which would help an enemy. The onus was from henceforth on the accused to prove his purpose was not prejudicial to the State.

S.2 of the Act was an innovation too. It makes it an offence for anyone to retain or communicate information which has been received whilst in the employment of the Crown or by virtue of contracts with the Crown or as a result of being an employee of a Government contractor. No offence is committed if the disclosure was authorised or if the communicant was under a duty to pass the information on. It is even an offence to receive information which one knows or has reasonable grounds to believe is communicated in contravention of the Act unless one can show that one was an unwilling recipient.

S.2 has been the subject of severe criticism and there has been sustained public outcry over the last five years since the cases of Sarah Tisdall and Clive Ponting. In the former case Sarah Tisdall was sentenced to six months' imprisonment for a breach of *s.2* when she divulged the date of arrival of Cruise missiles at Greenham Common to *The Guardian* newspaper. In Ponting's case Clive Ponting was prosecuted under *s.2* for sending to Tam Dalyell information relating to the sinking of the Argentine cruiser, General Belgrano, in 1982 which he considered should have been given by the Defence Minister in answer to the Parliamentary Question by Tam Dalyell, Labour MP for Linlithgow. Clive Ponting was acquitted by the jury in a perverse verdict, which amounted to a statement that they considered the section an unsatisfactory one.

These two cases provide examples of one of the main criticisms of the Act. In neither case, it could be argued, was the information divulged vital to present security. The revelations in both cases severely embarrassed the Government but did they really do much more harm than that? There are clear examples moreover when *s.2* has been used to prevent disclosures which can have had nothing to do with State security. In 1972 threats to use *the Official Secrets* Act were made to prevent publication of proposed changes to the rail network and the public hangman was, on another occasion, prevented from publishing his memoirs. Any type of information is covered by *s.2*, not just secret or confidential information.

A second criticism of *s.2* is that it is very vague. When is a person 'authorised' to make a disclosure? When is it his duty to do so? Clive Ponting argued that he had been under a duty to ensure the House of Commons received correct information. This argument did not receive much sympathy from the judge.

There have been various attempts to amend the law but the Conservative Government's Bill in 1979 failed and was withdrawn when it was realised it would have prevented disclosures that Blunt was a spy.

The *Franks' Committee Report* on *s.2* in 1972 described it as a 'catch all' and a 'mess'. It proposed that there should be criminal sanctions only where certain categories of information were divulged. These categories were:

(i)   information of major national importance in defence, security, foreign relations, currency and reserves if the information was classified as Secret or Top Secret. A minister's certificate that the classification was correct would be necessary to obtain a prosecution;

(ii)   Cabinet documents;

(iii) information facilitating criminal activity or violating confidential information supplied to Government by or about individuals.

The Committee would also have made the use of official information for private gain an offence and receipt of information would only have been an offence if there were reasonable grounds for belief there was a breach of the *Official Secrets Act*.

Even the proposals of the Franks' Committee have been criticised because:

(1)   no defence is provided that the disclosure in fact caused no harm to the interests of the State;

(2)   over-classification of information could still occur;

(3)   the Attorney-General would retain his discretion whether or not to prosecute which, many would argue, he has so unfairly operated recently.

In the 1987-1988 session a Conservative backbencher, Richard Shepherd, introduced a Bill to refer in Section 2 but the Government imposed a three line whip at Second Reading and the Bill was defeated. The Home Secretary promised reform of section 2 and a White Paper is to be published in June 1988 to lead to early legislation, probably in the next session of Parliament.

(f)   *Contempt of court*

The law of contempt seeks to balance the competing interest of fair and proper administration of justice with freedom of expression. Criminal contempt may take one of several forms, including scandalising the court by imputing improper motives to the judiciary (e.g. *R v Gray (1900))*; prejudicing either a fair criminal trial (e.g. *R v Thomson Newspapers ex parte Attorney-General (1968) 1 All ER 268)* or civil proceedings (*e.g Attorney-General v Times Newspapers (1974) AC 273* and contrast with the 1979 decision of the European Court of Human Rights on this case); identifying witnesses in defiance of a court ruling (e.g. *Attorney-General v Leveller Magazine Ltd (1979) AC 440);* and contempt in the face of the court (e.g. *Morris v Crown Office (1970) 2 QB 114).*

The law of contempt of course is now largely governed by the *Contempt of Court Act 1981.* This creates a strict liability offence of publishing anything which creates a *substantial risk* that the course of justice in *active proceedings* (civil or criminal) will be *seriously impeded or prejudiced (s.2).* There are few defences to this charge, e.g. a *fair and accurate report of legal proceedings held in public and published contemporaneously in good faith (s.4).* But the courts now have a power to order the postponement of such reports where it is thought to be necessary to avoid *substantial risk of prejudice to the administration of justice* – e.g. because it might prejudice a forth-coming trial of an alleged accomplice. A person who publishes matter offending the Act who, having taken reasonable care, does not know there are active proceedings is protected as is an innocent distributor who does not know the contents of the publication and having taken reasonable care distributes the matter.

The *Contempt of Court Act 1981* does not change the law of civil contempt of court, as discussed in *Home Office v Harman (1982)*.

(g)   *Parliamentary privilege*

This topic was considered earlier (see Lesson 3).

(h)   *Discovery of documents and other information*

As to the duty to make discovery, even (sometimes) imposed on innocent third parties, see *Norwich Pharmacal v Customs and Excise (1973) 2 All ER 943; D v NSPCC (1976) 3 WLR 124; London and County Securities v Nicholson (1980) 3 All ER 861; British Steel Corporation v Granada TV (1981) 1 All ER 417.*

As to the use which can be made of discovered information see *Riddick v Thames Board Mills (1977 3 All ER 677); Home Office v Harman (1982).*

As to the so-called *civil search warrant* see *Anton Piller v Manufacturing Processes Ltd (1976) 1 All ER 779; Yousif v Salama (1980) 3 All ER 405; Rank v Video Information Centre (1980) 2 All ER 273.*

92. FREEDOM OF ASSOCIATION AND ASSEMBLY

92.1 Freedom of association

The law generally does not restrict the freedom to join together for political purposes provided that no criminal conspiracy is involved, i.e. to do an unlawful act or use unlawful means to do a lawful act. However, it is illegal to belong to the IRA (Irish Republican Army) or the INLA (Irish National Liberation Army) which are proscribed organisations under the *Prevention of Terrorism (Temporary Provisions) Act 1984*. For a similar, Northern Irish, case see *McEldowney v Forde (1971) AC 632*. It is also unlawful to ask others to contribute to or make or receive a contribution for the IRA or the INLA and to address or arrange for a person to address a meeting to promote the IRA or the INLA.

The *Public Order Act 1936* imposes other important restrictions on freedom of association. *S.2* makes it an offence to organise, train or equip members of an association for the purposes of usurping the functions of the police or armed forces, or of using physical force in the promotion of a political object, or arousing reasonable apprehension that such force will be used (see, for example, *R v Jordan and Tyndall (1963) Crim LR 124*). This section is rarely used today. The consent of the Attorney General is needed for a prosecution.

S.1 of the Act makes it an offence to wear a political uniform in a public place or at a public meeting. It was held that an offence under *s.1* was committed when a group wore black berets to indicate association with a political body, the IRA *(O'Moran v DPP (1975) QB 864)*. The *Prevention of Terrorism (Temporary Provisions) Act 1984* makes it a separate offence to wear any item of dress or wear, carry or display any article in such a way as to cause reasonable apprehension that one is a member of a proscribed organisation.

92.2 Freedom of assembly

There is a multitude of statutory powers and criminal offences which affect freedom of assembly and private law measures may also be applicable, e.g. trespass. Only the principal restrictions will be examined here. It is important to note the very broad and largely uncontrolled discretions which the police and other authorities have in maintaining public order, also the important changes in the law made by the *Public Order Act 1986*, in force in its entirety from April 1987. Note that unless otherwise directed examination questions should be answered using the Public Order Act 1986 and not referring to the 1936 Act problem and common law provisions. These are included in this Manual in case a comparison is required

(a) *The prevention of public disorder*

There exist many statutory and administrative powers controlling the use of public parks and buildings as meeting places, e.g. the use of Trafalgar Square is governed by regulations made under the *Trafalgar Square Act 1944* and often byelaws apply to parks and public spaces requiring prior approval for meetings. The use of public buildings at election times is governed by the *Representation of the People Act 1983*, which provides that election candidates must be permitted to use schools and public halls for election meetings. At other times the local authority has a discretion as to whether to allow an organisation to use its property. The courts are very restrained in reviewing the exercise of these wide discretionary powers.

A selective form of preventive justice is binding over orders, whereby individuals are required to enter into an undertaking to be of good behaviour and keep the peace on pain of forfeiture of a pecuniary surety. Refusal to enter into such an undertaking may result in imprisonment for up to six months. Binding over orders are particularly effective in preventing public disorder where only a few people are involved: see, for example, *Lansbury v Riley (1914) 3 KB 229; Wise v Dunning (1902) 1 KB 167*.

Where the police reasonably apprehend that a meeting (whether in a public place or on private premises) or a public procession, is likely to give rise to a breach of the peace, they may take reasonable steps to prevent such an occurrence (see *Duncan v Jones (1936) 1 KB 218; Thomas v Sawkins (1935) 2 WB 249*). In one case, for example, a policeman's action in removing an orange lily being worn by a lady who walked through a crowd of Roman Catholics, was upheld as lawful *(Humphries v Connor (1864) 17 Ir CLR 1)*.

Another important statutory power encroaching upon freedom of assembly was *s.3 Public Order Act 1936* which empowered a chief of police (or in London the Metropolitan Police Commissioner) where he had reasonable grounds for apprehending that a public procession (i.e. not a public meeting) might give rise to serious disorder, to impose conditions on the procession, including the route to be followed. If he considered these powers were insufficient to preserve public order, there was available a procedure for obtaining an order prohibiting all or certain classes of public processions for a period up to three months. The procedure was as follows: outside the Metropolitan Police Area the chief officer of police applied to the local authority for such a ban and any such ban made by the local authority was subject to the Home Secretary's approval. Within the Metropolitan Police Area the MPC himself made an order subject to the approval of the Home Secretary. In *Kent v Metropolitan Police Commissioner (1981)* the court made it clear that it would not intervene to quash the MPC's order banning marches within the Metropolitan Police Area on the grounds that it was too wide as to area and too long in duration. This operational decision must, the court decided, be left to the MPC.

It is important to note that these powers were limited to marches, and did not extend to public meetings.

The preventive measures in *s.3 Public Order Act 1936* were added to and enhanced by the *Public Order Act 1986*. It made the following provisions:

(i)   By *s.11* of the Act advance written notice must be given to the local police if a public *procession* is to be held which will demonstrate support for, or opposition to, the actions of others or if the procession will publicise a cause or campaign or commemorate an event. The date, time and route of the procession is to be notified with at least six clear days' notice unless it is not reasonably practicable to satisfy this time limit. Exemptions from the requirement to give notice are available where the procession is customary or a funeral procession organised by an ordinary undertaker. Organisers of processions commit an offence if no notice or an incorrect notice is filed or if the procession deviates from the particulars in the notice unless this is through no fault of the organisers, being outside their knowledge or due to circumstances beyond their control.

(ii) *Ss.12 & 13* replace *s.3 Public Order Act 1936*. They make similar preventive powers available to control or ban *processions* in an extended range of circumstances. They can be used not only where serious public disorder is feared but also where there is reasonable fear of serious damage to property, or of serious disruption to the life of the community or that the purpose of the procession is to intimidate a person to carry out or refrain from carrying out something he is entitled to carry out or not as he chooses.

(iii) *S.14* is a new concept in that it allows control but NOT the ban of a public assembly. Only certain public assemblies are susceptible to this control – those which have 20 or more people gathered in a place which is either wholly or partially open to the air. Furthermore, before the controlling conditions may be placed on the assembly, a senior police officer must, having regard to the time or place, reasonably believe it will give rise to serious public disorder, serious damage to property, serious disruption to the life of the community or that the purpose of the assembly is intimidation. The conditions which may be used are on the place, the maximum numbers or the maximum duration.

(b) *Public order offences*

In prosecuting after public disorder the police may use what are seen as purely public order offences or they may utilise other laws, e.g. *s. 137 Highways Act 1980.* The two classifications of offence will be considered separately and, in order to simplify for the student's bene-fit, the pre-April 1987 law on public order offences will first be considered before the reforms of the *Public Order Act 1986* are set out in detail. This will be followed by the miscellaneous offences used some-times by the police in a situation of public disorder:

I Before April 1987

The common law offences of unlawful assembly, riot and affray and the statutory offences under *s.5 Public Order Act 1936* and *s.70 Race Relations Act 1976* are relevant.

(i) *Riot*

The essential ingredients of riot were (see *Field v Metropolitan Police Receiver (1907) 2 KB 853):*

(1) an assembly of three or more persons;

(2) those assembled must have a common purpose;

(3) there must be some execution or inception of execution of this purpose;

(4) there must be evidence of solidarity, i.e. intent to help one another against anyone who impedes them; and

(5) there must be a display of force or violence such that at least one person of reasonable courage must have been alarmed. However, there is no need to produce in the witness box a person to say that he actually was alarmed *(R v Sharp (1957) 1 QB 552).*

The offence of riot was not easy to establish. Nor, indeed, was the right to compensation for persons whose property has been damaged in a riot (granted by the *Riot (Damages) Act 1886).* It was necessary to show that the damage was caused by people *riotously and tumultuously* assembled. It was held in *Dwyer v Metropolitan Police Receiver (1967) 2 QB 970* that these two concepts are distinct and must be proved separately. Where claims under the Act succeed, the compensation is paid out of the local police fund.

(ii) *Affray*

This consisted of unlawful fighting or threats of force by one or more persons giving rise to alarm in the neighbourhood. There was no requirement of common purpose (see *Button v DRP (1966) AC 591; Taylor v DPP (1973) AC 946).*

(iii)   *Unlawful assembly*

This was the offence often used to restrain conduct which might develop into a riot. Once again, there had to be an assembly of three or more persons with solidarity between them, and a reasonable apprehension of a breach of the peace. It is critical to note, however, that where persons assembled for a lawful object without intending to cause a breach of the peace, the offence was not committed by them even though they realised that their meeting would be opposed by others and that a breach of the peace might ensue. This principle, that those who go about their lawful conduct ought not to be penalised because of threats by others acting unlawfully, emerged from the leading decision of *Beatty v Gillbanks (1882) 9 QBD 308.* In that case disputes had arisen between the Salvation Army and their opponents, the Skeleton Army, and two Salvation Army officers had been convicted of unlawful assembly. Their appeals were successful as they had acted lawfully and had not incited or intentionally provoked any breach of the peace. In *Wise v Denning (supra)*, Wise was convicted of disturbing the peace because, although he and his supporters committed no breach of the peace, he was deliberately insulting and provocative to Roman Catholics present and they committed breaches of the peace. Because of the difficulties in obtaining a conviction for unlawful assembly, frequently the police would prosecute for obstruction of the police in the course of their duty.

(iv)   *Threatening, abusive and insulting behaviour*

S.5 Public Order Act 1936 was very important. It provided:

Any person who in any public place or at any public meeting:

(a)   uses threatening, abusive or insulting words or behaviour; or

(b)   distributes or displays any writing, sign or visible representation which is threatening, abusive or insulting,

with intent to provoke a breach of the peace or whereby a breach of the peace is likely to be occasioned, shall be guilty of an offence.

The test was not whether the words or behaviour would have had the requisite effect on a *hypothetical audience of ordinary, reasonable citizens*, but whether the words or conduct used to the audience in question, however hostile, were likely to cause a breach of the peace (see *Jordan v Burgoyne (1963) 2 QB 744*). It was held in *Brutus v Cozens (1973) AC 854* that s.5 did not cover *vigorous, distasteful, and unmannerly speech* even though that might occasion a breach of the peace. The question is whether the speech was 'insulting', a word which must be given its 'ordinary meaning' or 'threatening' or 'abusive'.

II From April 1987

The *Public Order Act 1986* abolished the common law offences of unlawful assembly, rout, riot and affray and replaced them by statutory definitions. It also reformed *s.5 Public Order Act 1936.*

(i)   *S.1 – riot*

Riot is redefined in such a way as to recognise its seriousness. It is punishable on indictment by ten years' imprisonment or a fine or both. It occurs where *12 or more* present together use or threaten violence for a common purpose and their conduct, taken together is such as would cause a person of reasonable firmness present at the scene to fear for his personal safety. A common purpose can be inferred from conduct.

(ii) *S.2 – violent disorder*

This is punishable on indictment by five years' imprisonment, a fine or both and triable summarily by six months' imprisonment, a fine or both. It occurs where *three* or more present together use or threaten unlawful violence and their conduct taken together is such as would cause a person of reasonable firmness present at the scene to fear for his personal safety. Note there is *no* requirement of common purpose.

(iii) *S.3 – affray*

This is punishable on indictment by three years' imprisonment, a fine or both and summarily by six months' imprisonment, a fine or both. It occurs where a person uses or threatens unlawful violence towards another and his conduct is such as would cause a person of reasonable firmness present at the scene to fear for his personal safety. Where two or more use or threaten unlawful violence, their conduct must be taken together and a threat cannot be made by use of words alone. A power of arrest without warrant is given to a constable.

Note: The following rules apply to the three offences given above:

(1) Violence does not have to be threatened simultaneously.

(2) A person of reasonable firmness does not actually have to be or be likely to be present.

(3) The offences may be committed in a private as well as a public place.

(4) Violence, except for affray, includes violence towards property and is not for any of the offences restricted to conduct causing or intended to cause injury or damage.

(iv) *S.4 – replacing s.5 POA 1936*

The definition of the offence is altered so that threatening, abusive or insulting words, etc. are unlawful with intent to cause the victim to believe immediate unlawful violence will be used against him or another by any person or to provoke immediate use of unlawful violence to the victim or another or whereby the victim is likely to believe such violence will be used or provoked.

No offence is committed where it all occurs within dwellings. Constables are given the power to arrest without warrant. The offence is triable summarily and the maximum penalty is six months' imprisonment.

(v) *S.5 – new offence*

Similar to *s.4* in that it deals with threatening, abusive or insulting words, etc., but the offence occurs if these are used within the hearing or sight of a person likely to be caused harrassment, alarm or distress. It is a defence to show there was no reason to believe such a person was present or if the actions take place inside a dwelling and there is no reason to believe it was visible or audible from outside or the conduct was reason-able. A constable is given power to arrest without warrant but only if warning is first given which is unheeded. The maximum penalty is a fine.

Note: For all the above the mental element required is intention or awareness that one might be violent, etc. If one is intoxicated through drink, drugs or anything else, one is to be taken to be aware of what one would know without intoxication unless the intoxication is not self-induced or due to medical treatment only.

(vi) *Part III POA 1986*

By *Part III* the *Public Order Act 1986* reforms the law on racial hatred. This is defined as hatred against a group of persons in Great Britain defined by reference to colour, race, nationality (including citizenship) or ethnic or national origins *(s. 17)*. It is an offence to use threatening, abusive or insulting words or behaviour or display, publish or distribute such material with an intent to stir up racial hatred or whereby it is likely to be stirred up. The offence may occur in a public or private place but, if the action is committed by someone inside a dwelling who cannot be seen or heard from outside, there is no offence.

III Miscellaneous offences

(i) *Obstruction of the highway*

It is an offence under *s. 137 Highways Act 1980* wilfully to obstruct the free passage along a highway without lawful authority or excuse. It has been held that the obstruction need only be slight, and the prosecution need not establish an intention to obstruct *(Arrowsmith v Jenkins (1963) 2 QB 561)*. Again, the police enjoy considerable discretion, not only in deciding whether particular conduct amounts to obstruction, but also whether or not to prosecute for that, or any other offence.

(ii) *Miscellaneous*

There are many other criminal offences relevant to public order, e.g. conspiracy (see *R v Kamara (1974)* but see now *s.5 Criminal Law Act 1977); incitement to nuisance; obstruction of a police officer in the exercise of his duty; and others.

Civil law is also relevant, e.g. trespass, public nuisance and the so-called economic torts.

(iii) *Picketing*

Peaceful picketing in contemplation or furtherance of a trade dispute attracts certain immunities in the law of nuisance, conspiracy and obstruction (see *s. 15 Trade Union and Labour Relations Act 1974; Piddington v Bates (1960) 3 All ER 660; Broome v DPP (1974) AC 587; Express Newspapers v MacShane (1980) 1 All ER 65; Duport Steels Ltd v Sirs (1980) 1 All ER 529*. It should be noted, however, that secondary picketing is unlawful. In simple terms, secondary picketing occurs when a person (not being a trade union official) pickets outside a place which is not his present or immediately past place of work or, if he has none, his employer's head office.

It should be noted that this immunity does not extend to peaceful picketing for purposes other than in relation to trade disputes: see, for example, *Hubbard v Pitt (1976) QB 142* where a majority of the Court of Appeal regarded peaceful picketing by environmentalists outside a developer's office as an unreasonable use of the highway.

(c) *Freedom from government surveillance and the right to privacy*

Recently two issues of constitutional importance have generated much public debate among lawyers and academics, as well as the national press. These issues are so-called *jury-vetting* and *telephone-tapping.*

(i)   *Jury-vetting*

The traditional principle of a trial by jury is that the accused should be tried by *twelve good and true men* picked at random so as to avoid the risk of personal prejudice (either in favour of or against the accused). If, by chance, a juror appeared prejudiced then either the prosecution or the defence could challenge him and the court would ask him to stand down from jury service. Further, some people are disqualified from sitting on a jury (e.g. people with a recent criminal record). These may also be challenged. However, the problem is often in establishing either the bias of the juror or the disqualification of the juror. For this purpose *jury ~ vetting* might be employed by either the Crown or the defence to establish whether there is cause for challenge. For this purpose *vetting* means background inquiries on potential jurors, which may involve the questioning of neighbours. This practice was recently condemned as *unconstitutional* and a grave invasion of a juror's right to privacy by Lord Denning MR in *R v Sheffield Crown Court, ex p Brownlow (1980) QB 530.* Such vetting also, of course, contravenes the notion of random selection. However, the practice has not been declared illegal and recently a differently-constituted Court of Appeal approved the practice as essential in order to exclude disqualified jurors: *R v Mason (1981) QB 881.* The most controversial aspect, however, is vetting for political purposes, i.e. to discover the political sympathies of jurors who may serve in a *sensitive* trial with deep political overtones (such as those involving crimes of terrorism committed for political purposes). In response to the public disquiet on this issue, the practice is now regulated by guidelines issued by the Attorney-General but, because these are non-statutory, there is no guarantee that they will be observed or that sanctions are available if they are broken. All this is a salutary reminder that the individual has no settled *right to privacy* in English law.

(ii)   *Telephone-tapping*

Telephone-tapping involves the listening in to or recording of private telephone conversations. The practice is often employed by the police, who use Post Office facilities, in order to discover and apprehend criminals. In 1957 this practice was challenged in Parliament after the Home Secretary had disclosed to the chairman of the Bar Council information about the conduct of a barrister so obtained.

Subsequently a Committee of Privy Councillors was set up to investigate the issue and reported that the practice was legal if authorised by a Minister because of an ancient prerogative power to intercept communications between subjects. In any event, the offensive invasion of personal privacy is not yet recognised as an independent tort in English law (although telephone-tapping might be unlawful for other reasons, e.g. breaching the *Wireless Telegraphy Act 1949*). However, recently it was established that, provided certain requirements were satisfied, telephone-tapping was not unlawful, simply because there was nothing in English law to make it unlawful: see the judgment of Sir Robert Megarry V-C in *Malone v MPC (1979) 2 All ER 620.* Because this judgment did nothing to allay public anxiety, the Government announced an inquiry into the subject which was published as a White Paper. *The Interception of Communications in the UK,* Cmnd 7873, HMSO. New regulations were drawn up to govern telephone-tapping and the system was to be supervised by a senior Law Lord appointed by the Prime Minister (on 6 June 1980 Lord Diplock was appointed to the post). Only his first report was to be published. Because of the security issues, his subsequent reports will be secret, with Parliament being informed only of findings of a general nature or of any changes in arrangements. This reform failed to satisfy many MPs, who wanted to see legislation on the matter introduced as soon as possible. Indeed, in the *Malone Case*, Megarry V-C commented that this was a subject which *cries out for legislation*. Lord Diplock's first report claimed that there was no need for public concern as to the amount of telephone-tapping. After the decision of the European Court of Human Rights in the *Malone case* in 1984 the calls for legislation became irresistible and the *Interception of Communications Act 1985*, which received the Royal Assent in July, was the result. This Act came into force on 10 April 1986 and makes it an offence to intercept telephone or postal communications unless the Secretary of State has issued a warrant to intercept or the person intercepting believes on reasonable grounds that the person, whose communications are intercepted, agreed to the interception. Prosecutions require the consent of the Director of Public Prosecutions. The Secretary of State may also issue warrants to intercept if he considers it necessary in the interests of national security to prevent or detect serious crime or to safeguard the UK's economic well-being. Various safeguards to individual liberty are inserted so that a Tribunal and Commissioner are set up to monitor the working of the Act.

Jury-vetting and telephone-tapping are further illustrations that (apart from the law of trespass, nuisance, copyright and confidence) there is no 'right to privacy' in English law. Thus, in the nineteenth century case of *Penny v SE Railway (1857) 264 JQB 225* a landowner was unable to claim compensation for loss of privacy when a railway was built (upon an embankment) outside his window. It should be noted that *Malone v MPC* would have been differently decided had the invasion of Malone's privacy taken the form of trespassing in his house to 'bug' the telephone, instead of recording his telephone calls at the telephone exchange. The case would then have been on all fours with *Entick v Carrington (1765)* (in the absence of statutory authority).

93. *DISCRIMINATION*

By the *Race Relations Acts 1965, 1968 & 1976* discrimination, i.e. treating a person less favourably because of his colour, race or ethnic or national origins, was outlawed. Discrimination in respect of provision of goods and services, employment and housing was made illegal except where, for instance, employment in a private household or letting of residential accommodation in small premises was involved. Advertisements showing an intention to discriminate were also made illegal. The *Race Relations Board* was set up to receive complaints and to attempt to conciliate regarding them. Where conciliation failed the Board could bring civil proceedings. No action could be brought by the victim.

The efficacy of the provisions was adversely affected by various judicial decisions. In *Ealing v Race Relations Board (1972) AC 342*, for instance, it was held that discrimination on grounds of *nationality*, but not national origins, was legal and in *Race Relations Board v Charter (1973) AC 868* the statutes were held not to govern membership of private members' clubs. In *1976*, therefore, a new *Race Relations Act* was enacted to deal with some of the specific points raised in cases, and to provide greater protection for individuals. *Nationality* was listed as one of the grounds of illegal discrimination and discrimination in education was, for the first time, made unlawful. A new public corporation, the *Commission for Racial Equality*, was created to replace the Race Relations Board. The Commission has power to investigate on its own initiative, as well as to bring proceedings and to assist victims of discrimination preparing themselves to bring actions. Victims may now make direct complaint to the court, except in employment cases where complaint is to the Industrial Tribunals. The Act does not extend to discrimination on religious grounds: *Mandla v Lee (1983) 2 AC 548*.

The *Sex Discrimination Act 1975* is similar in scope and pattern to the Race Relations Acts. It outlaws discrimination on grounds of sex or marital status, except where a person's sex is a *genuine occupational qualification* in employment and subject to a number of special cases, e.g. ministers of religion. The *Equal Opportunities Commission* was created to enforce the Act and, as under the *Race Relations Act 1976*, rights to seek individual remedies were given.

The *Treaty of Rome*, which also prohibits sex discrimination in general terms, has direct effect, and is therefore part of English law, and goes further than both the *Equal Pay Act 1970* and the *Sex Discrimination Act 1975*. See *Macarthys Ltd v Smith (1981) QB 180* and *Garland v British Rail Engineering (1982) 2 All Er 402*.

Also see section 92.2b II on racial hatred.

94.   EMERGENCY POWERS

94.1   *Emergency powers – use of the armed forces*

The most usual reason for calling in troops to aid the civilian police has always been that troops are entitled to carry firearms whereas the police, as a general rule, are not. It was once the duty of local magistrates to call for assistance from the armed forces, where necessary, but now it is likely that such decisions would be taken at a much higher level, probably by the Home Secretary. Troops have very rarely been called upon to assist the police in maintaining public order but police/army operations, e.g. to deal with threats of terrorism at Heathrow, are becoming more common. As to the use of firearms to prevent crime, see: *AGNI's Ref. No. 1 of 1975 (1977) AC 105.* Where an emergency amounting to a state of war exists, the military authorities may impose restrictions on citizens in their own country and may set up military tribunals to deal with breaches of their directions. This is known as a state of martial law. It arises where for some reason Parliament cannot, or will not, give the usual statutory authority given to troops in emergencies and where, therefore, the armed forces take matters into their own hands. It has been held that where a state of war exists, martial law can be declared and the ordinary courts will then have no jurisdiction over the military authorities: *Marais v General Officer Commanding (1902) AC 109.* When the state of martial law ends the courts may then review the legality of acts done during it. Acts necessary, or perhaps simply deemed necessary at the time, to deal with the state of war would be considered justified on later review. It is usual, however, after the ending of martial law for an *Act of Indemnity* to be passed, giving retrospective protection to the armed forces. During conditions of war the maxim is 'between opposing armies, laws are silent'.

94.2   *Emergency powers in peace and war*

By the *Emergency Powers Act 1920*, amended in 1964, where the Crown proclaims that a state of emergency exists in that the community, or part of it, is about to be deprived of the essentials of life, a wide power to govern by means of statutory regulations is conferred on the *Executive.* Any regulations made must be laid before Parliament. A state of emergency lasts only one month, although it may be prolonged by a new royal proclamation.

In times of war it has been usual to pass statutes known as *Defence of the Realm Acts* or, in the Second World War, the *Emergency Powers (Defence) Act.* Under such statutes power to make regulations by *Order in Council*, for public order and safety and the defence of the realm, is conferred. Any regulations made cannot be examined by the courts to see whether they were necessary, but action allegedly taken under them may be declared illegal if not in fact authorized by the regulations (see *AG v Wilts United Dairy* earlier).

In *Liversidge v Anderson (1942) AC 206l* where the Home Secretary had power, under defence regulations, to order the detention of anyone he reasonably believed to come within certain specified categories, e.g. persons of hostile origin, it was held that the court would not enquire into the grounds of the Home Secretary's belief but would take it to be *reasonable* if he said it was. It is thus clear that the courts regard emergency regulations as being very different from other authorisations of ministerial action. Lord Atkin's dissenting judgment in this case is famous.

95. THE ARMED FORCES

95.1 Introduction

The control of the armed forces is part of the Royal Prerogative, but their maintenance during peacetime is a matter for statutory authority, as it was provided by the *Bill of Rights 1688* that *the raising or keeping of a standing army within the Kingdom in time of peace, unless it be with consent of Parliament, is against law.* It became the custom to legislate for the maintenance of the army on an annual basis in order that Parliament should have a chance to consider the matter every year. No legislation was ever needed to keep a standing navy, however, which was excluded from the *Bill of Rights* restrictions as having, historically, caused no threat to liberty.

95.2 Members of the armed forces

Officers are commissioned by the Crown, which may also dismiss them at pleasure. Other ranks join on the basis of contract, but may not sue for pay or for damages on wrongful dismissal. Members of the armed forces remain bound by the ordinary civil and criminal law as well as becoming subject to military law. Even where something unlawful is done at the command of a superior officer, the perpetrator of the unlawful act remains liable. There is a defence of obedience to superior orders but this seems only to protect a person who acted on orders which he did not realise were illegal. It was said in the South African case of *R v Smith (1900) SA 202* by Solomon J: *if a soldier honestly believes he is doing his duty in obeying the commands of his superior, or if the orders are not so manifestly illegal that he must or ought to have known that they were unlawful, the private soldier would be protected by the orders of his superior officer.* The defence is very limited for it seems that it will only protect where no reasonable person, rather than the defendant himself, who may have been an unreasonable person, would have believed the commanded act to be unlawful.

95.3 Military law

There is a system of *courts-martial* which try those subject to military law. All members of the armed forces are bound by military law, as are employed civilians in some circumstances. Military law covers the administration and discipline of military personnel.

Courts-martial have jurisdiction, first, to try some ordinary criminal law offences, when committed by members of the armed forces and, secondly, to try military offences created by *Part II Army Act*, over which they have exclusive jurisdiction. Members of courts-martial are judges both of fact and of law. Counsel may appear on either side and the ordinary rules of English criminal evidence are observed. There is a Courts-Martial Appeal Court to hear appeals from courts-martial. This court is equivalent to the Court of Appeal and appeal lies from it to the House of Lords.

Courts-martial are inferior to the High Court and therefore the High Court has a supervisory jurisdiction over them in the same way as it supervises administrative tribunals. Actions for *certiorari*, prohibition and *mandamus* may therefore be brought (see administrative law remedies – later). These remedies may be invoked quite apart from any right of appeal to the Courts-Martial AC 206

Further reading

(a) *General*

Wade and Bradley, Chapters 27, 29.
de Smith, Chapters, 23, 24 and 25.
Street, Chapters 3-6, pp.156-165.

(b) *Public order*

Wade and Bradley, Chapter 28.
de Smith, Chapter 24.
Bevan (1979), *Public Law* at p.163.
Supperstone (1982), *public Law*, 355. *Select Committee on the Parliamentary Commissioner for Administration.*
Gregory (1982), *Public Law*, 49.
The Times, 17 May 1985.

(c) *Official secrets*

Wade and Bradley, Chapter 30.
de Smith, pp. 491-497.
Williams (1968), *Not in the Public Interest.*
Street, pp.211-17.
Franks Report, Cmnd 5104, 1972.

(d) *Contempt*

Phillimore Report, Cmmd 5794, 1974.
Discussion Paper, Cmmd 7145, 1978.
New Law Journal, Editorial, 3 May 1979.
Whittaker, *New Law Journal*, 24 May 1979 at p.506.

(e) *Freedom of assembly*

Williams (1967), *Keeping the Peace.*
Street, Chapter 2.
Scarman Report on Red Lion Square Disturbances, Cmnd 5919 1975.
Williams (1970), *Cambridge Law Journal* 96.
Dicey, *Law of the Constitution* (10th edition), Chapter 7.
Wallington (1976), Picketing, *Cambridge Law Journal*, 82.

(f) *Right to privacy*

Younger Report, Cmnd 5012, 1971-72.
A-G's Guidelines on Jury Vetting, *The Times*, 11 October 1978.
Report on Telephone-Tapping, Cmnd 283, 1957 (The Birkett Report).
Morrick, *New Law Journal*, 14 June 1979 at p.575.
1980, *Public Law*, 431.

(g) *Discrimination*

Wade and Bradley, pp.574-578.
de Smith, pp.448-457.
Street, Chapter 12.

LLB

CONSTITUTIONAL LAW

LESSON 10 (REVISION)

101. REVISION OF LESSONS 6-9

102. *REVISION QUESTIONS*

101. REVISION OF LESSONS 6-9

Read through each section of Lessons 6-9, pausing at the end of each paragraph to recall what you have just read. If you cannot recall it adequately and in detail, read and check your knowledge until you are satisfied.

When you have completed this task and referred to the reading lists, test your knowledge further by working through all the questions on the next pages.

102. *REVISION QUESTIONS*

1. Is the Prime Minister simply the chairman of the Cabinet or is he its master?

2. What do you understand by the doctrines of collective and individual ministerial responsibility? What is their current constitutional importance?

3. 'The power, influence and authority of the senior members of the Civil Service have grown to such an extent as to create the embryo of a corporate state.' (Tony Benn MP)

    Discuss.

4. 'Nowhere has democracy worked well without a great measure of local government.' (Professor Hayek, *The Road to Serfdom*).

    Do you think that the 1984/85 legislative reforms relating to the structure and functions of local government in London and the Metropolitan regions undermine this political philosophy?

5. 'One of the constant elements over a long period of British political history has been the power of local public authorities to determine for themselves the level of their expenditure by virtue of their power to levy a tax on the occupation of property.'

    To what extent, if at all, does the *Rates Act 1984* affect this constitutional arrangement?

6. How are local funds audited? Consider the impact of recent reforms in the methods of local authority audits.

7. 'Those who argue that the Local Government Commissioners have failed to fulfil their role as champions of the citizen, ignore the value of their general supervisory role.'

    Discuss.

8. The Oxbridge branch of the British Nazi Party has organised a march through a part of Oxbridge with a high immigrant population in support of its demand that all coloured immigrants be compulsorily repatriated. All the marchers are to wear specially-made red, white and blue sashes, and to carry banners reading 'Wogs go home'. The Nazi Party's chairman, Adolf, has assured the police that his members intend to act peacefully, but the local Socialist Workers' Group have announced their intention to hold a counter-demonstration in the middle of the Nazis' route and to resist their progress by violence if necessary.

    Advise the police what steps may be taken to prevent the clash from occurring, and what offences will be committed by members of the Nazi Party if they march as planned.

9. There is a military coup in Ruritania and a new regime comes to power. Yorrick and Zygmund, two Ruritanian students, attend a tennis tournament at Wimbledon between England and Ruritania. Acting on a prearranged plan, they climb the barriers and walk onto the tennis court, where they sit down and unfurl a banner which proclaims 'Justice for Ruritania'. The crowd becomes restless at the disruption of play. Police officers start to carry the students from the court; as he is carried away, Zygmund shouts at the crowd 'You are all hired lackeys of the fascist Ruritanian junta'. Disorder breaks out among the crowd with fighting among rival factions.

    What offences, if any, have Yorrick and Zygmund committed?

10. 'In the last analysis personal freedom depends solely on the will of those in power to protect it.'

    Do you agree? Would your answer be different if we had a Bill of Rights?

11. Explain the changes to the law on public order made by the *Public Order Act 1986*.

LLB

CONSTITUTIONAL LAW

LESSON 11 (STUDY)

111. *ADMINISTRATIVE LAW*

111.1 *Introduction*

Administrative law is the law concerning *the administration*. The term, the administration, encompasses all authorities that are part of government. All sorts of government activities, both direct and indirect, are included. Thus administrative process covers:

(a)   direct public services, e.g. Department of Employment, Department of Health and Social Security;

(b)   indirect public services provided by public corporations, e.g. the Post Office, BBC, Forestry Commission;

(c)   control of local authority provision of services, e.g. by means of loan sanction, confirmation of byelaws;

(d)   ministerial delegated legislation;

(e)   specific ministerial powers, e.g. over immigrants, aliens;

(f)   special tribunals on particular matters.

111.2 *Controls over the administration*

The administration clearly has a very wide sphere of activity. It is necessary, therefore, that its activities should be subject to scrutiny and control. Control may be formal or informal and may occur either before or after a decision has been taken. Informal control before the decision stems from statutory provision for public participation and consultation in administrative decision-making processes. For instance, public corporations often have on their boards of management people from outside the world of public administration. These laymen are generally distinguished in other fields and so their appointment does not exemplify public participation in its widest sense. True public participation is most clearly to be seen in the sphere of planning. Local authorities in drawing up long-term plans for the development of their areas are now bound to consult with local amenity groups and other interested parties. Compliance with these requirements is ensured by the fact that the authority must give details of the participation processes used to the Secretary of State for the Environment. In 1975, the *Dobry Report on the Development Control System* advocated still greater public participation. It was suggested that registers of planning applications should be kept open in the evenings and that officers should always be available to explain the details of an application. Major planning proposals should be heralded by public meetings and exhibitions and efforts should be made to inform and to consult the *non-joiners* who did not attend meetings or read local newspapers. The Secretary of State was in broad agreement with the Dobry Report's conclusions, although he did not consider it possible, or necessary, to

enact all the recommendations. The need for participation in decision-making by those likely to be affected is, however, clearly accepted. Before most delegated legislation is made interested parties are first consulted and such consultation is sometimes made mandatory by the enabling Act.

However, formal controls over the administration are still of more significance than informal controls. There are three main types of formal control:

(a)   by the courts;

(b) by the Ombudsman; and

(c) by the Council on Tribunals.

Control by the courts will be examined in the next lesson.

112. ADMINISTRATIVE TRIBUNALS

112.1 What is a tribunal?

It is a body set up outside the ordinary court system to exercise a judicial function. On many occasions the phrase 'administrative tribunals' is used. This means no more than that the tribunal operates within the framework of an administrative scheme set up by the government, such as the National Insurance Scheme. Tribunals sometimes bear other names such as 'court', 'board', 'commission', 'referees' or 'umpires', but are no less tribunals for that reason. The vast majority are set up by statute although there is a well known exception – the Criminal Injuries Compensation Board.

112.2 The number and variety

Tribunals have proliferated recently, especially since World War II, and there are over 2,000 of some 50 different types. They operate in many different fields and some adjudicate between individual and State and others between two individuals. For example:

(a)   national insurance: individual and State;

(b)   employment law: industrial tribunals – two individuals;

(c)   rating: local valuation court and Lands Tribunal – individuals;

(d)   leases of land: rent tribunal – two individuals;

(e)   income tax and rating: individual and State;

(f)   copyright and patents.

112.3 Staffing and procedure

This varies from tribunal to tribunal. Often, however, a tribunal will have two lay members (not legally trained) with a professional lawyer, from a list compiled by the Lord Chancellor,as Chairman, e.g. Industrial Tribunal.

Sometimes there are fewer members or they may all be specialists in a particular field.

Members of tribunals may only be removed during their fixed term appointment with the Lord Chancellor's agreement although tribunal members may not be reappointed for a further period when their fixed term appointment expires if the relevant Minister does not so wish.

Procedure is more informal than in the courts but again it varies with the tribunal. Some tribunals have their procedures laid down in a statutory instrument, e.g. Industrial Tribunal.

112.4 The advantages of tribunals over courts

(a)   Cost of tribunals is lower than courts. No court fees. Legal representation is not required and may be discouraged.

(b)   By sitting on tribunal panels regularly, the members build up a level of expertise which is not available in the courts and their decisions tend to be consistent; e.g. Judges cannot be expected to be conversant with local land values for rating purposes whereas estate agents or surveyors on a tribunal would be.

(c)   The procedure is less formal than a court and less daunting to ordinary members of the public who might take a grievance to a tribunal where they would lack the courage (and money) to go to court, e.g. Supplementary Benefits Appeal Tribunal.

Tribunal members frequently assist lay applicants to put their case.

(d)   It saves time as court lists are notorious. Litigants and legal advisers may be kept waiting for a long time before the case is heard and no exact time for hearing is set. Tribunals set times for hearing and sit locally as business demands.

(e)   If the tribunal system did not exist the courts could not cope with the extra workload.

112.5 *The disadvantages of tribunals over courts*

It is argued:

(a)   that the formality of the court system protects the parties as the rules of procedure have been shown to work over many years;

(b)   that the proliferation of tribunals outside the court system is in opposition to the rule of law. Dicey said that cases should be heard by the ordinary courts rather than bodies outside that system;

(c)   that administrative tribunals infringe the doctrine of the separation of powers because the minister involved may, in certain circumstances, select the panel to adjudicate on a matter involving his department. Such a panel may include his civil servants;

(d)   Legal Aid is not available to assist an applicant except in the Employment Appeal Tribunal, Lands Tribunal or Mental Health Review Tribunal.

112.6 *Appeals and application for judicial review*

Most regulations setting up tribunals provide for an appeal to a higher tribunal or court on a point of law. Exceptions are the Immigration Appeal Tribunal and the Social Security Commissioner.

Sometimes there is also a provision for appeal on a question of fact.

Application may be made for judicial review if the tribunal has:

(a)   made an error of law;

(b)   acted *ultra vires* (without authority);

(c)   breached the rules of natural justice.

112.7 *The Franks Committee its proposals for reform and the Tribunals and Inquiries Act 1958, as amended in 1971*

The Franks Committee reported in 1957 making many proposals for the reform of the law on administrative tribunals. There had been public outcry at the obvious increase in the number of tribunals since 1945 and it was considered that safeguards should be introduced to protect the individual against a new form of body set up by the State which appeared a possible oppressor. It was for these reasons and more immediately because of the Crichel Down Affair that the Committee was appointed. It recommended that standards of 'penness, fairness and impartiality' should be adhered to by tribunals.

The Council on Tribunals was set up under the *Tribunals and Inquiries Act 1958* to supervise both the working of tribunals and inquiries. Its work is summarised at section 114 (below).

In addition the 1958 Act was important because by *s.12* it provided that the parties before a tribunal could request reasons for the decision of the tribunal, and by *s.14* provisions in earlier Acts of Parliament which sought to exclude judicial review of decisions were nullified.

113. *STATUTORY INQUIRIES*

113.1 *Introduction*

Very often when a public body has exercised its powers, it leaves behind a person or persons aggrieved by the decision, e.g. planning, supplementary benefits, council housing, discretionary grants for a multitude of objects, compulsory purchase and so forth. The list is almost as endless as the law granting these powers. To leave a large number of people seething with discontent, feeling badly done-by is bad administration. Parliament is aware of this phenomenon, and also of the fact that administrators, like everyone else, are prone to occasional error, bearing in mind the wide discretion given to them in statutes. As a step to minimising unrest and unease, and reducing errors, Parliament, where it sees fit, has provided two major means of appeal: first, the method of tribunals and, secondly, the statutory inquiry. Where Parliament is not concerned about the political consequences of a decision, so long as a fair one is made, the tribunal is resorted to as being judicial and independent. On the other hand, where Parliament wishes the final decision to remain in the hands of the administration, a statutory inquiry is used. A statutory inquiry occurs before the decision is taken and takes facts and opinions from interested parties after which a report is prepared. Thus the final decision is taken, usually by the minister or some-one in his department, on the basis of a report from the inquiry. Although the inquiry is independent and may recommend a remedy, the decision still remains in the hands of the administrators.

113.2 *Characteristics of inquiries*

The inquiries are called statutory because an Act setting up an administrative scheme often sets up at the same time the form of inquiry to deal with any potential difficulties. Inquiries are neither purely administrative nor purely judicial. The inquiry tests an issue in relation to the law and is therefore quasi-judicial. It is not judicial because the decision is not usually made by it. The purpose of the inquiry is not only to ascertain the facts but to grant those adversely affected the opportunity to object. In most cases there are two public bodies concerned – local and central – and an individual or corporation, who feel ill-treated by the authority. The inquiry ascertains the facts under a procedure similar to that in a court (e.g. witnesses may be examined, cross-examined and re-examined). Ultimately some central department makes the final decision on policy – final, that is, unless some act gives rise to review on the basis of *ultra vires* or breach of natural justice. The 'person appointed' is usually an inspector appointed and paid by a government department but who is independent of that department. Sometimes, however, a private practitioner, solicitor or surveyor may be involved. Although the inspector's reports are of great value and may sway the minister to change his mind, central government must have power to overrule the inspector's decision on broader national issues.

113.3 *The Franks Report, inquiries and the Council on Tribunals*

The Franks Committee recommended in respect of inquiries that the following points should be incorporated into the law:

(a)   an individual should be given full warning of the case he would have to meet;

(b)   any policies applicable by the government department involved should be divulged;

(c)   inspectors should be under the supervision of the Lord Chancellor;

(d)   the inspector's report should be attached to the minister's decision;

(e)   full reasons should be given on the decision;

(f)   it should be possible to challenge the decision in court;

(g)   if the minister decides to disagree with the recommendations of the inspector, then the inquiry may be reopened.

All these recommendations (except (c)) have, to an extent, been adopted.

The Council on Tribunals has functions in respect of inquiries which are similar to those for tribunals except that:

(i)   the Council has no general review powers relating to statutory inquiries; and

(ii)   it makes no recommendations as to the personnel who should conduct inquiries.

113.4 *Impartiality and inquiry procedure*

Inquiries arise in two different ways. They may arise as a result of objections to a proposal put forward by a minister or they may arise when a proposal by an individual is rejected by a local authority and the individual appeals to the minister.

It would be unrealistic to expect a minister, who is reaching a decision after an inquiry into proposals initiated by himself, to be as objective and as impartial as a tribunal. However, the minister is under a duty to cause a properly conducted inquiry to be held, to consider the objections and to ensure there is a fair report. This was established in *Franklin v Minister of Town and Country Planning (1947) All ER 289*. In this case the Minister, whilst the *New Towns Bill* was before Parliament, made a speech at Stevenage saying that it would be designated a new town once the Bill had been enacted. After enactment a local inquiry was held and the Minister made an order in respect of Stevenage. This was challenged in the courts by the objectors on the grounds of the Minister's bias evidenced by his speech and later matters. The court, in upholding the Minister's decision, made it clear that the Minister must act fairly by leaving himself open to the objectors' arguments but that he could not be expected to be totally objective.

In a triangular situation where a minister, after an inquiry into a dispute between an individual and a local authority, has to make a decision, the standards of conduct are rather different. Once objections have been lodged to a proposal, the minister must act judicially and the rules of natural justice apply. However, the minister may, in making his decision, seek advice from his own department without divulging this to the parties.

113.5 *Planning Inquiry Commission*

Where a local inquiry is not suited to the task, e.g. in a regional or national context, then under *ss.47-49 Town and Country Planning Act 1971* a Planning Inquiry Commission of three to five members may be established.

Under these provisions a number of alternative sites for the third London airport was considered by the Roskill Commission.

Whichever inquiry is used the Minister takes the decisions. Under the *Tribunals and Inquiries Act 1971* the minister must, if requested, give a statement, either written or oral, of the reasons for his decision. These reasons, of course, are part of the record and may give rise to challenge for 'error of law on the face of the record'.

113.6   *Other kinds of inquiry*

(a)   *Railway, air and factory accidents*

Some statutes establish formal official inquiries into accidents of various kinds, especially those above. This not only safeguards the public as to future incidents but also investigates allegations against drivers, pilots and others.

(b) *Professional conduct*

These are more in the nature of tribunals.

(c) *Ad hoc*

Set up to investigate a particular matter of importance, e.g. the *Crichel Down Affair (1954)*.

113.7 *Tribunals of inquiry*

Under the *Tribunals of Inquiry (Evidence) Act 1921* Parliament – in practice the government – may set up a special inquiry into matters of public importance. Examples of their use include Ulster's Bloody Sunday (the Widgery Inquiry) and the Aberfan Disaster Tribunal. The inquiries are inquisitorial and the tribunal reports to the Home Secretary. They are generally presided over by a High Court judge.

114. *THE COUNCIL ON TRIBUNALS*

The *Council on Tribunals* was set up following recommendations of the *Franks Committee* in 1957. It was intended to make the operation of tribunals more uniform and to exercise control over them. The Franks Committee had been appointed to examine the workings of tribunals and of inquiries, and had concluded that special tribunals and inquiries had been created in order to promote good administration. The essential characteristics of good administration, which must be present in these special procedures, were, according to the Report, *openness, fairness and impartiality*.

S.1 of the Tribunals and Inquiries Act 1958 (now the 1971 Act) provided that the Council on Tribunals should keep under review the constitution and working of tribunals and should report thereon. It was also to report on any matters referred by the Lord Chancellor and was to have a watching brief over statutory inquiries, i.e. inquiries held in pursuance of a duty, rather than discretionary inquiries. The Council must be consulted in making procedural rules for tribunals and inquiries and is also likely to advise on draft legislation for new tribunals. It makes an annual report to the Lord Chancellor.

The Council is composed of 10 to 15 members and has separate members for Scotland and Wales. Its chairman and the chairman of the Scottish committee of the Council work full-time, and receive salaries, but the rest of the members are part-time and can only claim expenses. Some members of the Council are lawyers and it does have legal advisers, but a criticism often levelled at the Council concerns its lack of legal expertise. Its chief work has been in formulating procedural rules for tribunals and it is therefore surprising that it receives so little legal help. Visits to tribunals are generally made by non-lawyer members.

Although the Council is more concerned with tribunal procedure than with the substance of tribunal decisions, it has the power to investigate individual complaints. However, its effectiveness in this area has been limited by its lack of sanction. The Council can merely give advice when it finds a complaint to be substantiated and so it cannot redress individual grievances.

The Council has been effective in setting standards for tribunals and in establishing a climate of opinion favourable to those standards. Its watchwords throughout have remained the Franks Committee triumvirate of *openness, fairness and impartiality*.

115. *DELEGATED LEGISLATION*

115.1 *Introduction*

As the tasks and activities of the administration have increased, so also have the agencies carrying out these activities. Tribunals have been set up in order that there should be continuity and uniformity of decision on subjects where once continuity and uniformity would have been ensured by the fact that one man, the Minister, made all the decisions. Thus, in some departments there is a system of hearing and appeal much like that to be found in the courts. A decision may initially be taken by an individual officer and is then open to appeal to a tribunal. In turn appeal may lie from the tribunal to the Minister himself.

Just as decision-making power may, for reasons of convenience, be delegated by the Minister to his tribunals and officers, so also legislative power may be delegated by Parliament. Delegated legislation may be of various types. It may be made by the Queen in Council, by ministers and heads of government departments, by local authorities or by public corporations. Public corporations and local authorities have power to make bye-laws within their spheres of concern. These bye-laws will be subject to confirmation by an appropriate Minister and are not classified as statutory instruments.

115.2 *Statutory instruments*

The more important kinds of delegated legislation are made by the Crown in Council and by ministers, and are known as statutory instruments (they may be labelled as rules, regulations or orders). The power to legislate on a particular matter must have been specifically delegated by Parliament in a statute. The statute is called the *enabling Act*. There are various ways in which the making and application of a statutory instrument are controlled:

A. *The Statutory Instruments Act 1946*

The enabling Act is likely to require that any statutory instruments made under it are *laid before Parliament* and it may require either that a negative,or that an affirmative, Parliamentary procedure is used. There are six different procedures for laying which may be adopted by the enabling Act. An *affirmative laying requirement* usually means that the instrument must be laid before Parliament and cannot come into force until it has been approved by affirmative resolution of each House of Parliament. The *negative laying requirement* is more commonly to be found in enabling Acts. The procedure for negative laying is laid down in the *Statutory Instruments Act 1946* and the most common form provides that the instrument laid takes effect immediately subject to annulment by resolution of *either* House. The prayer for annulment has to be made within the 40 day laying period provided for in the Act.

It is uncertain what the effect would be if a minister neglected to lay such an instrument before Parliament. There has, up to now, been no decision in the English courts as to its validity. *S.4(1) Statutory Instruments Act 1946* provides that an instrument which must be laid before Parliament after it has been made *shall be so laid before the instrument comes into operation* and that the Lord

Chancellor must be notified if it is essential that it should come into operation earlier. This provision seems to suggest that an instrument which is not laid might be invalid. However, in *Starey v Graham (1899)* Channel J expressed the opinion that a laying requirement in an enabling Act was probably no more than directory, i.e. as opposed to being mandatory or imperative and, therefore, if a laying requirement in an enabling Act may only be directory it would seem that *s.4(1)* might be directory also. See also *Springer v Doorly (1950)*. However, in *R v Sheer Metalcraft (1954) 1 QB 586* Streatfield J said:

> in my judgment the making of an instrument is complete when it is first of all made by the Minister concerned and after it has been laid before Parliament.

And in the earlier case of *Institute of Patent Agents v Lockwood (1894) AC 347* Lord Herschell emphasised the importance of delegated legislation being subject to annulment by Parliament and thus subject to Parliamentary control. The necessity for Parliament to retain some control even after it had delegated power, and the clear and imperative language of *s.4(1)* seem together to suggest that laying requirements would be held mandatory if the matter came to court.

Laying requirements were again considered by the House of Lords in *R v SS Environment, ex p Greenwich LBC (1985)*. The Lords rejected Greenwich's arguments that instruments were invalid because they had not been laid before 'Parliament' (as they had been laid only before the Commons) holding that for purposes of the *Rates Act 1984* 'Parliament' meant from its context the Commons. Greenwich also argued that,as a notice had been served on them before laying and not as soon as reasonably practicable after,it was a nullity. Even if this was the case and the Lords did not agree that it *was, certiorari* being discretionary would not be issued for such a technicality as that.

B. *Judicial review*

Unlike primary Acts of Parliament which are immune from judicial review, the validity of delegated legislation is subject to judicial review usually on the general grounds that it is *ultra vires*, or beyond the power of the enabling Act. Judicial review lies even if the delegated legislation has been approved by resolution of each House of Parliament, (see *Hoffman La Roche v Secretary of State for Trade (1975) 119 SJ 591)*. Much depends on the wording of the enabling Act as to whether delegated legislation is *ultra vires*. In the absence of clear wording in the enabling Act, the courts apply certain maxims or principles of interpretation in reviewing the validity of delegated legislation, e.g. there is no power to levy tax without clear Parliamentary authority *(A-G v Wilts United Dairies Limited (1921) 38 TLR 781; Commissioners of Customs and Excise v Cure and Deeley Limited (1962) 1 QB 340)*.

Certain procedural errors have already been observed, e.g. that not laying before Parliament might invalidate delegated legislation. The failure to comply with requirements of consultation might also produce invalidity where the duty to consult is a mandatory as opposed to a directory requirement. In *Agricultural Training Board v Aylesbury Mushrooms Limited (1972) 1 All ER 280* the enabling Act provided that the Minister should, when setting up a training board for a particular industry, consult with interested parties in advance. In organising a Mushroomgrowers Board the Minister first consulted the National Farmers' Union, of which the Mushroomgrowers Association formed a part. He also sought to consult the Mushroomgrowers directly but these letters failed to arrive. The court held that the statutory instrument made by the Minister did not apply to the Mushroomgrowers because the Minister by corresponding separately with their association had showed an intention to consult with them and, as this had failed, the mandatory requirements of the enabling Act had not been met.

A more recent case on consultation is *R v Secretary of State for Social Services, ex p Association of Metropolitan Authorities (1986) 1 All ER 164*.

The *Housing Benefits Act 1982* gave the Secretary of State power to make regulations and he had a duty to consult organisations representing local authorities first. The court held the duty to be mandatory and concluded that there was a requirement that the organisation be given adequate time to make an informed reply. A declaration was granted that the regulations were invalid.

A failure to publish a statutory instrument gives rise to a special defence under *s.3(2)* of the 1946 Act, which provides:

> it shall be a defence to prove that the instrument had not been issued by HMSO at the date of the alleged contravention unless it is proved that at that date reasonable steps had been taken for the purpose of bringing the purport of the instrument to the notice of the public or of persons likely to be affected by it, or of the person charged.

In *R v Sheer Metalcraft* it was established that the burden is on the Crown to prove that alternative reasonable steps had been taken to publish the instrument. There has recently been a trend for statutes to allow non-statutory documents to be consulted by the courts as a guide to interpretation. See, for example, *Fothergill v Monarch Airlines (1981) AC 251* and note the use of *Codes of Practice*, for example under the *Employment Act 1980*. Do these by-pass Parliament?

C.   *Joint Select Committee on Statutory Instruments*

There is in existence a Joint Select Committee of the Commons and Lords which considers statutory instruments. There are seven members of each House on the Committee and the Committee has a quorum of two. Every statutory instrument of a general character and other instruments laid or laid in draft before Parliament are considered to decide if the special attention of the House should be drawn to the instrument on any of the following grounds:

(i)   that it has a retrospective effect not authorised in the enabling Act;

(ii)   that it seeks to impose a charge;

(iii) that there is an attempt to immunise it from judicial review;

(iv)   if there has been unreasonable delay in publishing or laying the instrument;

(v)   for an unjustified delay in notifying the Speaker that the instrument came into force before laying;

(vi)   if it appears poorly drafted or in any other way unusual or if it appears to go beyond the scope of what was envisaged in the enabling Act.

115.3 *The advantages of statutory instruments*

Statutory instruments are seldom debated in Parliament and pass through no Committee Stage and some commentators are therefore concerned that they provide an avenue for the abuse of power but they are in reality advantageous and the controls mentioned in the last section work relatively well. The advantages are:

(a)   technicalities which many MPs could not understand can be reserved for debate by experts in the Government department and industry concerned, leaving Parliament free to consider the general underlying principles of legislation. This saves scarce Parliamentary time;

(b)   Acts of Parliament may be brought into operation by stages;

(c)   statutory instruments can be brought into effect much more quickly than legislation so that enabling Acts often provide for regulation by statutory instrument if new circumstances or a crisis occur.

Further reading

(a) *General*

Wade and Bradley, Chapters 32, 33 and 37.
de Smith, Chapter 26.
Justice and Administrative Law, Robson (3rd edition).

(b) *Tribunals and inquiries*

de Smith, Chapter 27.
Franks Report, HMSO, 1955.
Motorways v Democracy, John Tyme (McMillan Press).
The Big Public Inquiry, Outer Circle Policy Unit (from 4 Cambridge Terrace, London NW1).

(c) *Delegated legislation*

de Smith, Chapter 17.
The New Despotism, Lord Hewart, 1929.
Donoughmore Report on Ministers' Powers, HMSO, 1932.
Joint Committee on Statutory Instruments, First Special Report, HC 169. 1977-78.
Report of Select Committee on European Secondary Legislation, JC 642, 1977-78.
1983, *Public Law*, 43
1983, *Public Law*, 395.

LLB

CONSTITUTIONAL LAW

LESSON 12 (STUDY)

121. *JUDICIAL CONTROL OVER THE ADMINISTRATION*

    121.1   INTRODUCTION
    121.2   LACK OF JURISDICTION
    121.3   ABUSE OF POWER
    121.4   IMPROPER PROCEDURE

AN ANALYSIS OF ENGLISH ADMINISTRATIVE LAW

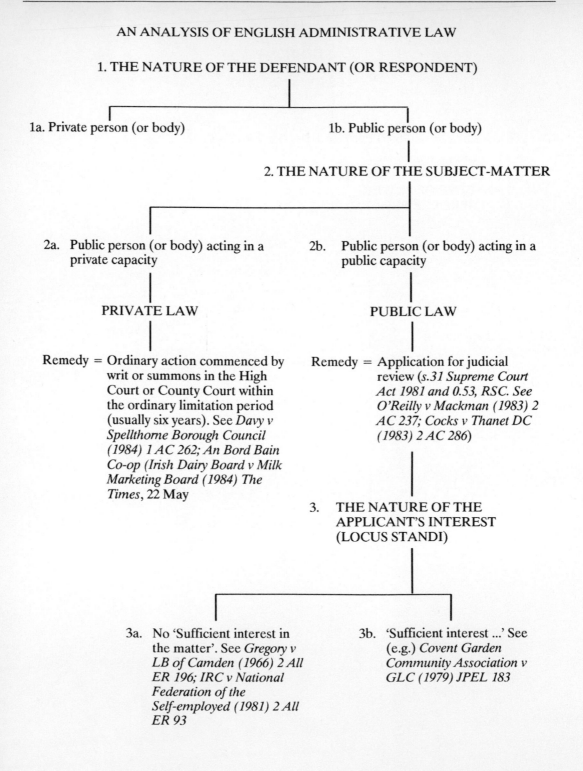

1. THE NATURE OF THE DEFENDANT (OR RESPONDENT)

1a. Private person (or body)

1b. Public person (or body)

2. THE NATURE OF THE SUBJECT-MATTER

2a. Public person (or body) acting in a private capacity

2b. Public person (or body) acting in a public capacity

PRIVATE LAW

PUBLIC LAW

Remedy = Ordinary action commenced by writ or summons in the High Court or County Court within the ordinary limitation period (usually six years). See *Davy v Spellthorne Borough Council (1984) 1 AC 262; An Bord Bain Co-op (Irish Dairy Board v Milk Marketing Board (1984) The Times*, 22 May

Remedy = Application for judicial review (*s.31 Supreme Court Act 1981 and 0.53, RSC. See O'Reilly v Mackman (1983) 2 AC 237; Cocks v Thanet DC (1983) 2 AC 286*)

3. **THE NATURE OF THE APPLICANT'S INTEREST (LOCUS STANDI)**

3a. No 'Sufficient interest in the matter'. See *Gregory v LB of Camden (1966) 2 All ER 196; IRC v National Federation of the Self-employed (1981) 2 All ER 93*

3b. 'Sufficient interest ...' See (e.g.) *Covent Garden Community Association v GLC (1979) JPEL 183*

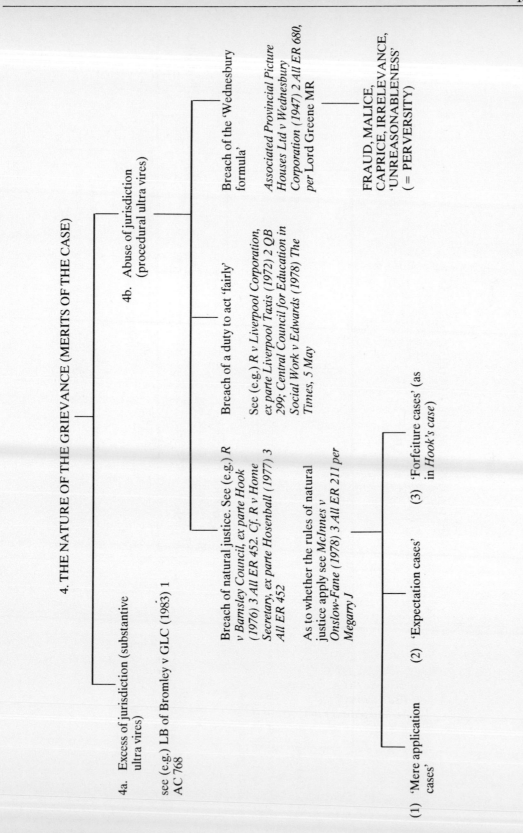

4. THE NATURE OF THE GRIEVANCE (MERITS OF THE CASE)

4a. Excess of jurisdiction (substantive ultra vires)

see (e.g.) LB of Bromley v GLC (1983) 1 AC 768

Breach of natural justice. See (e.g.) *R v Barnsley Council, ex parte Hook* (1976) 3 All ER 452. Cf. *R v Home Secretary, ex parte Hosenball* (1977) 3 All ER 452

As to whether the rules of natural justice apply see *McInnes v Onslow-Fane* (1978) 3 All ER 211 per *Megarry J*

(1) 'Mere application cases'

(2) 'Expectation cases'

(3) 'Forfeiture cases' (as in *Hook's case*)

4b. Abuse of jurisdiction (procedural ultra vires)

Breach of a duty to act 'fairly'

See (e.g.) *R v Liverpool Corporation, ex parte Liverpool Taxis* (1972) 2 QB 299; *Central Council for Education in Social Work v Edwards* (1978) *The Times, 5 May*

Breach of the 'Wednesbury formula'

Associated Provincial Picture Houses Ltd v Wednesbury Corporation (1947) 2 All ER 680, per Lord Greene MR

FRAUD, MALICE, CAPRICE, IRRELEVANCE, 'UNREASONABLENESS' (= PERVERSITY)

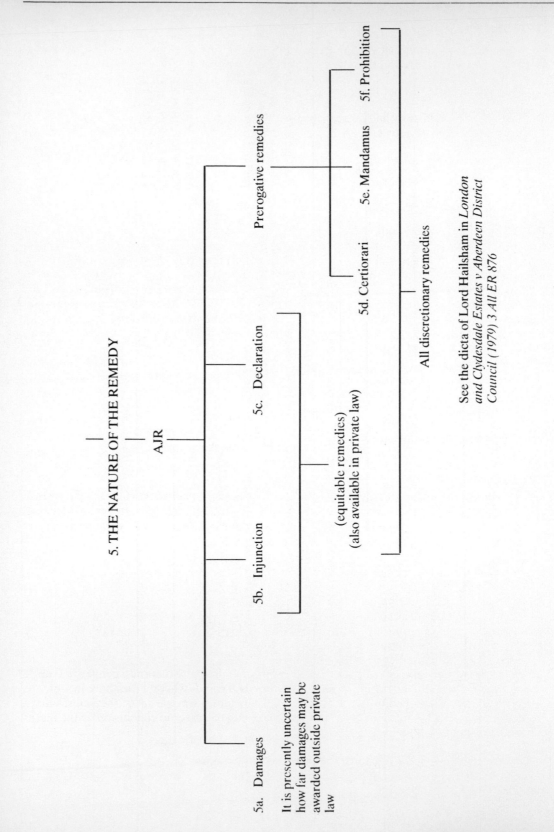

5. THE NATURE OF THE REMEDY

AJR

5a. Damages

It is presently uncertain how far damages may be awarded outside private law

5b. Injunction

5c. Declaration

(equitable remedies)
(also available in private law)

Prerogative remedies

5d. Certiorari

5e. Mandamus

5f. Prohibition

All discretionary remedies

See the dicta of Lord Hailsham in *London and Clydesdale Estates v Aberdeen District Council (1979) 3 All ER 876*

121.1 *INTRODUCTION*

The courts will control acts of the administration and will overturn them as being *ultra vires*, literally beyond the powers and therefore void on three main grounds. These are:

(a)   that the authority did not have jurisdiction to perform the act in question;

(b)   that whilst the authority had jurisdiction over the act in question, it abused the power which it had been given, e.g. by exercising it for an unauthorized purpose;

(c)   that the authority did not observe the required procedure in performing the act.

Each of these factors will be examined in turn.

121.2 *LACK OF JURISDICTION*

Jurisdiction means, simply, *authority to decide*. It might appear to be a simple matter to discover whether an administrative body or tribunal has authority to decide a particular matter. The tribunal's rules will be listed somewhere and if the matter in question is of a nature stated to be within the jurisdiction, then the tribunal has authority to decide over it. It was always said that the question whether a tribunal had jurisdiction does not depend on the truth or otherwise of the facts into which it must enquire nor upon the correctness of its findings on those facts, but rather upon the nature of them. Whether a tribunal had jurisdiction could be judged at the commencement of its hearing. As Lord Reid said in *R v Governor of Brixton Prison ex p Armah (1966) 3 All ER 177*:

> if a tribunal has jurisdiction, it has jurisdiction to go right or to go wrong. The court will not be concerned with what decision the tribunal makes, provided that it had jurisdiction to make the decision.

The question whether or not a tribunal has jurisdiction is, however, not one purely for the tribunal to decide. As Farwell LJ said in *R v Shoreditch Assessment Committee ex p Morgan (1910) 2 KB 859*:

> no tribunal of inferior jurisdiction can by its own decision finally decide on the question of the existence or extent of such jurisdiction ... it is a contradiction in terms to create a tribunal with limited jurisdiction and unlimited power to determine such limits at its own will and leisure – *such a tribunal would be autocratic, not limited.*

Thus the court will always review a decision by a tribunal as to its jurisdiction.

The distinction between the nature of the matter before the tribunal and its facts, is not always clear cut, and therefore the question of jurisdiction cannot always be decided before the facts of the dispute are examined. In *R v Fulham Rent Tribunal ex p Zerek (1951) 1 All ER 482*, Devlin J offered guidance to tribunals faced with such a problem:

> When at the inception of an enquiry by a tribunal of limited jurisdiction, a challenge is made to their jurisdiction, the tribunal have to make up their minds whether they have jurisdiction or not. If their jurisdiction depends on the existence of a state of facts, they must inform themselves about them, and if the facts are in dispute, reach some conclusion on the merits of the dispute.

Thus the tribunal may have to examine the facts in order tn see whether they have jurisdiction to examine the facts: The same enquiry may be conducted by the court in some cases.

In *White and Collins v Minister of Health (1939) 3 All ER 548*, for instance, the court had to decide whether the minister was right in confirming a compulsory purchase order on certain land. It was provided by statute that no compulsory purchase order could be made in respect of land forming part of a park. Said Luxmore LJ:

> the jurisdiction to make the order is dependent on a finding of fact; unless the land can be held not to be part of a park there is no jurisdiction in the borough council to make, or in the minister to confirm, the order. In such a case it seems almost self-evident that the court which has to consider whether there is jurisdiction to make or confirm the order must be entitled to review the vital finding on which the existence of the jurisdiction relied upon depends. If this were not so, the right to apply to the court would be illusory.

But contrast the attitude of the courts in such cases as *R v Preston Supplementary Benefit Appeal Tribunal, ex parte Moore (1975) 2 All ER 807* – (meaning of *house-holder*).

Although the distinction between jurisdiction and facts had clearly become more complex than early judges had supposed, the principle that once a tribunal had jurisdiction, it could reach a right or a wrong decision and would not lose jurisdiction if it reached a wrong one, continued to be accepted. However, in *Anisminic v Foreign Compensation Commission (1969) 2 AC 147*, Lord Reid in an important judgment, explained that principle, which he himself had propounded in *ex p Armah, supra*, and showed that it did not provide a simple answer to jurisdictional questions. He said that in some cases although the tribunal had jurisdiction to enter on its enquiry, it either did or failed to do something in the course of the enquiry so that its decision was a nullity. It might have acted in bad faith, or failed to observe the requirements of natural justice or taken into account something which it had no power to take into account. He gave various other examples of the sort of errors that he had in mind. But if a tribunal committed none of these errors then it was indeed entitled to decide the question rightly or wrongly.

Thus, according to Lord Reid, the word *jurisdiction* does not have the narrow compass that had earlier been assigned to it. A tribunal reaching a decision in bad faith or failing to comply with rules of natural justice can be said not to have had jurisdiction. The *ultra vires* categories of acting in excess of a given power and abusing that power become almost indistinguishable. However, it must be emphasized that there still is a

difference between questions of jurisdiction and questions of abuse of power (which will be examined shortly) for, as Lord Reid said, provided that a tribunal acts in accordance with the stringent procedural rules that he listed, provided that it does not act in bad faith or in breach of natural justice, provided that it takes into account all that is relevant and ignores all that is irrelevant, and so on, its final decision cannot be attacked. The court will not examine the reasons for the decision and will not strike it down on the ground that it is unreasonable. Cf. abuse of power at 121.3 below.

To sum up, therefore, the court may declare the decision of an administrative body to be void as being made without jurisdiction if that body either was not initially competent to decide the matter or lost its authority to decide by acting in breach of the accepted standards of procedure during its deliberations. Jurisdiction is judged as a matter of law, but a decision as to jurisdiction may involve an initial examination of the facts of the case.

121.3 *ABUSE OF POWER*

Powers which are delegated to administrative bodies are often discretionary powers. No duty is imposed on the body to decide in a particular way, but rather the body is left with a wide discretion and is free to reach its own decision on the facts before it in each case. Where the court is invited to review such a decision, it must guard against usurping the power of the tribunal and substituting its own decision for that of the tribunal. The courts have therefore trodden a precarious path between intervention and non-intervention and their attitude to discretionary power is still not absolutely clear. Some rules have, however, been formulated:

(a) The court will not permit sub-delegation of a delegated power unless further delegation of that power is clearly authorised. A delegate cannot generally himself delegate *(delegatus nonpotest delegare)*. In *Allingham v Minister of Agriculture (1948) 1 All ER 780* the minister had, during the war, delegated powers to county agricultural committees to control agriculture by telling farmers what to grow and where. One such committee delegated decisions as to where sugar beet should be grown to their executive officer. It was held by the court that this sub-delegation to the executive officer was *ultra vires*. Again, in *Ellis v Dubowski (1921) 3 KB 621*, a county council, which was statutorily empowered to license films to be shown in their area, decided to allow any film with the British Board of Film Censors' certificate to be shown. It was held that this amounted to sub-delegation to the BBFC and was therefore *ultra vires* and void.

(b) The court will attempt to ensure that delegated power has been used for its proper purpose. Thus, in *Webb v MHLG (1965) 2 All ER 193*, where a local authority had power to acquire land compulsorily only for the purposes of coast protection, the court quashed a compulsory purchase order where they found that the land in question was not needed for *bona fide* coast protection work but rather for the building of a promenade. Again in *Hall v Shoreham UDC (1964) 1 All ER 1*, where a planning authority had used its power to annex conditions to grants of planning permission to require the applicant to build on his land a road to be used as a public highway, the court held that the requirement was *ultra vires* and stated that the normal *Highways Act* procedures, under which the applicant would have been entitled to compensation,should have been used by the Council. In *R v LB Hillingdon, ex p Royco Homes (1974) 2 All ER 643* the Council attached conditions to the grant of planning permission requiring Royco Homes to give homes to persons on the Council's waiting list and to afford security of tenure. These requirements were considered *ultra vires* and void because they amounted to an attempt by the Council to avoid its statutory duties. Where an authority appears to have exercised a power both for an authorised and for an unauthorised purpose, the court will try to discover which of the two purposes was dominant and will only uphold the action where the dominant purpose was authorised. There have been two recent cases on this point.

In *R v GLC and ILEA, ex p Westminster City Council (1984) Times 27 December* both the ILEA and the GLC loaned employees to a body set up to coordinate between the boroughs and trade unions. This was in order provided that the Wednesbury formula was not breached. Here the ILEA were in the clear, having lent only the one employee but the GLC were acting *ultra vires* lending seven who were to undertake duties campaigning against central government's plans to abolish the GLC and Metropolitan authorities. The point was that a major objective of the plan was to further a political motive. This was an irrelevant consideration.

In *R v ILEA, ex p Westminster City Council (1986) 1 All ER 19* the ILEA had retained an advertising agency to produce material to inform the public about rate-capping. This was challenged as unlawful and the High Court adopted de Smith's test of unlawfulness in these circumstances. The questions to be answered were what was the true purpose of the appointment and was such a purpose unauthorised? If so, then if the actor's conduct was materially affected by it there was an invalid exercise because irrelevant factors were taken into account. The ILEA had acted invalidly.

This approach was again followed by the court in *R v LB Lewisham ex pl Shell UK Ltd (1987)*.

The Borough Council decided to boycott Shell products, where there were available reasonable alternatives on reasonable terms, allegedly because this would promote harmonians race relations in the borough as Shell was involved in international trade with South Africa. Shell sought a declaration that the vote was invalid, certiorari to quash it and an injunction to prevent the policy being carried out. The court considered it must decide on the dominant purpose of the Council, was it to promote race relations under s.71 Race Relations Act 1976 or to sever like with South Africa? The court decided the latter prevailed and therefore although the decision was not unreasonable within the meaning of the Wednesbury formula (see below (e)). It was nevertheless void for an unauthorised purpose.

(c) A not dissimilar ground of review for abuse of discretionary power is that the decision-maker either took into account irrelevant considerations, or disregarded relevant considerations. In *Padfield v Minister of Agriculture (1968) AC 997* proceedings for *mandamus* were brought against the Minister because he had refused to appoint a committee of investigation to consider milk prices when requested by the South-East milk producers to do so. The Minister refused on the grounds that to appoint such a committee would give rise to many complaints by other regions. This, decided the House of Lords, was an irrelevant consideration and the Minister had abused the discretion invested in him. *Mandamus* was, therefore, granted to compel him to make the appointment.

A recent example is *R v Ealing LBC, ex p Times Newspapers (1986)*. The court held that local authorities who during the Wapping dispute banned any of Rupert Murdoch's papers from their libraries were taking into account irrelevant factors and their decision was illegal, irrational and unfair. A discretion must not be used to undermine the purpose of an Act.

(d) Often an authority exercising delegated power will formulate rules of policy to guide its decisions. Thus, for instance, a planning authority may make a policy to refuse applications to build houses other than of local materials, e.g. Cotswold stone in Gloucestershire and so on. In operating such a policy the authority may well fetter the free discretion which has been delegated to it and therefore the courts are careful to ensure that, where discretionary power has been delegated, a true discretion operates in each case. In *R v Port of London Authority, ex p Kynoch (1919) 1 WB 176* Bankes LJ explained the difference between proper and improper use of policy rules.

He said:

> ... there are, on the one hand, cases where a tribunal in the honest exercise of its discretion had adopted a policy, and, without refusing to hear an applicant, intimates to him what its policy is, and that after hearing him it will in accordance with its policy decide against him, unless there is something exceptional in his case.

Such a use of policy was acceptable, he considered. But he continued:

> on the other hand, there are cases where a tribunal has passed a rule, or come to a determination, not to hear any application of a particular character by whosoever made.

In those cases the court would intervene to protect the applicant's right to a proper determination.

In *Sagnata Investments v Norwich Corporation (1971) 2 QB 614* an application for planning permission to open an amusement arcade in Norwich was refused, for the corporation considered that such places were likely to corrupt the young. It was held that the corporation's fixed and rigid policy against the existence of amusement arcades had so fettered their discretion that they had not truly considered the application before them. Similarly in *Stringer v MHLG (1971) 1 All ER 65*, where a planning authority refused planning permission for the erection of some houses near the Jodrell Bank telescope merely because they had agreed in writing with Manchester University, which operated the telescope, to discourage building in the area, it was held that the authority had acted improperly in reaching a decision purely on the basis of their rule of policy.

The classic view on policy rules was restated in *R v SS Home Dept, ex p Findlay (1984) 3 All ER 801*. The facts were that the Home Secretary announced a new parole policy which was to be stricter but about which he had not first consulted the Parole Board. Four prisoners in open prisons who were pending parole challenged the policy change when they were replaced in closed institutions. However, the House of Lords decided that there was no statutory duty to consult the Parole Board and the factors taken into account such as retribution and public opinion were relevant so there was no unreasonableness. It was quite in order for a general policy to be formulated provided it was not followed slavishly so that exceptions to the rule were never admitted. In each case the merits of the position must be reviewed.

(e)   Apart from specific grounds of attack of administrative decisions, such as sub-delegation, and use of a fixed policy, the courts have another and wider basis of review. For, as Lord Greene said in *Associated Provincial Picture Houses v Wednesbury Corporation (1948) 1 KB 223*, even where an authority has kept strictly within the four corners of the matters which they ought to consider, it may still be possible to say that *they have nevertheless come to a conclusion so unreasonable that no reasonable authority could ever have come to it*. In such cases the court should intervene, not to substitute its own decision for that of the authority, but rather to see whether the authority has acted so unreasonably as to be abusing the powers delegated to it.

The court's use of this wide basis of review was at one time unrestrained. Thus, in *Roberts v Hopwood (1925) AC 587*, where the Poplar Council had resolved to give their male and female employees equal pay, acting under delegated power to pay such wages *as they thought fit*, the House of Lords held that they were only entitled to pay such wages as they *reasonably* thought fit and that their resolution must therefore be quashed as being unreasonable. In the more recent case of *Prescott v Birmingham Corporation (1955) Ch 210* the corporation's scheme to provide old age pensioners with free bus passes was stigmatised by the courts as unreasonable. However, the courts have recently shown themselves unwilling to intervene unless an authority's decision clearly is such as no reasonable authority could have reached. In *Luby v Newcastle (1965) 3 All ER 169* Diplock LJ warned:

> the court's control over the exercise by a local authority of a discretion conferred upon it by Parliament is limited to ensuring that the local authority has acted within the powers conferred. It is not for the court to substitute its own view of what is a desirable policy in relation to the subject matter of the discretion so conferred. It is only if it is exercised in a manner which no reasonable man could consider justifiable that the court is entitled to interfere.

In *Secretary of State for Education v Tameside (1976) AC 1014*, therefore, the House of Lords held that the defendant authority was not acting unreasonably in scrapping plans for comprehensive education drawn up by its predecessors because, it was said, its decision was nor such as no reasonable authority could have taken. Properly operated, the test is clearly a stringent one and findings of unreasonableness should thus be rare. Nevertheless, in *London Borough of Bromley v GLC (1983) 1 AC 768* the House of Lords quashed the decision of the Greater London Council to raise extra money from ratepayers to subsidise a 25% reduction in bus and tube fares. The GLC was held to be acting in breach of its statutory duty to provide an 'economic' transport system, i.e. a transport system in accordance with ordinary business principles. After the GLC drew up a new policy, 'Option

II – the Balanced Plan' for London's transport which would, if implemented, result in a 25% fare cut, it sought declarations that these plans were valid and these were granted. The GLC had now considered all points of view, those of the ratepayers as well as travellers. They were not simply attempting to impose an election manifesto regardless of the *Transport Act 1969*. The new plan was balanced and was a genuine effort to reconcile competing interests. It was not, therefore, unreasonable and the GLC's plans were permitted to be put into force (*R v London Transport Executive, ex parte GLC (1983) 2 All ER 262*).

In *Pickwell v Camden LBC (1983) 1 All ER 602* a discernably more respectful attitude was struck by the court towards the exercise of local authority discretion. In that case Camden Council had agreed to a local settlement with its manual workers who were striking for higher pay and reduced working hours. That local settlement turned out to be more favourable to the workers than was the case with the national settlement reached at a later date. Ratepayers complained that the Council had given in too easily to industrial pressure, and that the Council was notoriously sympathetic towards the employees. The District Auditor, relying on these and other arguments, applied for a declaration that the money voted by the Council for the local settlement was *ultra vires*. The application failed. The judgment of Forbes J is striking for its cautious approach to judicial interventionism. He said (at pp.621-24):

> ... when applying the principles of Wednesbury, which is to say, when exercising its supervisory jurisdiction, the court it not concerned with whether due or proper weight is given to a material consideration: the weight to be given to such a matter is for the body exercising the discretion to determine: the Court will no more substitute its own view of the importance of any relevant matter than it will do so for any other matter of statutory discretion. In considering whether it is right to conclude that ineluctably the only inference is that a relevant matter has been ignored the court should I think be very wary of coming to that conclusion: to weigh up a relevant matter and to conclude that the weight to be accorded to it is nil lies within the scope of discretion and is not necessarily to be equated with ignoring it ... while such a conclusion mighty sometimes be justified, despite the reluctance of the court to interfere in the exercise by a statutory authority of discretionary powers, where the decision is taken freely, voluntarily and under no pressure, the position may be very different where an emergency dictates a rapid solution to an urgent and pressing problem.

Forbes J went on to conclude that, since the Council was faced with a position where vital services had been so disrupted that real hardship was being caused to the community, it could not be inferred that they had acted unreasonably and illegally by giving way to such pressure, even though others might think the settlement was excessive, bad for ratepayers or should have been resisted despite the possible future repercussions for industrial relations in Camden.

In *R v Greenwich BC, ex p Cedar Transport Group Ltd (1983) The Times, 3 August (QBD)* the applicants, who were commercial ratepayers, argued that the expenditure plans of the Council were unreasonably excessive and *ultra vires*, being in breach of the fiduciary duty which the Council owed to the ratepayers. But the only evidence adduced in support of this argument was the fact that the proposed expenditure would exceed targets imposed by central government and expose the Council to a possible penalty of a £5.7 million cut in its block grant from central government. Such a cut would have to be made up by an increase in the rates. The court refused to draw the inference that the Council had acted illegally from those bare facts. Griffiths LJ pointed out that, by the very nature of things, local authorities being political animals, what the majority of the Council considered reasonable expenditure would probably appear unreasonable to the minority. It might even appear wrong to the court; but to be wrong was not the same as acting unreasonably in the legal sense of that word.

There are two recent politically controversial examples showing the judges' attitudes. In *R v Liverpool City Council, ex p Ferguson and Others (1985)* declarations were granted that the decision of the Council to issue dismissal notices to its teachers was invalid. An illegal rate had been declared and no attempt made to balance the budget and the decision to dismiss was a direct result of this. The dismissals were not in furtherance of the Council's duty as an education authority and it was irrational to take a decision so flawed by illegality.

In *R v SS Environment, ex p Notts CC (1985)* the House of Lords had to decide two points: first, whether guidance given by the Secretary of State could be said to be framed by reference to principles applicable to all authorities and, secondly, whether it was unreasonable under the *Wednesbury* formula to have criteria discriminating against high spending authorities because the effect was disproportionately disadvantageous. Lord Scarman said the court should intervene only in exceptional cases where the incidence of the monetary burden was adjusted by the Secretary of State and the Commons between taxpayers and ratepayers. There was no *prima facie* evidence of bad faith or improper motive on the part of the Secretary of State and the evidence did not show that he had taken leave of his senses, so his guidance should stand.

121.4 *IMPROPER PROCEDURE*

Where the procedural rules by which an administrative body must operate are mandatory (as opposed to directory), failure to abide by those rules will be *ultra vires* action and subject to judicial review. It is important to note however, that procedural rules are not exclusively to be found in the particular legislation, since the courts may insist on compliance with other implied procedural requirements, known as the principles of natural justice.

Before proceeding to examine those principles, attention will be given to the question whether there is a duty to provide reasons for administrative decisions. Although it may seem obvious that a good decision should be accompanied by reasons, there is nothing in the common law to compel a judge to give reasons for his decisions. *S.12 Tribunals and Inquiries Act 1971* imposes a duty on certain listed tribunals to give reasons for their decisions if requested to do so. There is no automatic duty that reasons should be stated unless there has been a request that they should be. Otherwise only a sufficient indication that the relevant questions have been examined is needed. Increasingly, however, the courts have imposed a duty to give reasons, even on bodies not listed in the *Tribunals and Inquiries Act*. In *Padfield v Minister of Agriculture (1968) 1 All ER 694 (supra)* it had been argued that since the minister had given no reasons for a decision, that decision could not be questioned. But Lord Pearce in the House of Lords said that where it appeared that the minister's decision was contrary to the policy of the statute and no reasons for it were given, the court would infer that he had no good reasons and would quash the decision accordingly. To assume where no reasons are given that there are none is clearly to create strong incentive for the giving of reasons. See further *Congreve v The Home Office (1976) 1 All ER 697*.

Apart from a duty to give reasons, the most usually implied procedural requirements are the two rules of natural justice. These are:

(a)   *nemo judex in causa sua:* let no man be a judge in his own cause;

(b)   *audi alteram partem:* let the other side be heard.

The term 'natural justice' is used because the rules are indeed considered to be *natural* as being indispensable to justice. Their history has been traced to Greek and Augustine jurisprudence and even where they have been held not to apply, there may still be a *duty to act fairly* which is a diluted version of them.

The rules of natural justice do not apply to all situations. Their content alters according to context. In order for them to apply at all it seems that there must be some *judicial* element in the decision. Thus, for instance, the rules will apply where there has been a *hearing* or a dispute between two parties argued before a *judge* or where someone's livelihood was at stake, but not where the decision was purely legislative in character: *Bates v Lord Hailsham (1972) 3 All ER 1019*. To see more clearly where and how the rules are applied, it is necessary to examine each of them in turn.

(a) *Nemo judex in causa sua*

This rule is otherwise known as the rule against bias and it has two sub-rules:

(i) where the party making the decision has a direct financial interest in the decision he is disqualified. The leading authority for this proposition is the decision in *Dimes v Proprietors of the Grand Junction Canal (1852) 3 HLC 759*. In this case Lord Cottenham made a decision relating to a company in which he, himself, held shares. Despite the fact that there was no suggestion that his decision had been in any way affected by his shareholding the court set it aside, stressing the importance of the fact that justice be seen to be done. This rule is operated rigidly and the only occasions where it may be waived are when the parties knowing the full facts agree to a waiver, where statute exempts from the rule or where everyone qualified to make the decision has a direct financial interest in it;

(ii) where the party making the decision has a non-financial interest in the decision. This rule is rather less strictly applied than the rule against adjudicators with a direct financial interest. It seems that if there is a reasonable suspicion that the party making the decision is biased the decision will be set aside. Again the court places emphasis on the idea that justice should be seen to be done. Several cases are set out below to illustrate this. In *R v Sussex Justices, ex p McCarthy (1923) All ER 233* the decision of a magistrates' court to convict a driver of criminal offences was set aside because their clerk, who had retired with the magistrates but not given any advice, was senior partner of a firm of solicitors advising a client who was suing the convicted driver for damages as a result of the accident out of which the criminal charges arose. In *Metropolitan Properties v Lannon (1969) 1 QB 577* Lannon, chairman of a rent assessment committee occupied a flat (in a block of flats) which his father leased from Metropolitan Properties. Lannon's committee assessed the rent for a similar block of flats nearby also owned by Metropolitan Properties. Since the rental value of that block of flats might in future affect the rental value of Lannon senior's flat the court found a reasonable suspicion of bias and set aside the rent assessment committee's decision. Another example of bias is shown in *R v Barnsley MBC, ex p Hook (1976) 3 All ER 452*.

(b) *Audi alteram partem*

This Latin phrase means 'let the other side be heard' and this rule of natural justice requires that both sides to a dispute be given reasonable notice of any hearing and of the case to be answered and a fair and adequate opportunity to present their cases. The exact detail of what this means varies from case to case according to the circumstances. For example in cases where a person's liberty or livelihood is at stake, the rule will require that an oral hearing occur but in less serious cases it may be sufficient for the parties to set out their cases in writing. The different content of the audi alteran pattern rule according to circumstances can be demonstrated by reference to *Currie v Barton (1988) Times 12 February*. In this instance a player who disagreed with his county ranking to play in a tennis tournament stormed from the court. He was banned by the County Tennis Committee from playing for the county for a period of three years. The plaintiff failed to obtain review on the grounds that he had already placed his views at length in a letter to the decision making committee and since his livelihood did not depend upon the licence there was no requirement on the Committee to award the plaintiff an oral hearing. Again the rule may require that legal representation of the parties be permitted. In *R v Board of Visitors of Wormwood Scrubs Prison, ex p Anderson (1984) 1 All ER 799*, although the court held that the prisoners had no *right* to legal representation, it recognised the Board's discretion to allow such representation and concluded that in serious cases where prisoners were accused of complicated offences carrying severe penalties of loss of remission of sentence, the only reasonable conclusion the Board could reach would be to allow the prisoners legal assistance. In *R v Prison Board of Visitors of the Maze Prison ex p Hone and McCarton (1988)* the altitude in Anderson was captured. The court held there was no automatic right to legal representation before a Prison Board of Visitors as there was before a criminal court.

The *audi alteram partem* rule applies to the following situations:

(i)   courts of law;

(ii)   tribunals which resemble courts of law;

(iii)   bodies with discretion to deprive a person of property, liberty, status or livelihood or to do anything else which would severely prejudice the legally recognised interests of the person affected.

The growth of this last category started with the celebrated case of *Ridge v Baldwin (1964) AC 40.* The facts were that the Chief Constable of Brighton, although acquitted of criminal charges, was dismissed by the Watch Committee in Brighton without notice either of the hearing or of the allegations against him. On his application for a declaration to quash the decision of the Watch Committee the House of Lords upheld his contentions on the ground that the duty of the Watch Committee was not purely administrative but judicial or quasi-judicial and the rules of natural justice, which clearly had not been satisfied, were therefore applicable. Since 1964 decisions of licensing authorities, local authorities and prison boards of governors have all fallen within this last category to which the rules of natural justice apply on certain occasions. Some examples follow.

In *McInnes v Onslow-Fane (1978) 3 All ER 211* the plaintiff applied on six occasions for a licence to become a boxing manager, each time unsuccessfully. He had previously held licences for other boxing positions from the Board of Control but these had been withdrawn for his conduct on a particular occasion. On his final application for a manager's licence the plaintiff asked for an opportunity to present his case at an oral hearing and prior notice of matters which might prevent issue of the licence. This was all refused and the plaintiff applied for a declaration that the Board's action was in breach of the rules of natural justice. The court refused to grant the declaration on the grounds that where there was not a legitimate expectation of receiving a licence, the rules of natural justice did not apply. Here there could only be a 'hope' that a licence would be granted rather than an expectation as the plaintiff had not previously held a *manager's* licence. As the Board had acted fairly without bias and honestly the court concluded that the plaintiff could not succeed. An application for parole too is considered to arouse only a 'hope', not a legitimate expectation, so the rules of natural justice do not apply.

In cases where the decision of a body may have a very adverse effect on an individual in some other aspect of life than his livelihood, for example his freedom, the rules of natural justice will also be applied. *R v Hull Prison Board of Visitors, ex p St Germain (1979) 1 All*

ER 701 arose out of hearings and consequent sentences by the Hull Prison Board Visitors after serious riots at the prison. The Board of Visitors is a tribunal of lay people, appointed from outside the prison service, who are supposed to act as impartial adjudicators between prisoners and prison officers when the former face serious disciplinary charges under the prison rules. In this particular case the applicant was a prisoner who claimed breaches of the rules of natural justice at his hearing before the Board. The preliminary point arose of whether such a tribunal was bound to observe natural justice. The Divisional Court held that the proceedings were purely administrative and that natural justice was inapplicable but, on appeal the Court of Appeal held that the board was under a duty to observe natural justice and the case was remitted to the Divisional Court to determine whether breaches had in fact occurred (it was found that some breaches of natural justice had occurred and the sentences imposed on the prisoners in question were set aside: *R v Hull Prison Board of Visitors (No. 2) (1979) 3 All ER 545*).

The Court of Appeal in the *Hull Prison (No. 1) case* took the view that a domestic disciplinary tribunal has a duty to observe natural justice if it is sitting to determine issues of guilt and to award punishments, even if it has other purely administrative functions.

However, in *R v Deputy Governor of Camp Hill Prison (1984) 3 All ER 897* the Deputy Governor had ordered a prisoner to lose 14 days' remission after a hypodermic syringe was found in a cell occupied by four men. The court considered that the Deputy Governor had wrongly construed the prison rules but nevertheless concluded that he had been exercising a managerial and not a judicial function and that public policy demanded that a prison governor's authority should not be undermined by making every decision he made reviewable by the courts. The aggrieved prisoner's remedy was to apply to the Prison Board or to the Secretary of State.

The decision in this case is explicable on the grounds that the court had taken a policy decision for practical reasons that the prison system of discipline would become unworkable if all disciplinary decisions could be challenged on the grounds of a breach of the rules of natural justice. In R v Deputy Governor of Parkhurst ex p Leech and R v Deputy Governor of Long Lartin Prison ex p. Prevote (1988) the House of Lords reversed earlier decisions by providing that, like prison Boards of Visitors' decisions, those of a disciplinary nature made by a Governors or Deputy Prison Governor were susceptible to judicial review as there was in logic no reason for them to be treated differently. A further example of the courts' practical approach is the decision in *R v Prison Board of Visitors of Frankland Prison, ex pte. Lewis (1986) 1 All ER 272*. In this case it was argued that as Prison Boards of Visitors gained background knowledge about prisoners as part of their administrative visits, this disqualified them from sitting on a disciplinary hearing about a prisoner whose background was familiar to them. The chairman of a disciplinary board had previously heard a parole application in relation to a prisoner alleged to have been in possession of drugs and would therefore have known of his drug-taking history but he testified that by the time of the later disciplinary hearing he no longer had the details in his mind. Although the court was prepared to accept that there could be cases where it would not be proper for someone from a Prison Board of Visitors to sit on a disciplinary hearing this was not one and the position of magistrates and members of a Prison Board of Visitors was different.

The Court of Appeal also adopted the practical approach in *R v Chief Constable for South Wales, ex p Thornhill (1986)*. A deputy chief constable who had investigated disciplinary charges against a sergeant made a private visit to the Chief Constable on another matter during the course of an adjournment of the disciplinary hearing and it was argued that this constituted a breach of the rules of natural justice and invalidated the decision to dismiss the sergeant. The Court of Appeal said all the circumstances must be taken into account and from affidavit evidence the disciplinary hearing had not even been mentioned at the meeting. Therefore, there was no breach of the rules.

In *R v Wear Valley District Council, ex p Binks (1985) 2 All ER 699* an oral licence existed between the Council and a caravan owner by which she was allowed to park a caravan on Council ground to which the public had access. From the caravan she sold hot take-away food and this was her only livelihood. The Council without warning told her they were terminating her licence because it was undesirable to have street sales and because of litter. The Council argued there were only three types of licensing case where there were statutory powers which must be exercised honestly, where there was a street market and the applicant was a stall-holder (inapplicable here) and where a person's living was at stake, which they argued was not the case here because she only had a licence for the positioning of the caravan. However, the court decided that the public position and the threat to the livelihood of the woman took the case into the realms of public law so the woman should have been given warning of the proposals and an opportunity to be heard.

Two recent cases can be contrasted to illustrate the point that the rules of natural justice are applicable only where an individual's rights, interests or legitimate expectations are affected by an administrative decision. In *Hood v McMahon (1986)* the district auditor did not give the Liverpool councillors an oral hearing when he was deciding on the issue of certificates of sums due from them. This was unfair because the certificates of sums due could be enforced against the councillors' personal assets and could therefore have a very detrimental effect on the councillors' financial status, even causing bankruptcy. By contrast in *R v Secretary of State for the Environment ex p Southwark LBC (1987)* the court held that the Secretary of State did not have to consult a local authority before calling in the local plan under the *Town and Country Planning Act 1971.* The court held that to attract the rules of natural justice an administrative decision must be capable of affecting rights, interests or expectations of individuals.

The rules of natural justice do not apply in the following cases, although there will in these cases be a requirement that the decision-making body achieves the lower 'duty to act fairly'.

(i) where a body merely undertakes a preliminary enquiry or investigation as in *Moran v Lloyds (1983) 2 All ER 200* where a Lloyds underwriter challenged the investigation of a Committee of Lloyds investigating improprieties but was unsuccessful because the Committee merely was required to report rather than take a decision;

(ii) where scarce resources such as council houses or university places are being allocated. In *McInnes v Onslow-Fane (1978) 3 All ER 211* the duty to act fairly required only that an honest decision be reached without bias.

　　However, once a scarce resource has been allocated if it is withdrawn without an opportunity being given to the potential recipient to allow him to state his case, there may be a breach of the rules of natural justice. In *R v Secretary of State for Transport, ex p Sherriff & Sons Ltd (1987)* the Minister had agreed to make a grant for rail freight facilities orally. The undertaking was later withdrawn without warning and this was a breach of the rules of natural justice.

In the following situations there is no duty to follow the rules of natural justice or to act fairly:

(1) where the act complained of is legislative in nature;

(2) possibly where the power exercised is a prerogative power but this may change following the GCHQ decision;

(3)   where national security is at stake;

(4)   where private law only is relevant such as in employer/employee dismissal disputes where there is no element of public office;

(5)   where the applicant's own poor conduct has made compliance with the rules inappropriate. In *Cinnamond v British Airports Authority (1980) 2 All ER 368* the authority had banned six mini-cab drivers from Heathrow Airport because of their repeated breaches of the Authority's bye-laws. The drivers argued that they should have been given a hearing before being banned. It was held that the ban was lawful because the drivers had abused the authority given to them by law and had not been deterred by the criminal law because, although they had been convicted many times, the machinery for collecting fines was so time-consuming and fruitless that the drivers could ignore it with contempt. Further (per Lord Denning), not every administrative decision called for a hearing. If mini-cab drivers were of good character and came into the airport under a licence, it would only be fair that they should have a chance of putting their case before being banned. But the six drivers here had convictions and outstanding fines. It was not a necessary preliminary that they should be given a hearing; they could have made representations when they received the letter. Lord Justice Shaw agreed that, on the question of unfairness, the drivers had put themselves 'outside the pale' in their conduct at the airport and their disregard of the penalties of the law.

Further reading

(a)   *General*

Wade and Bradley, Chapter 34.
de Smith, Chapter 28.

(b)   *Jurisdictional error*

Rawlings (1979), *Public Law*, 404.
Wade (1979), 95 *LQR*, 163.
Public Law (1977) 293.
Student Law Reporter, Summer 1979, Article 9.
Wade (1980) 96 *LQR*, 492.

(c)   *Natural justice*

Alexis (1979), *Public Law*, 143.
Casey (1979), *LQR*, pp.469-70.
42 *MLR* (1979) 467.
Student Law Reporter, Spring 1979, Articles 17-20.
Hull, *NLJ*, 23 August 1979 at p.825.
Rawlings (1979), 95 *LQR*, 326.
Student Law Reporter, Autumn 1979, Article 11.
Report on the Affairs of the Peachey Property Corporation Ltd, HMSO, 1979.
Jackson (1980), 96 *LQR*, 497.
Samuel (1981), 97 *LQR*, 19.
Griffiths (1982), *CLJ*, 6 and 216.

LLB

CONSTITUTIONAL LAW

LESSON 13 (STUDY)

131. *REMEDIES AGAINST PUBLIC AUTHORITIES*

131.1 *Introduction*

Where a public authority acts unlawfully in any of the ways described in the previous lesson or acts contrary to the ordinary law, e.g. by committing a nuisance or trespass, the citizen may seek a number of different remedies. Each remedy must be dealt with in turn as they differ in availability and efficacy. The main remedies are:

(a)   *certiorari* and *prohibition;*

(b)   *mandamus;*

(c)   injunction;

(d)   declaration;

(e)   damages.

Certiorari, prohibition and *mandamus* are prerogative orders with a long history. They have been used in the field of public law for a considerable time. By contrast the injunction and the declaration (which is really a twentieth century phenomenon) have been adapted for use in administrative law although they were originally private law remedies. This helps to explain the different conditions applying to *certiorari, prohibition* and *mandamus* from those applying to the injunction and damages (see below). Until 1978 a plaintiff had to select the remedy he sought and make a specific application to the court following a very formal procedure, which was different for each of the remedies sought. In 1978 by *Order 53, Rules of the Supreme Court* (now *s.31 Supreme Court Act 1981*) the application for judicial review was introduced and now a plaintiff may make one application seeking several remedies at once. *Certiorari, prohibition* and *mandamus* may only be sought by making an application for judicial review but, although an injunction and declaration in a public law context must now usually be sought in this way, there may also be circumstances in which they may be sought separately.

The application for judicial review takes place in two stages:

(a)   an application is made for leave to bring the proceedings to the Divisional Court. A hearing takes place at which the court considers whether *prima facie* the applicant has a 'sufficient interest' to justify the proceedings. What is a sufficient interest differs according to the remedy sought (see below). If there is a sufficient interest, then

(b)   a hearing takes place to consider the merits of the application and, if it is satisfied as to the plaintiff's case, the court awards a remedy or remedies. At this stage the court may still reject the application on *locus standi* grounds.

131.2 *Certiorari and prohibition*

(a)   *Introduction*

These are complementary remedies. *Prohibition* will be granted by the court where a tribunal or court is acting or is about to act in excess or abuse of its powers. It is only available before a body has reached its decision and will not lie unless something remains to be done which the court can prohibit. *Certiorari* is granted to quash a decision which *has been made* in excess or abuse of power. *Certiorari* is a very much more common remedy than *prohibition*.

(b)   *The grounds*

Certiorari or *prohibition* may be granted where the decision was:

(i)   made *ultra vires;* or

(ii)   reached contrary to the rules of natural justice; or

(iii) procured by assertions shown to be fraudulent; or

(iv)   flawed by an error of law.

(c)   *To whom do certiorari and prohibition issue?*

The remedies are *NOT* available where the tribunal against which they are sought is a domestic tribunal. Domestic tribunals include committees of clubs or trade unions or an employer's disciplinary tribunal.

The remedies *ARE* available against any public authority determining questions affecting the rights, legitimate expectations or interests of individuals.

(d)   *The locus standi of the applicant*

As stated above the applicant must show he has a sufficient interest in the matter, otherwise the court will dismiss the application or use this factor as grounds for refusing a remedy. The test of sufficient interest is more liberal for these remedies than for *mandamus*, injunction or the declaration. Provided the applicant can show a substantial personal interest to vindicate or that he is a part of a local community and has by virtue of membership of that community a special grievance, the court will accept that there is a sufficient interest.

In *R v GLC, ex p Blackburn (1976) 3 All ER 184* the applicants, husband and wife, lived in the Greater London area and the husband was a ratepayer. The GLC proposed to exhibit films considered by the applicants to be pornographic and the Blackburns applied for prohibition to prevent the exhibition. Lord Denning and the Court of Appeal considered that, as citizens of London and a ratepayer, there was a sufficient interest. However, in *Barrs v Bethell (1982) 1 All ER 106* ratepayers were held to have insufficient *locus standi* when challenging a Council decision to freeze Council rents, thus losing the Rate Support Grant from the Government.

(e)   *Bars to the grant of certiorari and prohibition*

Certiorari and *prohibition* are discretionary remedies and the court may refuse the remedies if:

(i)   there has been unreasonable delay in seeking a remedy. There is normally a three month time limit to an application seeking *certiorari*;

(ii)   the applicant has waived or acquiesced in an excess of jurisdiction or breach of natural justice or has conducted himself improperly.

In *Ex p Fry (1954) 2 All ER 118* a fireman refused to clean a senior officer's uniform and sought *certiorari* after a disciplinary hearing. The court considered he should have carried out the order and pursued his grievance through the fire service procedural regulations;

(iii) there is a more suitable alternative remedy.

In *R v Secretary of State for Social Services, ex p Association of Metropolitan Authorities (1986) 1 All ER 164* the court, in deciding that the Minister had acted invalidly in issuing regulations, granted a declaration rather than *certiorari* because the decision affected the law of the land, not just the rights of an individual or locality and furthermore, as the regulations under review had now been consolidated into others, *certiorari* was no longer appropriate;

(iv) the application is made in respect of an area in which the courts consider they should not intervene.

For example, the Court of Appeal refused in 1975 to award *certiorari* against a Supplementary Benefit Appeal Tribunal where there had been an error of law. It took the view that only in the grossest of cases would it be appropriate to award *certiorari* against this class of tribunal. This policy has recently not been followed.

131.3 *Mandamus*

(a) *Introduction*

Mandamus lies to ensure that the duty of a tribunal, Minister or local authority is carried out. It is an exceptional remedy and this is reflected in the discretionary bars and *locus standi* conditions.

(b) *The grounds*

There is quite a wide range of situations in which it can be used, including:

(i) to compel a tribunal or court to hear a matter where it has wrongly declined jurisdiction;

(ii) to obtain public accounts withheld by local authorities;

(iii) to compel a body to provide reasons or adequate reasons for a decision where it is under a duty to do so;

(iv) to compel a body to exercise a discretion where it has fettered its powers to do so or has failed to do so because, for example, it took into account irrelevant matters.

(c) *To whom does it issue?*

It does *not* lie against the Crown or against a Crown servant if the duty, the subject of the proceedings, is owed only to the Crown. It cannot be used to compel a local authority or nationalised industry to provide a public service unless the applicant is a Minister.

Subject to the above it will lie against Ministers, local authorities, etc.

(d) *The locus standi of the applicant*

The applicant must show a sufficient interest which, in the context of *mandamus*, has been discussed in detail by the House of Lords in the 'Mickey Mouse' case, *Inland Revenue Commissioners v National Federation of Self-Employed and Small Businesses (1981) 2 All ER 93*. The facts were that print workers in Fleet Street had been avoiding tax on casual work they performed by the use of false names such as 'Mickey Mouse' or 'Donald Duck'. The Inland Revenue offered a tax amnesty to these workers in respect of tax over part of the period which had passed in return for the regularisation of the tax position for the future.

The National Federation of Self-Employed and Small Businesses sought a declaration that the amnesty was unlawful and *mandamus* to compel the Inland Revenue to collect back tax from the workers.

The House of Lords said that *locus standi* could in suitable cases of a straightforward nature be considered as a preliminary matter but in other cases should be dealt with at a hearing into the merits of the case. It went on to decide that the definition of the duty alleged to have been broken or left unperformed was important as one had to decide whether it expressly or impliedly entitled the plaintiff to complain. As far as tax matters are concerned there is a public interest in maintaining them as a confidential matter between the individual taxpayer and the Inland Revenue and the Revenue had in any event properly been exercising their discretionary powers. On this basis there was no sufficient interest to justify the grant of *mandamus*.

131.4 *Injunction*

(a) *Introduction*

An injunction is an order by the court which is either prohibitory or mandatory in nature. However, mandatory injunctions are comparatively rare.

An injunction may be an interim or interlocutory one or it may be final. An interim or interlocutory injunction is granted by a court pending a full hearing of the merits of the case in circumstances where it appears to the court that in the absence of such an order there may be a wrongful act likely to do serious harm if it is permitted to continue.

(b) *The grounds*

It lies to restrain a public nuisance, a breach of statutory duty or an *ultra vires* act.

(c) *To whom does it issue?*

An injunction cannot be obtained against the Crown which means that an injunction will not be issued against Government departments, public corporations which are Crown servants, Ministers or other officers of the Crown for acts done in the purported exercise of statutory functions but may be obtained against other public authorities.

(d) *The locus standi of the applicant*

Unless the applicant can show that he suffers special damage over and above that suffered by the rest of the community he must bring his proceedings by a relator action. This means that the applicant must bring the proceedings in the name of the Attorney-General, having first obtained the Attorney-General's consent to this course of action. If this permission is not forthcoming, that is an end of the matter and the applicant cannot proceed, for the courts will not question the Attorney-General's decision. The principle is clearly set out in *Gouriet v National Union of Post Office Workers (1977) 3 All ER 70*. In that case the Union of Post Office Workers was preparing to 'black' (i.e. not to handle) mail to South Africa. Gouriet decided to take action to prevent this but he had no greater interest in the dispute than any other member of the general public. When the Attorney-General refused his consent to the proceedings Gouriet nevertheless commenced the action. It failed on the issue of standing in the House of Lords which concluded that the courts will not question the Attorney-General's exercise of his discretion in deciding whether to permit relator proceedings and that a member of the public who has no special interest over and above that of the public at large cannot proceed by means of a relator action without the Attorney-General's consent and cannot continue in his own right.

(e) *Bars to the grant of an injunction*

It is not available if the injury is trivial or where there has been acquiescence in the injury or behaviour of the applicant.

131.5 *The declaration*

(a) *Introduction*

As the name of the remedy suggests this order is one which simply declares what the law is and how it applies to the facts of the particular case. No one is ordered to do anything but a public authority normally abides by the statement of the law.

Although the declaration was originally adapted from private law and is therefore in some respects similar to the injunction it differs in that no interim relief is available.

(b) *Grounds*

Declarations are sought to test the validity of administrative or judicial decisions, to declare rights and to establish the existence or scope of public duties.

A wide variety of situations can be covered. For example, in *Hall v Shoreham UDC (1964) 1 All ER 1* it was used to determine the validity of conditions attached to a planning consent and it was also used in *Ridge v Baldwin (1964) AC 40*. It can be used (instead of *certiorari* which will not lie) in respect of domestic tribunals if there has been a breach of natural justice.

(c) *To whom does it issue?*

Unlike the injunction it can be obtained against the Crown as well as local authorities, domestic tribunals, etc.

(d) *The locus standi of the applicant*

The same rules apply for *locus standi* as apply to the injunction.

(e) *Bars to the grant of a declaration*

A declaration will be refused if there is a more suitable remedy, for example, if a decision needs quashing, then *certiorari* is a more appropriate remedy. It will also be refused if the issue at stake is really one of morals or hypothetical. For example, in *Blackburn v A-G (1971) 2 All ER 1380* Blackburn challenged the United Kingdom's entry to the EEC on the grounds that membership would give rise to a permanent loss of sovereignty of the UK Parliament. The court refused declarations and said that the permanency of the loss of sovereignty was a hypothetical question and that such questions could not be dealt with by the courts.

In *R v Hillingdon LBC ex p Tinn (1988) Times 14 January* Mrs Tinn sought a declaration as to whether the Council would have a duty to rehouse her were she to sell her council house for which the mortgage payment were too high. She did not have a sufficient interest for the award of a declaration.

In *R v Notts County Council (1987)* the court said that a declaration could be granted unless it was of some use now or in the future and was not just a comment on events in the past, which had now been rectified by statute.

This confirmed the attitude of the courts in *R v Secretary of State for the Environment, ex p GLC (1985)* where the court held that a declaration under *s.31(2) Supreme Court Act 1981* could be made even where one of the prerogative remedies would not be available.

However, the court also stated that it should only use its discretion to obtain a declaration of the reasons of a public body for its decision where they involved a matter of general public importance and this was not established in this case since all that the GLC had wanted was extra detail about the reasons behind the reasons stated in a planning inspector's report.

131.6 *Damages*

Damages are available where the individual's person or property is injured by reason of the unlawful act of the public authority. An action will lie against a public authority in circumstances where it would lie against a private individual. The most usual actions would be in negligence or nuisance. Any breach of a duty laid upon an authority by statute would also be actionable provided that an individual suffered injury and provided that individual suit is not statutorily excluded (see *Anns v London Borough of Merton (1978) AC 728*).

131.7 *The decision in O'Reilly v Mackman (1983) 2 AC 237*

The facts of this case were that a prisoner sought to challenge the validity of a decision of the Board of Visitors by seeking a declaration in proceedings by way of originating summons in the Chancery Division; other prisoners brought actions by writ in the Queen's Bench Division seeking declarations for the same purpose. It was held that all the proceedings should be dismissed on the ground that they were an abuse of the process of the court. In general the correct procedure for a person seeking to challenge the decision of a public authority was by way of an application for judicial review in the Queen's Bench Division. The reasons for the decision were that public authorities were entitled to the safeguards provided by the procedure of an application for judicial review (AJR), namely:

(a)   the requirement for the applicant to obtain leave before asking for judicial review;

(b)   the right of the court to order security for costs from the applicant if it gave such leave;

(c)   the requirement for the applicant to produce his evidence on affidavit, thereby deterring knowingly false statements of fact which could be punished as perjury;

(d)   the requirement that such affidavits must contain full and candid disclosures of all material facts; and

(e)   the guarantee of a speedier hearing than in a private law action.

Those safeguards were designed to deal with groundless, unmeritorious or tardy harassment of public decision-making bodies. The latter were entitled to special protection on grounds of public policy, namely good administration, in the sense that public authorities and third parties should not be kept in suspense as to the legal validity of a decision for any longer period than was absolutely necessary in fairness to the persons affected by the decision.

Before the introduction of *Order 53 RSC* in 1977 there had been good reasons for using private law procedures against public bodies (i.e. to obtain discovery of documents, or administer interrogatories, or cross-examine deponents to affidavits; or to obtain damages/injunctions or declarations in addition to the prerogative orders of *mandamus, certiorari* and *prohibition*). Those reasons disappeared with the reforms introduced by *Order 53* (now *s.31 Supreme Court Act 1981*). Consequently private law actions should now be brought against public authorities only in special cases (e.g. where private law rights were also involved or where none of the parties objected), and it is for the court to decide whether such an exception exists on a case-to-case basis.

In the present case remission of sentence under the Prison Rules was not a matter of right but of indulgence, so that the prisoners' only remedy lay in public law in respect of their legitimate expectation to be heard fairly. Accordingly the Board was entitled to insist on use of the AJR procedure by the prisoners, for the safeguards under that procedure were not available in procedures by writ in the Queen's Bench Division or by originating summons in Chancery. Further, if, under an AJR, it should appear that only private rights were involved, the court could order the proceedings to continue as if begun by writ; there was no converse power to permit an action begun by writ to continue as if it were an AJR.

The decision in *O'Reilly v Mackman* has been criticised for making it necessary to distinguish between public law and private law issues, for it is questionable whether this distinction can be made and whether it is desirable to do so. To deny a right because of the form of action which the plaintiff has chosen could be seen as a retrograde step.

The plaintiffs in *O'Reilly v Mackman* had chosen the ordinary action because of the substantial delay in bringing the action which meant that it was unlikely that an *Order 53* application would be successful. There was also a substantial dispute on the facts, and in ordinary actions oral evidence and cross-examination is a matter of course whereas in an application for judicial review the normal procedure is evidence by affidavit only.

The next case to be decided after *O'Reilly v Mackman* illustrated the difficulty of making the distinction between public law issues and private law issues. In *Cocks v Thanet District Council (1982) 3 All ER 1135* the House of Lords decided that because a public law decision of a housing authority was a condition precedent to the establishment of a private law duty under the *Housing (Homeless Persons) Act 1977*, the proper route to challenge the decision was via *Order 53*.

It follows from *O'Reilly* that the procedure of judicial review under *s.31* of the 1981 Act is wholly inappropriate where a claim is based on alleged private law rights only, or even mixed public law and private law rights, if the plaintiff is able to establish his claim on the private law without the court having a discretion as to whether or not to refuse relief, because the procedure by way of AJR was geared specifically to the grant of *discretionary* relief, and aspects of public policy influenced the exercise of such discretion: *An Bord Bainne Co-op Ltd v Milk Marketing Board (1984) Times 22 May*.

It will be remembered that in *O'Reilly* it was recognised that, if private law rights were also involved, a private law action could be brought without being a misuse of the process of the court, so the decision in *An Bord Bainne Co-op* is fully in accordance with the policy laid down in *O'Reilly*. Similar 'case-by-case' exceptions to the general rule in *O'Reilly* were made in *Davy v Spelthorne BC (1984) and Wandsworth LBC v Winder (1983) 3 All ER 278*. In both cases

private actions were permitted against public authorities because private law rights were involved and it was recognised that it might cause the plaintiffs in those cases injustice if they were required to use the AJR procedure. However, in both cases it was emphasised that the private law rights were independent of the public law decisions that were being challenged (thereby distinguishing *Cocks v Thanet DC*) and that it would not be contrary to public policy to allow those actions to proceed. Thus in *Wandsworth LBC v Winder (1984) 3 All ER 976* the defendant had challenged the council's decision to increase council rents, including his own, under its powers and duties conferred by the *Housing Act 1957*. When sued for the rent he raised the issue that the council's decision was *ultra vires*. The Council, relying on *O'Reilly* argued that such a defence must be struck out, since such a claim must be brought by way of AJR. However, the House of Lords held that the tenant was entitled to raise the *ultra vires* defence, even though this was an issue of public law, because the tenant could rely on his pre-existing private law rights arising from his occupation of his council flat and from the previously established rent, and those private law rights were not dependent on the public law decision which was being challenged.

Since *Wandsworth LBC v Winder* there have been further examples of applications for declarations and injunctions by the wrong procedure and confusion between public and private law. These help to clarify the position after that case so they are set out below.

In *R v Coal Board, ex p NUM (1986)* the court held that judicial review was not the appropriate means to challenge a decision of the Coal Board to close Bates Colliery because the decision was a business or management one such as a private company would have to take. It was not a part of its duties as a public body.

In *R v IBA, ex p Rank Organisation (1986)* Rank was a shareholder in Granada and the IBA refused to allow Rank to vote more than 5% of the Granada shares. Rank challenged by judicial review but the court concluded that the refusal was on the basis of the articles of association of Granada and did not arise out of powers accorded the IBA by the *Broadcasting Act 1980* and therefore judicial review was not available.

In *Ettridge v Morrell (1986)* the court held that a candidate's right to hold a meeting in a school room during a local election campaign could be enforced by an action which was not brought under *Order 53* but under the ordinary method of seeking a declaration.

In *R v Secretary of State for the Home Department, ex p Dew (1987) 2 All ER 1049* the Queen's Bench Division considered when proceedings begun by an application for judicial review could be transferred to continue as if begun by writ under *Order 53 rule 9(5) Rules of the Supreme Court*. Mr Justice McNeill held that such a transfer was not permitted where the proceedings disclosed no right of complaint in public law. Dew alleged that on arrest he had suffered a bullet injury in an arm and this had not been properly medically treated but by the time the case reached court treatment had been received and the court held that Dew simply had a claim in damages in private law. *S.31 Supreme Court Act 1981* did not allow a transfer where there was no element of public law right involved.

In *Guevara v Hounslow LBC (1987)* the court took the view that if substantial public law rights were at stake the proper procedure was the application for judicial review, even if private law rights were also involved.

131.8 *Error of law, the decision in Anisminic (1969) and ouster or privative clauses*

(a)   *Error of law*

The classic exposition of the law on judicial review was that it was available to correct excesses of jurisdiction, decisions where there had been a breach of the rules of natural justice and cases where an error of law within jurisdiction could be corrected provided it appeared on the record. The record had a technical meaning, and included in the nineteenth century barely more than the magistrates' decision which normally had no reasons appended. The review for error of law on the face of the record was thought by many to be obsolete in the twentieth century but was revived by a decision in 1944 and further revitalised by the *Tribunals and Inquiries Act 1958* which provided by *s.12* that, upon request by the parties, a tribunal was required to give reasons for its decision. Such reasons became a part of the record, thus making review easier. Nevertheless the position remained that a jurisdictional error would be reviewed but an error of law within jurisdiction could only be corrected if it was on the record.

In 1969 the case of *Anisminic Ltd v Foreign Compensation Commission* was decided. The case was important from the point of view of its interpretation of jurisdictional error (which has given rise to much academic argument) and because of its judgment in relation to privative or ouster clauses, i.e. clauses designed to remove the jurisdiction of the courts to review decisions.

(b)   *Anisminic Ltd v Foreign Compensation Commission (1969) 1 All ER 208*

The facts were as follows. Anisminic was a British company which, during the Suez Crisis in 1956, suffered expropriation of its Egyptian assets by the Egyptian Government. These assets were later purchased by an Egyptian company, TEDO, but Anisminic reserved its rights in respect of any compensation later paid by the Egyptian Government. In due course a lump sum was paid by the Egyptian Government to the British Government which passed it to the already existing Foreign Compensation Commission for distribution in accordance with the *Foreign Compensation Act 1950*, set up to distribute post-World War II payments. *S.4(4)* of the Act had a provision that the decision of the Commission was final and 'not to be called into question in any court of law'. The FCC refused the application submitted by Anisminic because TEDO was Egyptian and the Foreign Compensation regulations provided a complicated formula to prevent payments being made to non-British nationals. As Anisminic's successor in title was Egyptian the FCC concluded that Anisminic was excluded from receiving compensation. Anisminic sought review of the decision of the FCC.

The House of Lords held the ouster clause effective to prevent review of errors within jurisdiction but not those which fell outside juris-diction. Furthermore, the error of law committed by the FCC was jurisdictional because the tribunal had asked itself the wrong question or applied the wrong test. The Lords also indicated that errors of law committed by administrative tribunals were likely to be classified as jurisdictional because the members of such bodies are not trained lawyers and cannot therefore be presumed to intend that their errors should not pass uncorrected.

(c)   *Ouster clauses*

Privative clauses take various forms:

(i)   wordings such as 'if the Minister thinks fit'. This type of clause has been considered in the work on *ultra vires* and the courts' powers of review of such powers is dealt with in such cases as *Tameside* or *Padfield*;

(ii)   clauses phrased so that the decision is described as 'final' or 'not to be questioned in any court of law' – the *Anisminic* type of clause – as to the affect of these in respect of the decisions of inferior courts (see below);

(iii)   clauses which provide a time limit within which any decision must be challenged. These clauses too are considered below and their treatment by the courts is different from that meted out to the *Anisminic* type clause.

(d)   *Anisminic type ouster clauses and the decisions in Pearlman v Harrow School and Re Racal Communications Ltd*

In the *Anisminic case* the House of Lords seemed to retain the distinction between errors of law within jurisdiction and those outside jurisdiction for inferior courts. Ouster clauses would effectively prevent review for errors of law within jurisdiction but not for those errors taking the court beyond its jurisdiction.

In the Court of Appeal during the 1970s Lord Denning seemed to take a different approach. He indicated that he thought any error of law which caused injustice should be reviewed and that privative clauses would be ineffective to prevent such review even where the error was within jurisdiction according to the normal tenets. Lord Denning was prepared to treat all errors of law as jurisdictional errors.

It was this sort of reasoning that led to the decision in *Pearlman v Harrow School (1979) 1 All ER 365*, a decision of a majority of the Court of Appeal later disapproved by the House of Lords in *Re Racal Communication Ltd. (1980) 2 All ER 634*. The facts in *Pearlman* were that the *Housing Act 1974* made the decision of a County Court judge final as to whether works amounted to 'structural alterations' for the purposes of the Act. The judge decided that the installation of central heating was not a structural alteration for the purposes of rate relief. Other County Court judges had taken the opposite view and review of the decision was sought in the Court of Appeal. Eveleigh LJ took the view that the judge's error had been jurisdictional so the privative clause did not work. Lord Denning indicated that he regarded the error as jurisdictional because he thought the judge had reached a wrong decision. This line of reasoning would totally remove the difference between errors within and errors outside jurisdiction. Both these judgements were disapproved in *Re Racal* and the dissenting judgement of Geoffrey Lane LJ preferred. He took the view that if the judge in *Pearlman* was acting outside jurisdiction then no errors of law were ever within jurisdiction. If this were so then a right of appeal was, in effect, created. That could not have been intended as there was an express finality clause in this case. Although the judge's decision was doubtful on its merits nothing could properly be done about this, because the judge had not embarked upon an unauthorised extraneous or irrelevant exercise.

In *Re Racal* the facts were that a High Court judge may under the *Companies Act 1948* order an investigation into the books of a company and his decision is under the Act described as 'not appealable'. The DPP had applied for an investigation of the company as he suspected fraud. The High Court judge refused to authorise investigation of the books and the DPP sought review on the basis of the decision in *Pearlman*. The Court of Appeal reviewed the decision but this time there was an appeal to the House of Lords who reversed the decision of the Court of Appeal unanimously. The Court of Appeal had no original supervisory jurisdiction over the High Court and it was not appropriate to treat the decisions of the High Court judges in the same way that those of administrative tribunals were treated. Thus, for them the distinction between jurisdictional and non-jurisdictional errors remains. Unfortunately the position of the decisions of inferior courts was not finally decided but it seems that for them too the distinction remains. The difficulty may now be to decide whether the decision-making body was a court or a tribunal. In 1980 in one case the Lords took 27 pages to decide if a valuation court was an inferior court or a tribunal in connection with the *Contempt of Court* rules. Much may depend on the construction of the relevant statute in any case. There are presently several conflicting cases as to whether the *Anisminic* principles apply to coroners' courts or not.

(e) *Time limit clauses*

In planning statutes a six week time limit is often provided within which any remedy must be sought. In *Smith v East Elloe (1956) 1 All ER 855* and *R v Secretary of State, ex p Ostler (1976) 3 All ER 90* the courts recognised the effectiveness of such clauses to exclude judicial review even when the decision challenged was tainted with fraud, breach of the rules of natural justice or other serious defect. The basis of such decisions seems to be the particular public policy considerations inherent in planning law. No review is permitted after the six weeks have expired.

132. *CROWN PROCEEDINGS: CIVIL ACTIONS IN TORT AND CONTRACT*

132.1 *Historical background*

The feudal belief that the King ruled by Divine Right and could do no wrong had the consequence that there could be no person or court which could declare that the King was in error. The courts acted in the name of the King who could sue but not be sued. However, by the time of Edward I subjects were permitted to sue the Crown by the use of an extremely formal procedure called a 'petition of right' but only in cases where the subject was land or a contract. The procedure had many flaws. Where the cause of the dispute was a tort (or civil wrong) committed by the Crown or one of its servants, the unfortunate subject had no remedy whatsoever available to him. In more recent times the injustice of this position was recognised so that the Crown would in practice nominate a defendant, who was a civil servant, and would then pay any damages and costs awarded against him. In the twentieth century there were calls for reform. In 1921-27 Lord Hewart prepared a Bill but it became law as the *Crown Proceedings Act* only in 1947. To summarise, it had the effect of reforming and simplifying the complicated proceedings for cases in contract or land and it also provided that in certain circumstances the Crown could be sued in tort. Further details are set out below.

132.2 *The law of tort*

(a) *Before the Crown Proceedings Act 1947*

The Crown was not liable in tort and was not regarded as being responsible (as an ordinary employer would be) for the wrongs of its servants. In *Viscount Canterbury v Attorney-General (1842)* the house of the Speaker of the House of Commons was burned down due to the negligence of workmen employed by the Crown. The Speaker's claim failed on the ground that the Crown could do no wrong. Nevertheless the man who committed the wrong was not absolved from liability and could be sued. In practice the Crown defended proceedings brought against its servants and, if the latter lost, the Crown paid damages and costs.

(b) *After the Crown Proceedings Act 1947*

The Act preserves the personal immunity from suit of the Monarch but *s.2* states:

> The Crown shall be subject to all those liabilities in tort to which, if it were a private person of full age and capacity, it would be subject: (a) in respect of torts committed by its servants or agents; (b) in respect of any breach of those duties which a person owes to his servants or agents at common law by reason of being their employer; (c) in respect of any breach of those duties attaching at common law to the ownership, occupation, possession or control of property.

In respect of (a) the Crown is liable vicariously for the torts of its employees acting in the course of their employment, and the torts of its agents which the latter have been authorised to commit. In the case of (b) some common law duties owed by an employer to his employees are the provision of safe equipment and tools; a safe system of work; and the employment of competent workmen. Common law duties relating to employees and to property have largely been provisions of a particular statute or not will depend on whether this is Provided expressly or by necessary implication in the statute. There is a modern tendency for statutes to bind the Crown, e.g. the *Health and Safety at Work Act 1974*, the *Occupiers' Liability Acts 1957 & 1984* and the *Fatal Accidents Act 1976*.

An example of an Act where Crown liability is not laid down is the *Town and Country Planning Act*. Thus the Crown has no need for planning permission to develop its land though invariably it consults the local authority before doing so.

Who is a Crown servant

One who is directly or indirectly appointed by the Crown and paid wholly out of the consolidated fund, moneys provided by Parliament or a fund certified by the Treasury as its equivalent.

Policemen are not servants of the Crown as they are not paid wholly out of the consolidated fund; part of their remuneration comes from local rates. However, under the *Police Act 1964* the chief officer of police of any area is made liable for torts committed by constables under his control in the course of their duties. The police fund meets any damages and costs awarded as a result of their torts.

Public corporations are not part of the Crown, though new town development corporations may be.

Exclusion of judges

Judges are paid from public funds (defined above) but they are excluded when discharging judicial functions or executing judicial processes:

> No proceedings shall lie against the Crown by virtue of this section in respect of anything done or omitted to be done by any person while discharging ... any responsibilities of a judicial nature vested in him, or and responsibilities which he has in connection with the execution of judicial process.

Even High Court judges themselves cannot be sued but the judges of inferior courts may be where they act without jurisdiction.

The reason for the immunity of the Crown in these matters is that judges cannot truly be said to be servants of the Crown. The independence of the judiciary is essential to freedom.

HM Forces

Under the *Crown Proceedings Act 1947* there was a wide exclusion of the Crown's liability for the death or personal injury caused by a member of the armed forces to another member of the armed forces where the former was on duty and the latter was on duty *or* was on any land, premises, shia or vehicle used by the armed forces *and* the Secretary of State certified that the death or injury is attributable to service for pension purposes. The member of the forces responsible is himself immune unless the court is satisfied that his act or omission was not connected with the performance of his duties. Similarly, where the death or injury to a member of the forces is caused by the condition or nature of any land, premises, ship or vehicle used by the forces or any equipment supplied for use by the forces.

The certificates of the Secretary of State are conclusive evidence. In *Adams v War Office (1955) 3 All ER 245* a serviceman was killed by the firing of a live shell. His parents, not entitled to a pension under the regulations in force, sued for damages as personal representatives. As the Secretary of State had certified that death was attributable to service for pension purposes the parents could not sue the Crown in tort.

A recent case is a good illustration of the operation of *s. 10* CPA *1947*. In *Bell v SS Defence (1985) 3 All ER 661* a soldier indulging in 'horseplay' received head injuries in Germany whilst on army property and was left by Army doctors without proper attention for over an hour. He was subsequently sent to a civilian hospital but without sufficient information to enable them properly to treat him and he died. *s. 10 CPA 1947* was invoked to absolve the Crown from liability in damages on the ground that the doctors were on duty and at all times acting on army premises.

In *Pearce v Minister of Defence (1987)* a Royal Engineer on Christmas Island successfully claimed damages for personal injury from the Government despite the Secretary of State's certificate under *s.10*. This decision was reached by the court on the ground that those who carried out the tests were not members of the armed forces but of the Atomic Energy Authority.

In May 1987 a Private Member's Bill, the *Crown Proceedings (Armed Forces) Act 1987* received the Royal Assent. Its effect is to mitigate the harshness of *s.10* during time of peace. It provided that in time of peace service personnel or their dependants could seek redress for death or injury caused by their fellows whilst on duty but that s.10 could be restructured in the event of actual or impending hostilities or at any time of great national emergency.

132.3 *Contract law*

(a)   *Before the Crown Proceedings Act 1947*

At this period it was essential for a litigant seeking to sue the Crown in contract or in connection with a land claim first to obtain the consent of the Home Secretary, who acted on the advice of the Attorney-General. Without such consent no claim could proceed. The petition of right had a very complicated procedure which was abandoned after 1947 but nevertheless the 1947 Act did not change the old rules of substantive law in relation to contracts, which are still extant. These rules are dealt with in sub-section (b) below.

(b)   *After the Crown Proceedings Act 1947*

The Act provides:

> Where any person has a claim against the Crown ... and the claim might have been enforced by petition of right, or by a proceeding provided by a statutory provision repealed by this Act, then ... *the claim may be enforced as of right ... by proceedings taken against the Crown in accordance with the provisions of this Act.*

The procedure for claims against the Crown therefore changed considerably. The reference to 'statutory provisions' is to express rights of action given by the statute concerned, e.g. 'the minister can sue and be sued'. Now the procedure is in the Act and described later. Thus, contract cases may be brought under the Act.

The substantive rules setting out which contracts are binding on the Crown were not altered by the *Crown Proceedings Act 1947*. There are a number of points of importance:

(i)   The general law on agency needs to be understood before the position on government contracts is clear. A summary follows.

Under the general law of contract a person, A, may authorise another, B, to enter into contracts on his behalf with a third party, C. If B acts within his authority, then C can enforce the contract against A and *vice versa*. However, problems may arise in some circumstances:

(1)   if B enters into a contract with C, telling C that he acts on behalf of A, when in fact A has never given B any such authority and has never told C that B had such authority. Here C cannot enforce the contract against A but he may sue B for damages for breach of warranty of authority. In other words, the law considers that to induce C to contract B made a promise to C that he was authorised by A to act on A's behalf, which has been broken. A right to damages therefore arises;

(2) if B, although properly appointed as agent for A, goes beyond what A has authorised him to do when entering a contract with C. If C knew that B overstepped his powers, he will have no remedy, but if he was ignorant of this he can recover from A who in turn has a remedy against B for breach of the terms of the agency.

These rules have to be modified where the Crown is a contracting party. The Crown, being an artificial person, must contract by an agent. If an agent contracts on behalf of the Crown in circumstances where he was not authorised to do so, the Crown is probably bound unless:

(A) the person contracting with the Crown could reasonably be expected to know the limits of the agent's authority; or

(B) the limit on the authority to contract was laid down by statute; or

(C) the Crown was precluded by statute from entering into the contract.

It should also be noted that there is no action for breach of warranty of authority by an agent for the Crown. In *Dunn v MacDonald (1897) 1 QB 401* Dunn had been appointed for a fixed term to serve the Crown in Nigeria. He was dismissed before the three year period ended and sued the Crown unsuccessfully for damages for breach of contract. The court held the contract invalid. Dunn then sued the civil servant who had appointed him, again unsuccessfully. It was stated that no action lies against a public servant upon any contract he makes in that capacity and an action will lie only on an express personal contract.

This decision was applied in the *Prometheus (1949)*.

(ii) In the *Amphitrite Case (1921) 3 KB 500* it was established that the Crown cannot by contract fetter its freedom of action in matters concerning the welfare of the State. However, the exact scope and applicability of the doctrine is uncertain and it has rarely been invoked. The case concerned a breach of contract by the Government in wartime and it may therefore be that the principle is a narrow one, for war is clearly a special situation. However, although it has not been used as authority in later decisions, it does seem that a wide spectrum of executive action is covered.

(iii) A petition of right was not available where a contract was concluded on the basis that it was dependent on the grant of funds by Parliament and no funds were in fact given. This was decided in *Churchward v R (1865) 1 QB 173* where the plaintiff had contracted to run a mail service between Dover and the Continent, in return for an annual sum to be provided by Parliament. If the contract is not dependent on a special allocation of funds where, for instance, it is simply an employment contract of a civil servant, a petition of right could have been used and so action under *s.1* is now possible.

132.4 *Procedure*

The Crown is not in name a party to the proceedings but sues and is sued in the name of the appropriate government department or the Attorney-General. The Treasury issues a list of names and addresses of the government departments. If the case does not appear to relate to one of these, then the action is brought against the Attorney-General *(s.17 Crown Proceedings Act)*.

The Act states that no execution or attachment or process shall issue to enforce payment by the Crown, i.e. the department or Attorney-General. Similarly, no injunction, order for specific performance or delivery of property may issue. In other words, a successful plaintiff cannot force the Crown to pay on a judgment of the court. All the court can do is to make an order declaratory of the rights of the parties *(s.21)*. This would appear to defeat the whole purpose of the Act but in practice the orders and judgments of the court are obeyed without question. The government department pays the amount ordered out of moneys provided by Parliament *(ss.25(3) 6 37)*. This does, of course, leave us with a problem of injunctions (an order prohibiting some unlawful act) but the reasoning behind this is that the work of government cannot be stopped by such means and damages are awarded instead.

132.5 *Crown privilege (or public interest immunity) in the law of evidence*

The general principle

Although under *s.28 Crown Proceedings Act 1947* the Crown may be ordered to make discovery of documents and answer interrogatories (i.e. provide the plaintiff with documents essential to his case; and to answer pertinent questions), it can withhold such a document or refuse to answer a question on the grounds that to do so would harm the public interest. This is known as *Crown privilege* and the leading case for many years was *Duncan v Cammell Laird (1942) AC 624 – The Thetis Case.*

The submarine, HMS Thetis, sank during its maiden voyage and employees of the shipbuilders were drowned. Their dependants claimed that their deaths were caused by negligence on the part of Camnell Laird, the shipbuilders. To prove their case the plaintiffs required discovery of the contract between the Admiralty and the defendants, and the salvage reports which gave the evidence of the cause of the disaster. The Admiralty intervened and the First Lord of the Admiralty testified in his affidavit that the disclosure of the documents would be contrary to the public interest. In fact, as we now know, there was highly secret apparatus on board and it is not surprising that the House of Lords upheld the minister's privilege. Lord Simon LC said that in any event whether his reasons were good or bad, there was no limitation in law on the absolute right of the minister to decide what should be privileged from disclosure in the public interest.

This ruling covers not only documents but oral evidence as well so that witnesses cannot be called to state orally what could not be disclosed by the documents. Moreover, the privilege can be claimed with similar success in proceedings to which the Crown is not itself a party.

The above principles were applied in *Ellis v Home Office (1953) 2 QB 135* where no question of national security arose. Ellis, awaiting trial in a prison hospital, was assaulted by a convicted man, a suspected mental defective. The plaintiff claimed negligence for failure to guard the dangerous man properly. The plaintiff required a sight of prison documents and medical notes to substantiate his claim. The Home Office claimed Crown privilege and, though the judges could see no harm to the public interest, held themselves bound to accept the Home Office decision.

Present administrative practice

The above case highlighted the frequent claims of Crown privilege which were used to ensure unnecessary secrecy for matters which did not truly involve national security. Additionally, cases in the Commonwealth were making inroads into the principle starting with *Robinson v South Australia (No. 2) (1931) All ER 333.*

In 1956 the Lord Chancellor made a statement in the House of Lords committing the executive to follow practice rules as follows.

Crown privilege will not be claimed for the following classes of documents:

(a) medical reports, including prison reports, where the Crown or the doctor is sued for negligence;

(b) reports of witnesses of accidents on the roads or on government premises, or of accidents to government employees;

(c) statements of witnesses to the police;

(d) documents needed by the defence in criminal charges;

(e) documents in contract cases which relate to fact, not to comment or advice.

Present position in common law

Since the Lord Chancellor's statement the Lords have made important decisions in *Conway v Rimmer (1968) AC 910.* Here a former probationary police constable brought an action for malicious prosecution against his former superintendent. In the course of pre-trial proceedings the defendants disclosed the existence of documents written by the superintendent and one by the Chief Constable. The Home Secretary claimed Crown privilege for these, stating that they fell within the class of documents,the production of which would be injurious to the public interest. The court held that the documents should be produced for its inspection with a view to the court making a decision as to disclosure. Subsequently, the Lords held that the documents would not prejudice the public interest and ordered them to be produced to the plaintiff. The Lords made it clear, however, that they would seldom dispute a claim of Crown privilege upon the specific contents of a document concerning Cabinet decisions, criminal investigations, national defence and foreign affairs. In every case the court had the duty to weigh the public interest of justice against the public interest asserted by the government.

In 1972 the Law Lords in *R v Lewes JJ, ex p Home Secretary (1973) 2 All ER 1057* described the term 'Crown privilege' as 'wrong', 'misleading', 'not accurate', and 'a misnomer'. In this case, however, they upheld a claim of Crown privilege for a confidential report of a police authority to the Gaming Board which the plaintiff required to prosecute the police officer for libel.

In *Compton (Alfred) Amusement Machines Ltd v Customs & Excise Commissioners (No. 2) (1974) 2 All ER 371* the documents were refused as contrary to the public interest. Compare with *Norwich Pharmacal Co v Customs & Excise Commissioners (1974) AC 133* where discovery was allowed as they were not highly confidential and would relate to persons who were probably tortfeasors. Most of the Lords inspected documents in *Burmah Oil Co Ltd v Bank of England (1980) AC 1090* – although Lord Wilberforce refused to do so on the grounds that the claim was a class claim of a clear sort where those seeking to overcome the claim of Crown privilege had not shown a counteracting interest to justify their call for disclosure. The Lords took the view that the documents should not' be disclosed because they were unnecessary or alternatively that, although relevant, the public interest required non-disclosure. The decision in *Conway v Rimmer* was subjected to some criticism and it was suggested that no body of rules could be deduced from that decision.

In *Continental Reinsurance Corporation (UK) Ltd v Pine Top Insurance Co (1986)* the plaintiffs were a company carrying on business as reinsurers. They had agreed to reinsure the business of Nelson Stevenson Bloodstock Ltd, a proportion of whose risks were reinsured by the defendants. The defendants pleaded misrepresentation and non-disclosure of material facts because the plaintiffs had failed to disclose correspondence with the Department of Trade, which had criticised the plaintiffs manner of underwriting. The defendants required production of these confidential documents and discovery was granted by the High Court after inspecting them. The Secretary of State appealed against disclosure. On the issue as to whether the High Court judge was right to inspect the documents, Oliver LJ made the following preliminary points:

1. Where the court finds *prima facie* the grounds for immunity are weak, they should inspect 'low level' documents before ordering production as in *Conway v Rimmer*.

2. The court generally ought not to inspect 'high level' documents, e.g. Cabinet minutes.

3. Where there is a close balance between the conflicting public interests of justice and confidentiality, the court should inspect. *(Air Canada v Secretary of State for Trade (1983) 1 All ER 910).*

Having regard to the judgments of Bridge LJ in *Burmah oil v Bank of England and Attorney-General (1970) AC 1090* and Lord Diplock in *Lonrho v Shell Petroleum (1981) 2 All ER 456* it was held that the judge was right to inspect the documents himself but disclosure was not allowed.

This judgment, like the *Lonrho* decision, distinguishes class and contents claims and, although the court has gone behind the class claim to inspect the documents, the refusal to disclose them is based not on contents but on class.

Consideration must be given to the fact that disclosure of certain documents might lead in future to the composer being less candid, e.g. *R v Gaming Board, ex p Benaim and Khaida (1970) 2 QB 417* and *Collymore v Att-Gen (1970) 2 All ER 1207* and in

Williams v Home Office (1981) 1 All ER 1151 the following factors were stated to be important:

(a) whether harm would be done to the public service by disclosure;

(b) whether the administration of justice would be harmed by the withholding of the document;

(c) whether the documents were necessary; and

(d) whether there was a reasonable probability that the documents contained material which would give substantial support to a contention in the civil action.

In *Blackpool Corporation v Locker (1948) 1 KB 349* it was held that Crown privilege could not be claimed by local authorities. Now, following *Re D (Infants) (1970) 1 All ER 1088* – local authority case-records of children under care – the authority may object to the introduction of evidence on the ground of public interest and the material need not even emanate from central government.

133. PUBLIC CORPORATIONS

133.1 *Introduction*

In addition to the various Crown departments under ministerial control, there are also independent public corporations, created by statute and subject to ministerial and Parliamentary scrutiny.

These bodies are of various types. They may have been set up to manage nationalized industries, e.g. the National Coal Board, the Post Office, gas and electricity boards; or other services, e.g. the BBC, the Housing Corporation; or to regulate private enterprise activities, e.g. the Independent Broadcasting Authority, the Livestock Commission. The powers and status of each public corporation are laid down in the relevant statute for the corporation. The members of their boards are generally appointed by a minister and the minister may often set up advisory committees or councils to advise him. Apart from this, the minister's powers are generally indirect and the day-to-day running, especially of the commercial corporations, is left to their boards and staff. Closer scrutiny is maintained of those corporations financed entirely by public money.

133.2 *Parliamentary scrutiny*

Public corporations must submit annual reports and accounts to Parliament, where they are subject to debate. A Select Committee scrutinizes those reports from nationalized industries and may make direct enquiries without the intervention of the relevant minister. Question time in the Commons provides further opportunity for examination of particular points.

133.3 *Liability to action*

Where it is sought to bring an action against a public corporation, the question will arise whether or not that action should be governed by the *Crown Proceedings Act*. Where the corporation is a *servant or agent of the Crown* the 1947 Act, and its attendant privileges, does apply. But if the corporation is not a servant or agent of the Crown, action can be brought in the usual way and all the usual statutory duties will apply (see earlier).

It is now usual for statutes setting up public corporations to state expressly what the status of the corporation is to be. Thus the *Electricity Act 1957* states in *s.38*:

> it is hereby declared for the avoidance of doubt that neither the Electricity Council nor the Generating Board nor any of the area Boards are to be treated as the servant or agent of the Crown, or as enjoying any status, immunity or privilege of the Crown, and no property of the Council or any of those Boards is to be regarded as the property of, or held on behalf of, the Crown.

See further: *Post Office Act 1969, s.6(5)* and *Transport Act 1968, s.52(5)*.

Statutes setting up public corporations which pre-date the *Crown Proceedings Act* do not usually state whether the corporation is a servant or agent of the Crown. In *Tamlin v Hannaford (1950) 1 KB 18* the Court of Appeal decided that the British Transport Commission was not such a servant or agent after having examined at length the *Transport Act 1947* which set it up. Denning LJ remarked that the question was not whether the Board was *an emanation of the Crown* for quite clearly it was, but rather whether it was truly a servant or agent. In deciding this the relationship between the minister and the corporation was vital, for the degree of direction which the minister could give would show whether the corporation was relegated to the position of agent.

It would not now be usual for a modern corporation to be a Crown servant or agent and therefore corporations can generally be sued in their own name and are unable to take advantage of the provisions of the *Crown Proceedings Act*.

Further reading

(a) *Remedies*

Wade and Bradley, Chapter 35.
de Smith, Chapter 29.
Law Commission's Working Paper, October 1971, HMSO.
Glover, *NLJ*, 5 April 1979 at p.347.
Student Law Reporter, Autumn 1979, Article 10.
Student Law Reporter, Summer 1978, Article 8 (on RSC, p.53).
1978, *LAR*, 1979.
1978, *Cambridge Law Journal*, 205.
Law Commission Report (Law Comm. 73), Cmnd 6407.

(b) *Crown proceedings*

Wade and Bradley, Chapter 36.
de Smith, Chapter 30.
Estoppel: *Student Law Reporter*, Spring 1980, Article 6, and
New Law Journal, 15 February 1979 at p.161.
1980, *Public Law*, 263.
1981, 97 *LQR*, 525.

(c) *Public corporations*

Wade and Bradley, Chapter 36.
de Smith, Chapter 11.

LLB

CONSTITUTIONAL LAW

LESSON 14 (STUDY)

THE PARLIAMENTARY COMMISSIONER FOR ADMINISTRATION

141. 'THE OMBUDSMAN'

    141.1 INTRODUCTION
    141.2 CRITICISMS OF THE FILTER SYSTEM AND
            JURISDICTIONAL BARRIERS
    141.3 CONDUCT OF INVESTIGATIONS
    141.4 THE EFFECTIVENESS OF THE OMBUDSMAN
    141.5 THE SELECT COMMITTEE ON THE PARLIAMENTARY
            COMMISSIONER

142. OTHER OMBUDSMEN

    142.1 HEALTH COMMISSIONERS
    142.2 LOCAL GOVERNMENT COMMISSIONERS
    142.3 INSURANCE AND BANKS OMBUDSMEN
    142.4 THE FRENCH OMBUDSMAN ('MEDIATEUR')

143. NATIONAL SECURITY

144. BREACH OF CONFIDENCE

141. 'THE OMBUDSMAN'

141.1 *Introduction*

The *ombudsman* system, under which an appointed individual could investigate complaints about government action and could secure redress of grievances against the State, originated in Sweden in the nineteenth century but had achieved sudden and widespread popularity in the 1950s and 1960s, when many administrations throughout the world spawned ombudsmen.

It was often said that Britain had no need of an ombudsman because all the MPs acted as ombudsmen. However, it came to be recognised that questions in Parliament and the possibility of court action were not always sufficient to ensure high standards of administration. After World War II an administrative scandal occurred which became known as the *Crichel Down Affair* (for the facts read the *Report of the Inquiry into the Disposal of Land at Crichel Down*, Cmnd 9176). The report on the affair exposed the rigid and high-handed attitudes of some administrators. Shortly afterwards, New Zealand, a country with a similar parliamentary and administrative system to our own, appointed its first ombudsman. The combined effect of these events was that the idea of a British ombudsman was, for the first time, seriously mooted.

In 1965 the Labour Government published a White Paper advocating the appointment of a British ombudsman, or *Parliamentary Commissioner* as he was to be called, to investigate cases of maladministration. In the subsequent debate on the *Parliamentary Commissioner Bill* in the House of Commons, Richard Crossman admitted that the government had been unable exhaustively to define maladministration but, he said, its characteristics included such things as *bias, neglect, inattention, delay, incompetence, ineptitude, perversity, turpitude, arbitrariness and so on.* This list has come to be known as the *Crossman catalogue* and its interpretation has been a matter of some dispute. *S.12(3) Parliamentary Commissioner Act 1967* provides that *nothing in this Act authorises or requires the Commissioner to question the merits of a decision taken without maladministration.* The first Commissioner, Sir Edmund Compton, concluded from this provision that his task was to examine the procedure by which a decision had been reached and that he could not look at a decision on its merits. Maladministration was a matter of procedure not of substance. However, it is clear that the *Crossman catalogue* would allow examination of decisions on their merits, for such words as 'perversity' and 'arbitrariness' point to matters of substance rather than of form.

Indeed, the Select Committee on the Parliamentary Commissioner took this view in their 1967 Report (see HC 350, 1967-68, para.14). Since then the Ombudsman has criticised discretionary decisions which were perverse or arbitrary on their merits.

By *s.1* of the 1967 Act the Commissioner is appointed by the Queen and holds office until he is 65, unless he resigns or is removed under that age. Complaints are referred to him by MPs. This was intended merely to be a transitional provision to safeguard the Commissioner from being overwhelmed with complaints, but it has yet to be repealed. When the Commissioner receives a complaint he must decide whether the complainant has any alternative remedy, for all available avenues of appeal must first have been exhausted. He next must decide whether he has jurisdiction over the matter. *Sch.3* of the Act lists a number of matters not subject to investigation. These include matters of foreign policy, state security, extradition, employment of public servants, honours and awards, the hospital services and government commercial transactions. The exclusion of complaints about employment and other conditions of public servants is unusual. Other European ombudsmen receive and investigate many complaints from public employees.

The Commissioner conducts his investigations in private. He may interview civil servants and may require the production of any documents other than Cabinet papers. If he finds maladministration, he may make recommendations as to appropriate action to redress the grievance, but he does not himself provide remedies. Since the Commissioner is thus ultimately powerless, his effectiveness may be questioned. However, the report of his findings is sent to the MP who first forwarded the complaint and he will generally raise the matter in Parliamentary Questions. Also the Commissioner may himself lay a special report before Parliament if he considers that the injustice to the person aggrieved by the maladministration has not been, or will not be, remedied. The main sanction against government inaction is therefore publicity and indeed ombudsmen have gradually learnt to use the Press to ensure that their findings are not ignored. In addition to any special reports the Commissioner must also lay an annual general report before Parliament in which he summarises his activities during the year. These reports show the patterns of complaint and investigation and students should look at some of them, particularly the more recent ones. There are now also commissioners to investigate local government and the health service. Their powers and jurisdiction are somewhat similar to those of the Parliamentary Commissioner.

Until the appointment of Sir Cecil Clothier QC, the Ombudsman had always been a former civil servant. Although it is arguable that a former civil servant is more likely to be familiar with administrative processes and may be liable to conduct his investigations more speedily and critically as a result, it can also be argued that former civil servants might appear to take the departmental view on any dispute, and be more likely to be lenient to their ex-colleagues than an outsider would be. It has even been argued by some that the appoint-ment should be a political one, with the Commissioner having ministerial status. He would be answerable to the electorate on his record of the redress of grievances. On the other hand, making the office a political appointment would bring many disadvantages. Indeed, the office of Parliamentary Commissioner operates now to strengthen the doctrine of individual ministerial responsibility by exposing maladministration for which a minister may have to accept responsibility. And while the minister is effectively limited by the information which his department decides to provide him, the Ombudsman has independent investigative powers (see *s.8* of the Act).

Whoever the Commissioner may be, it is clear that his function is parallel to that of the courts (see, for example, *Congreve v Home Office (1976) 1 All ER 697* and HC 680, 1974-75 (special report of the PCA)). Investigations may take place after something has allegedly gone wrong in the administration and the Commissioner remains separate from the courts for he will not investigate matters which could be brought before them unless he is satisfied that it is not reasonable to expect the person aggrieved to pursue his remedy at law. The Commissioner has wider powers of investigation than a court,for his is an inquisitorial role. But he cannot provide formal remedies, he cannot award damages or grant an injunction. Thus also he is not limited to particular categories of remedy but can instead suggest complex and sophisticated forms of remedy, remedies which will truly redress the individual grievance of the individual complainant.

141.2 *Criticisms of the filter system and jurisdictional barriers*

The 'filter system' and the jurisdictional barriers outlined above have been severely criticised in recent years. In 1978 the Commissioner adopted a new policy on the handling of complaints from the public: when he receives a complaint direct, instead of returning it to the complainant, he sends it to the latter's MP and asks whether he may deal with it. Of the first 49 complaints dealt with by this means, 42 were returned to the PCA by the MP. It has been argued that the adoption of such a convoluted procedure under-lines the absurdity of persisting with the 'MP filter' ... a device which can only have the effect of distancing the PCA from the public he is intended to serve. However, if the filter system were abolished it would undermine the position of MPs as the traditional champions of their constituents' grievances against powerful bureaucracy (see further G Drewry, *New Law Journal*, 21 June 1979, at p.605).

Organisations such as 'Justice' (the British section of the International Commission of Jurists) have recommended that the public should have direct access to the Ombudsman, and this reform has also been urged by the Ombudsmen themselves, including Sir Cecil Clothier QC, in his retiring report in March 1984 (considered later, below).

There appear to be two main reasons for the jurisdictional barriers in *Sch.3* to the Act. The first is public policy, based on the ground that the 'public interest' would not be served by a revelation of these matters. The second is that other redresses are available. Thus the matter of government contracts and commercial transactions is protected because much of the work is confidential and politically inflammable, while another institution, the in this field.

Yet despite these reasons the jurisdictional barriers erected around the Parliamentary Commissioner clearly limit his potential for redressing administrative grievances. The Act itself has been described by Professor Street as 'a half-hearted affair hedged about by restrictions and exceptions'. There is also little doubt that the large areas of administration which are excluded are the very ones that provide most problems, namely, commercial dealings with the government, and the activities of the police and public corporations.

141.3 *Conduct of investigations*

The Commissioner has a discretion upon whether to initiate, continue or discontinue an investigation.

In *Re Fletcher's Application (1970) 2 All ER 527* the applicant asked the Court of Appeal for leave to move for an order of *mandamus* requiring the PCA to investigate a complaint. Leave was refused by the Court of Appeal because the *Parliamentary Commissioner Act 1967* confers a discretion on the PCA whether to investigate any allegation or not; the court has no jurisdiction to order him to investigate any matter.

The Commissioner conducts his investigations in private. He may interview civil servants and may require the production of any documents other than Cabinet papers.

The effect of an unjustified refusal to give evidence to the Commissioner is a contempt of him, and he may report the refusal to the High Court, which may deal with the matter as if the person in question had been guilty of contempt of court.

It has been said that the ultimate strength of an independent ombudsman is his power to get at the relevant departmental files; when that is frustrated his ability to serve the aggrieved citizen is negated.

For this reason it has been argued that the Commissioner should have the right of access to Cabinet papers, except where the Attorney-General certifies that such access would be prejudicial to the safety of the State or otherwise contrary to the public interest. On the other hand, it is not the function of the Ombudsman to be a 'court of appeal' to whom those dissatisfied with the political judgment of the Cabinet may turn for a second opinion. He is an officer of Parliament, not the source of a higher jurisdiction than Parliament. Redress should be sought either in political action or through the courts where the legislative authority for the policy is at issue.

141.4 *The effectiveness of the Ombudsman*

The effectiveness of the Ombudsman is well illustrated by contrasting two famous cases which were investigated by the Commissioner. The first is the *Sachsenhausen Concentration Camp Affair*

(1969). Under the *Anglo-German Agreement 1964* the German Government provided £1 million for compensating UK citizens who had suffered from Nazi persecution during World War II. Distribution was left to the discretion of the UK government and the Foreign Office made rules for the distribution. Later the Foreign Office withheld compensation from 12 persons who claimed to be within the scope of these rules because of their detention within the Sachsenhausen Concentration Camp. A complaint of maladministration was referred to the PCA, who investigated and subsequently reported defects in the administrative procedure by which the Foreign Office had reached its decisions, and that this maladministration had damaged the reputation of the complainants. Though the Foreign Secretary (George Brown) maintained that the decisions were correct, he nonetheless accepted the findings and made available an additional £25,000 in order that the claimants might receive the same rate of compensation as successful claimants on the fund (which had, by that time, been exhausted).

Note: At no time were any legal rights of the claimant involved, for the Foreign Office rules were not enforceable in law, so that no judicial remedy was possible. Moreover, parliamentary pressure alone, without the PCA's report, would not have been successful. (Indeed, the report was based on information which traditional parliamentary procedures could not have discovered.)

Unfortunately the Ombudsman did not meet with similar success in the *Court Line Holiday Company Affair (1975)*.

The facts of this case were that the Court Line Holiday Company had run into serious financial troubles, so that a number of advance-booked holidays were placed in jeopardy. In response to the national outcry, the government nationalised part of the company's operations and the Industry Secretary (at that time Mr Tony Benn) gave assurances in the House of Commons which were taken by many people as guaranteeing those holidays already booked. Court Line eventually collapsed and many prospective holidaymakers lost their money' Maladministration was alleged and the PCA (at that time Sir Alan Marre) eventually upheld the holidaymakers' complaints. However the government rejected those findings of maladministration and the complainants saw their champion floored by greater political might.

Mr Benn successfully persuaded Parliament that the issues involved were policy matters and that he had been exercising his judgment *as a minister* in determining how far in his statements he could qualify his confidence in Court Line without putting the company's continued existence in jeopardy. Therefore, said Mr Benn, under *s. 12(3)* of the Act, this was not maladministration and hence was no concern of the Commissioner!

141.5 *The Select Committee on the Parliamentary Commissioner.*

This is a Committee of the House of Commons appointed to examine the reports laid before the House by the Parliamentary Commissioner and matters in connection therewith. The Committee does not act as a court of appeal from the decisions of the Commissioner but, since he is an officer of the House, they are competent to give him general advice as to the exercise of his discretions under the Act.

In a report published by the Select Committee on the PCA, the present system of Ombudsmen was deplored for being 'untidy' and 'uncoordinated' and the Committee recommended greater cooperation between the various Ombudsmen (HC Report no. 254, 1979-80).

On 3 January 1985 Mr Anthony Barrowclough QC was appointed as the new Parliamentary Commissioner for Administration, to take over from Sir Cecil Clothier QC, who has become the first Chairman of the new Police Complaints Authority. As Mr Barrowclough's appointment was announced, the Select Committee of the PCA issued a report recommending that his powers should be widened to enable him to investigate allegations of maladministration by the 'quangos' (quasi-autonomous, non-governmental organisations), such as the Arts and Sports Councils, the Scottish and Welsh Development Agencies, and the Monopolies and Mergers Commission, which spend millions of pounds of taxpayers' money each year but which at present are not within the PCA's jurisdiction. Although the all-party Select Committee thought that the nationalised industries should continue to be excluded from the PCA's jurisdiction, it made an exception in the case of the Civil Aviation Authority because of frequent complaints about airport noise. Whether these recommendations will be accepted by the government remains to be seen.

The Office of the PCA is at present at Church House, Great Smith Street, London SW1P 3BW (Telephone: 01-212 7676).

142. OTHER OMBUDSMEN

142.1 *Health Commissioners*

In 1973 a Health Service Commissioner for England, Scotland and Wales was established by the *National Health Service Reorganisation Act 1973*. At present the holder of the office is the same person who holds the office of Parliamentary Commissioner.

The duty of the Health Service Commissioner is to investigate any alleged failure in a service provided by a health authority, or an alleged failure to provide a service which should be provided, or any other action taken by or on behalf of such an authority, in any case where there is a complaint of injustice in consequence of the failure or in consequence of maladministration. Complaints may be made direct to the Health Service Commissioner, though they must first be brought to the notice of the relevant health authority. The merits of a decision taken without maladministration may not be questioned and certain matters, such as those connected with the diagnosis of illness, are specifically excluded from the Ombudsman's jurisdiction.

142.2 *Local Government Commissioners*

See section 82 above.

142.3 *Insurance and banks ombudsmen*

The insurance industry has had an established ombudsman for some years with the power to make compensation awards to those who have suffered maladministration from insurance companies. A similar ombudsman for bank customers was appointed in 1985; services covered include all personal banking including complaints about cash dispenser machines and bank charges. The main exclusion is that customers will not be able to challenge a bank's decision to reject a loan application.

142.4 *The French Ombudsman ('Médiateur')*

The concept of an Ombudsman had already found favour in many other countries before the British adaptation in 1967, but perhaps its adoption in France in 1973 is the most striking because it is France which has the most highly developed system of administrative law (*droit administratif*). The French Ombudsman, known as the *Médiateur* (or 'Mediator') was introduced in response to what was believed to be the dangers presented by the incessant growth of the administrative machinery of a modern industrial and welfare state. The need was felt for a simple, free and readily accessible remedy for injustice caused by maladministration or bad rules, thereby rendering the bureaucracy less oppressive and more human in character. Judicial review remained too technical for ordinary citizens to trust completely, with the result that the French administrative courts had become too remote from ordinary citizens. Further, minor errors of administrative procedure were not suitable for the weighty and lengthy consideration of such courts. Many French academics and administrative lawyers resisted the introduction of the officer of Mediator in 1973 on the ground that his essential functions were already performed by the administrative courts, notably the *Conseil d'Etat*. This resistance proved so strong that the Mediator, although enjoying a wide jurisdiction over most of central government (including the nationalised industries), is in a weaker position than his British counterpart, since he was not set up with the aim of increasing the power of MPs over the Executive. Thus there is nothing, for instance, comparable to the British Select Committee on the Parliamentary Commissioner.

Consequently, the creation of the office of an 'ombudsman' in France should not be taken as an admission of the inadequacies of a developed system of administrative law. In a country such as France the tendency to dispute any action of the administration is very common and so the creation of the Mediator was in a sense a psychological reassurance to ordinary French people that, if they were put off by the expense or delays or formalities of the administrative courts, there was another door to knock at, where they could express their grievances to someone in an easy and simple way. The office of Mediator was therefore the consequence of 'cool logic being swept aside by emotional and political forces' (Neville Brown and Pierre Lavirotte, *Law Quarterly Review*, April 1974).

143. *NATIONAL SECURITY*

For Sedition, Official Secrets Acts 1911-1939 'D' Notices see Lesson 9 of the Manual.

There are today many statutes which include provisions to the effect that where notional security is at stake the position shall be treated as an exception to the normal rules.

> eg.   there is no appeal against deportation where the Secretary of State certifies that deportation is conductive to the public good in the interests of national security. (*Immigration Act 1971 s.15*) the parliamentary commissioner is not permitted to investigate matters where national security is at stake. (*Parliamentary Commissioner Act 1967 sched. III*)

The common law too has developed so that cases where national security is at stake are treated as exceptions.

> eg.   The rules of natural justice do not apply if national security is at stake (*R v Secretary of State for Home Office ex p. Agee and Hosenball (1977)* and the *GCHQ case (1984) 3 All ER 452*).

There are many statutory provisions allowing a Minister himself to decide that national security is at stake but Lord Scarman in the GCHQ case gave a very important survey of the law on national security in which he concluded.

That where a question as to the interest of national security arises in judicial proceedings the court has to act on evidence. In some cases a judge or jury is required by law to be satisfied that the interest is proved to exist; in others, the interest is a factor to be considered in the review of the execise of an executive discretionary power. Once the factual basis is established by evidence so that the court is satisfied that the interest of national security is a relevant factor to be considered in the determination of the case, the court will accept the opinion of the Crown or its responsible officer as to what is required to meet it, unless it is possible to show that the opinion was one which no reasonable minister advising the Crown could in the circumstances reasonably have held. There is no abdication of the judicial function, but there is a commonsense limitation recognised by the fudges as to what is justiciable; and the limitation is entirely consistent with the general development of the modern case law of judicial review.

In reading this conclusion he took notice of the fact that in the Zamora decision, despite the often quoted speech of Lord Parker:

> 'Those who are responsible for the national security must be the sole judge of what the national security requires. It would obviously be undesirable that such matters should be made the subject of evidence in Court of law or otherwise discussed in public'.

The court took notice of the fact that no evidence of urgent necessity was given and refused to declare the requisition of a vessel to be valid.

He also took not of the decision in *Chandler v DPP (1962) 3 All ER 142* where Lord Reid in the House of Lords said he did not 'subscribe to the view that the government or a minister must always or ever as a general rule have the last word 'about the safety or interests of the State.

Evidence was produced from a senior air force officer that obstruction of the airfield would cause a danger to the safety or interests of the State but he could not be cross examined on this evidence.

The position the courts will take today is that evidence must be produced to show that national security is at stake but once the court is satisfied on that point it will not enquire into the action that the Executive has taken to meet the national interest since it has insufficient information and expertise to make such a judgement. In the *GCHQ case (1984) 3 All ER 935* the Government produced an affidavit by Sir Robert Armstrong (head of the civil service) as to the dangers of disruption to work at GCHQ had consultation taken place prior to the decision to ban and the House of Lords accepted this as sufficient evidence that national security was at stake.

144. *BREACH OF CONFIDENCE*

As indicated in Lesson 9 the Courts will, in suitable circumstances, restrain breaches of confidence by injunction. This intervention originated in cases of marital confidence *(Argyll v Argyll)* and was extended first into cases of employers' confidential information and them into the public sphere by *A.G. v Jonathan Cape (1976) 1 QB 752*. In that case the court acknowledged that an injunction could be granted to prevent disclosures of confidential information by former Cabinet Ministers but refused an injunction to prevent publication of the Crossman diaries because the information disclosed in the Diaries was not sufficiently sensitive to warrant protection by the court. This area of the law is once again topical because of the Spycatcher case *(AG v The Observer Ltd (1988) Times 11 February*, where Peter Wright, a former M15, employee has written his memoirs and proposed to publish men in Australia. The UK Government wished to prevent publication and sought an injunction to his effect in Australia but the Supreme Court of Australia has now refused such relief. Publication of Peter Wright's memoirs (Spycatcher) has now gone ahead in many countries throughout the world and many copies have been imported into the UK.

In February 1988 the Court of Appeal considered an appeal against refusal by the High Court of the Attorney General's application for an injunction to restrain the newspapers from publishing information from Spycatcher and an appeal is now (in June 1988) pending before the House of Lords.

The Court of Appeal acknowledged that, as recognised in Jonathan Cape case, confidentiality could arise not only out of a contract but also out of a relationship and that the courts 'must have power to deal with publication which threatens national security'. The Crown had an enforceable right to the maintenance of confidentiality from the very nature of the information and the likely consequences of disclosure. However the Court concluded that no injunction would be granted to the Attorney General to restrain third parties, such as newspapers, from serialising information from Spycatcher because Spycatcher had now been dissenimated worldwide. The Court of Appeal accepted the view of the High Court that in respect of an application for an injunction against Peter Wright himself the position would be different so that an injunction could be granted against publication of Spycatcher in this country. The grounds for this view were that the Courts accepted that it was in the national interest that secrecy be maintained about operations within M15 and that employees of the service were bound without limit in point of time to preserve secrecy.

This obligation was not relieved by widespread knowledge about the information for which State of affairs Wright himself was responsible.

LLB

CONSTITUTIONAL LAW

LESSON 15 (REVISION)

151. *REVISION OF LESSONS 11-14*

152. *REVISION QUESTIONS*

151.1 *REVISION OF LESSONS 11-14*

Read through each section of Lessons 11-14, pausing at the end of each paragraph to recall what you have just read. If you cannot recall it adequately and in detail, read and check through your knowledge until you are satisfied.

When you have completed this task and referred to the reading lists, test your knowledge further by working through all the questions on the next pages.

152. *REVISION QUESTIONS*

1. Describe and justify any reforms you would make to the Parliamentary Commissioner Act 1967.

2. Is delegated legislation satisfactorily controlled?

3. Wagga County Council has statutory powers to run buses, and to fix the route for bus services. Shortly before the council elections are due to take place, the council announces the creation of six new bus routes, each of which serves a ward represented by a member of the majority party with a narrow majority. The council also announces that a new dial-a-bus service is to be created.

   Members of the minority party believe that these services are being introduced solely to win votes at the election and without regard to any need or commercial justification. Local taxi-drivers, whose trade will be threatened by it, also believe that the dial-a-bus service is beyond the council's statutory powers.

   Assuming that these contentions are correct, who should apply for what legal remedies and in what manner?

4. Suppose that the Water (Expropriation of Welsh Valleys) Act 1975 empowers specified Water Boards to take necessary steps to convert Welsh valleys into reservoirs 'if the appropriate Water Board is satisfied that, having regard to the need for water supplies, environmental and amenity considerations and the interests of the inhabitants of the valley, the balance of advantage favours the conversion'. The Birmingham City Water Authority (which is one of the specified boards) commissions a survey of three Welsh valleys for this purpose. The surveyors report that Cymtwth is the least suitable of the three valleys. The Water Authority hold a public enquiry in Birmingham (one hundred miles from the valleys) and the inspector reports that Cymtwth is the most heavily populated and environmentally important of the valleys. He advises that Cymllannel should be used for the purpose. The Water Authority decides to convert Cymtwth into a reservoir.

   Advise Euean Moran who farms in Cymtwth, and who suspects the fact that Sir John Smith, the Chairman of the Water Authority, has a weekend cottage in Cymllannel may have affected the decision, on the steps he may take to seek to set aside the decision.

5. Describe and explain the main provisions of the Crown Proceedings Act 1947.

6. Pipsqueak, a junior civil servant in the Department of Education and Science, commissions Rook, a well-known sculptor, to undertake a sculpture for the foyer of the Department's new offices, at a fee of £25,000. An MP raises the matter in the Commons as an example of wasteful public expenditure, and the Department receives many complaints from members of the public. The Minister announces that the contract cannot be justified in the current economic climate and has been cancelled. Rook demands compensation but this is rejected on the ground that Pipsqueak had no authority to contract for the Department.

   Advise Rook. Would your advice be any different if the cancellation had been part of the systematic cut in public expenditure by 5% imposed by the incoming government after an election?

7. What are public corporations? How much control do ministers and Parliament have over them?

8. You are asked by the government of a newly independent member of the Commonwealth to advise it on the creation of the office of Ombudsman.

    Drawing on the experience gained in this country of that office, what recommendations would you make?

9. Comment on *s. 12(3) Parliamentary Commissioner Act 1967* which provides that:

    'It is hereby declared that nothing in this Act authorises or requires the Commissioner to question the merits of a decision taken without maladministration by a government department or other authority in the exercise of a discretion vested in that department or authority.'

10. 'Granted the very limited jurisdiction and powers accorded to the Parliamentary Commissioner for Administration by statute, it is remarkable how successful the experiment has been; but it is time that the office was made closer to that of an Ombudsman so that he can do his job properly.'

    Discuss.